The Syndicate Seri<

GW01219223

# Black Mirror Cult

by Mark Cunnington

**Trio Publishing**

Also by Trio Publishing

The Syndicate
The Syndicate 2nd Edition
The Syndicate (R.I.P.) Part II
Return of The Syndicate Part III
Running The Syndicate Part IV
Revenge of The Syndicate Part V
The Ransom and The Syndicate Part VI
The Syndicates Part VII
The Fear

First published 2016

Published by Trio Publishing


ISBN 978 0 9537951 9 2

Printed and bound in Great Britain by Clays Ltd, St Ives plc

# Introduction

In the beginning, I never wanted you to read my story, but having had my hand forced by events outside of my control, eventually, instalment by instalment, all – as they say – was revealed. What is gratifying is you enjoyed it, thousands of you, a situation which I cannot deny continues to thrill me. From that initial negative there has emerged a huge positive, something I could never have imagined at the outset – and I have you, the readers, to thank for it. Your enthusiasm is gratefully received. That said, I know you're not here to accept my heartfelt gratitude. You're here to read the next bit. The bit after so much time has passed. The bit I told myself would only ever come into being if Something Happened.
And after all those years, something did.

Our story doesn't really start from where we left it because it's a new story. One where time has passed, life has moved on, perspective has shifted and one where we are all older – but not necessarily any wiser.

# Chapter 1

"I'm glad you popped by," Pup told me as he lifted the recently boiled kettle and poured its contents into a couple of mugs, "because there's something I need to tell you."

I nodded absent-mindedly. Pup had probably found a new and quicker way of indenting boilies – a design application he had come up with years ago allowing anglers to draw and fade boilies when using a throwing stick. Either that or he had some other snippet regarding the minutiae of bait-making to tell me. I was in his house of a thousand rampaging flavours purely by way of a social call. I had no bait to pick up, wasn't going fishing until the following day, and had decided to nip in and visit him purely on a whim. It had been nearly a month since I had last seen him.

As Pup bullied the two tea bags, I gazed out of the kitchen window and saw Wilton's gravestone standing sombrely to attention in the right-hand border running the entire length of the back garden. His bait testing cat, the original one, had died many years ago – peacefully from old age, not from eating a prototype boilie that had caused superbug-like internal organ disintegration.

"Rambo's taking Sylvester on an overnighter this week," I said. "On The Lake. More likely to see some action on there than on The Pit at this time of year."

Pup smiled. "How old is he now? I lose track of the years."

"Nearly ten. He's a big lad for his age, mentally well advanced, too. What else would you expect having Rambo for a dad? They're bringing him up bilingual," I added, by way of more personal information concerning Rambo's son. "German and English."

Pup rolled his eyes at me as he gave me a steaming mug of builder's tea. "Well, I certainly didn't imagine Steffi would talk *French* to her son."

I was going to say something witty to patch over my previous stating-of-the-bleedin'-obvious faux pas when Hobbes padded into the kitchen and distracted me. The ginger ninja was the only cat Pup had kept from all the ones Wilton had sired, the rest had been given away to good homes when they had failed to be of use. Only Hobbes had inherited the specific genes affording the ability to grade carp bait like his father. As such, the feline was now defined by the encumbering job title, 'Head of New Product Viability' within Pup's bait business. The feisty ginger moggy nuzzled around my legs for a few seconds and I stroked his head, tickling him under his ears. The cat and I were on good terms now and our 'relationship' was far removed from the antagonism of years long past. The cat had become a major fixture in Pup's life, mine too to a lesser extent, and I always enjoyed seeing him when visiting Pup.

Social niceties concluded and job done on the greetings front, Hobbes wandered over to his old blanket-lined wicker basket and parked himself on the grubby blanket. As cats are prone to do, especially in human company, he started to lick his arse with no shred of self-consciousness.

"He's at something of a crossroads in his life at the moment," Pup informed me, eyeing the cat. "I guess we both are."

"So... Got anything new in the pipeline bait-wise?" I asked, trying to move the conversation along before Pup got the chance to elaborate on his bizarre utterance.

Pup scoffed. "New! I think I can safely say we're well beyond 'new' now. Reinvented more like... or perhaps *recycled*," he added, contemptibly. "We're more on a par with the fashion industry. Picking a bit from here and a bit from there, a bit from this line of thinking and a bit from another. Everyone's raiding their own back catalogue to get this year's latest product."

I smiled at this. "Yeah, but where would capitalism be without a latest, must-have product?"

Pup shrugged. "Huh. I know where I *won't* be," he said, taking the ever-present micrometer from the back pocket of his trousers.

Disdainfully, he tossed it on the kitchen table before sitting down on one of the two non-matching chairs parked under its battered surface. This second hand furniture 'set' was a relatively new addition – rumour had it he'd swapped twenty kilos of bait and five tubs of his legendary pop-ups for it. Pup took a swig of his tea and I noticed he wasn't wearing his normally ever-present surgical rubber gloves.

"What do you mean?" I asked, joining him at the table by sitting on the other non-matching chair.

"It's the reason why I'm glad you popped by. This is what I need to tell you."

"Pass me the micrometer," I said, nodding at the tool. Pup obliged by sliding it across the kitchen table. I picked it up and scrutinised it. "Set at eighteen point five millimetres," I said.

"Nought point five tolerance on an eighteen miller. Freezer baits, naturally. Air-dried shrink back a tad coming up more like seventeen to seventeen point five," Pup explained with little enthusiasm.

There was something in Pup's demeanour that jolted. It suddenly struck me he didn't seem his normal self – if a full-on baithead like him could ever be described as 'normal'.

"Sorry. You were saying... You know where you *won't* be. What did you mean by that?"

Pup took in a deep breath, his chest suddenly wobbling with emotion. "I won't be *here*," he stated, solemnly pointing an index finger at the floor. "Because... I'm-quitting-the-bait-game." The words came rushing out of him, almost tripping over each other, as they gushed from his mouth.

Now, there were lots of things I wasn't expecting Pup to say at that precise moment. 'I've been headhunted by NASA to be an astronaut on the first manned flight to Mars', was one. 'I've been asked to write an amusing and diverting weekly column for a broadsheet revolving around the metropolitan chattering-classes, where every third article will be about property prices and the importance of getting one's offspring into private education', was another. But the most unlikely thing I wasn't expecting him to say was he was quitting the bait game.

"Wow! I wasn't expecting you to say that," I admitted, completely shell-shocked. What I didn't add although it was my uppermost thought was, 'Who's going to sort out our bait if you don't?'

Quickly, as is my default setting when confronted by any major situation, I tried to analyse what was going on. Pup declaring he was quitting the bait game, after dedicating his whole life to the pursuit of boilie perfection, was a genuine out-of-the-blue bombshell. Something must have gone spectacularly amiss for him to make this fundamental life-altering decision. To my mind, this choice could only have been formulated as a direct consequence of some kind of psychological meltdown. What was also clear was the impact it would have on my carp fishing and Rambo's carp fishing. In short, from a purely selfish perspective, losing our boiliemeister to retirement was catastrophic news. In the few giddy seconds after Pup's revelation, I reminded and then chastised myself our bait concerns were of secondary importance when set against the implied traumatic mental state of my friend. Even so, I thought disconsolately, who the fuck was going to sort our bait if he didn't?

"I've already put the house on the market. I've had the estate agents round to value it," Pup gabbled, his terse tone confirmation there was to be no back-pedalling regards the gargantuan decision he had made.

"*And?*" I asked, incredulously. This was getting more intense and out of hand by the second. I now had 'Where the hell will he go?' to sit alongside 'What the hell will he do?'

"Do you know what they had the fucking cheek to say?" Pup asked, the fury suddenly brimming up in him and spilling over like an overheated saucepan of bile.

I shook my head and out the corner of my eye I saw Hobbes stop licking his arse and look up in concern at the recently self-proclaimed ex-boiliemeister. Pup rarely swore, only when deeply agitated.

"That it smelt," he continued, answering his own question. "That they couldn't sell it in its current condition because it stank! They said anyone interested in buying it would be put off by the terrible odour." Pup laughed a long hollow guffaw. "I ask you! What do they know?"

Hobbes, perhaps sensing his owner had eased back from some point of self-endangerment, one beyond my powers of detection, returned to the task in tongue. I, on the other hand, didn't move on to telling Pup the estate agent's analysis was spot on seeing as you could probably hair-rig a piece of his carpet and catch on it; or that walking into his house was the equivalent of undergoing an olfactory barrage, a blitzkrieg of fantastical fragrant fumes; or that if you were foolhardy enough to lick the bare walls of his boiling room, it was a racing certainty you would taste either

Monster Crab, Milky Toffee, Pineapple, Cream Cajouser or Cranberry at some point. Perhaps a combination of them all. I was also willing to bet somewhere in that room there was a small area still tasting of Tutti-Frutti – a patch behind the back of the fridge perhaps. All in all, I surmised, there seemed to be lots of things I wasn't telling Pup this morning.

"Estate agents. Too right. Masters of misrepresentation. Bastards!" I scoffed, going along with Pup's withering assessment of one of our nation's most loathed vocations while secretly agreeing. "But quitting the bait game? Why? *And* selling your house! What are you going to do? Where are you thinking of going?" I asked, genuinely bemused.

"The fact is Matt, I'm all mixed, rolled and boiled out," Pup answered with apparent honest candour. "I just can't face it anymore. So many, many, many, *fucking* many, tiny rolled balls. Some a bit tinier than others and some a bit tinier than that. Some that sink, some that float and some that waft somewhere in between. I mean, how many *millions* of them have I made? Day in day out, the same process over and over and over and over again and again and again. The measuring, the mixing, the rolling, the boiling, the drying and the bagging…" Pup wagged a finger at me. "Oh, I loved doing it, don't get me wrong, loved being the best…" Pup's finger stopped and he locked eye contact with me across the divide of the tabletop. In that instant I caught a glimpse of a certain wildness in his soul, the essence of someone teetering on the very edge. "But now I don't. I actually hate it. Hate it with a passion."

"Passion… *fruit?*" It was out before I could stop myself.

Pup was indignant. "I'm deadly serious, Matt. You can crack flavour jokes all you like. I mean it. It's over. I'm selling up and shipping out…" Pup stopped dead in his tracks and for the first time in my life I actually saw somebody's eyeballs boggle, a split second before they narrowed. Pup's head started to oscillate from side to side with a barely contained anger. "Wait! Wait! Hold on a minute… You think the same, don't you? *You* think my house smells? You're siding with them, aren't you? My God!" Pup sneered. "Go on, admit it!" he goaded with rising resentment. "Admit you think it stinks. You think I've been here so long, been so…" Pup's hands lifted above the tabletop and his fingers flickered as he tried to find the right word. "Been so… *incarcerated* within these four walls that I don't notice it? That I've become *immune* to it!"

Put on the spot, I did my famous impression of a gulping carp on an unhooking mat in non-answer.

After several seconds I managed to tease out one word. "Well…"

"Oh, for fuck's sake!" Pup declared, pulling both his cheeks down with the palms of two sliding hands as realisation hit. "It *does* smell! I *don't* notice it anymore. Does it really?" Pup's voiced lifted an octave as he asked me the question.

Sheepishly, I nodded. "It does smell quite a bit."

Pup stared at the micrometer for a good five seconds before snapping out of it.

"Well. It only goes to show I've made the right decision."

With that he got up out of the non-matching chair, walked over to the kitchen window and flung it open.

"Fresh air!" he shouted out of it. "This house needs fresh air!" Pup turned to me. "And so do I!" He made an expansive gesture, sweeping his right arm in a wide arc. "Come on down, air molecules!" he shouted.

Over the next few minutes, Pup completed the task of converting his house into a three bedroom wind tunnel. Every aperture connecting the house to the great outdoors was opened with gusto. Windows were jammed wide open and the front and back doors were wedged back on their hinges. When Pup had opened up the front door, the huge brass doorknocker – three golf ball-sized boilies attached by thick wire to a giant hook – had crashed violently against its hardwood. I followed like a little lap dog, saying nothing, as Pup strode into every room in the house determined to send its air change per hour rate spiralling upwards.

Once this was done to his satisfaction, with the house temperature plummeting thanks to the influx of chilly spring air, he returned to the 18-22mm room and started peeling off all the fish capture photos adorning the entire room. These were stuck to every plastered surface, not a gap between them there were so many – a repetitive themed wallpaper of proud anglers holding their prize. They were even all over the ceiling.

"Do you mind if I keep one?" I asked, as Pup continued to yank them off like a diligent Eastern European farmhand plucking feathers from a chicken.

"Be my guest," Pup answered, not diverting for a nanosecond from ripping down the photos. "I'm burning the fucking lot!"

I nipped back to the 25mm plus room and, still there after all those years, just below the light switch, was the picture of me and the fifty-five twelve mind-meld mirror from Lac Fumant (first time). I carefully popped it in my jacket pocket.

"Just for old time's sake," I whispered to myself and returned to Pup.

By then, Pup had stopped pulling off the photos by hand – too inefficient – and instead was blasting them off with the air blow gun connected to the compressor he used to power his sausage guns. Eight bar of oomph, I clocked the pressure gauge, and a long hose was more than enough to part 6 x 4 and 7 x 5 prints from the Blu-Tack holding them to the wall. The effect was bizarre. The room was raining carp trophy shots like a ticker tape parade.

Mirrors, commons, leathers and fully-scaled carp (not in equal ratios, obviously, *and* most were snapped long before the days of Simmos), clasped by an assortment of human misfits of all shapes, ages and sizes fluttered down from above where gravity had successfully overcome compressed air. Others, those still pneumatically charged, soared upwards, careening haphazardly towards the ceiling and the still-attached fledgling photos not yet able to fly.

Prints zigzagged down around my ears in ever increasing numbers as Pup continued to blast away. One of them see-sawed down and hit me, edge on, across the bridge of my nose. I caught it on the rebound, glanced at the photo of a middle-aged, bald-headed man holding a scraper twenty common and turned it over. On the back, written in biro, were the words, 'The Beast 22.11. 17th June 1992. John Dawes. Caught on Pup's pop-ups.'

"Whatever," I said, tossing it over my shoulder. I knew all I needed to know about catching twenties in the nineteen nineties.

Pup was now grappling with gaffer tape which he used to hold the air blow gun in a permanently 'on' position and attached to the end of a broom handle. With this makeshift extendable air blaster he started to take down the ceiling prints. A fresh blizzard of matt and gloss snowflakes fell to earth and settled as a layer of trophy-shot snow on the floor. So chaotic was the scene, Pup waving his pneumatic wand, Expelliarmusing (™ J K Rowling) the crap out of the photos, sending them cascading across the room, the gloss ones twinkling in the watery sun flooding through the open windows, I started to laugh hysterically.

Pup, who was already hysterical in the first place, joined in. As I held my sides, convulsing with laughter and bent double with tears of mirth running down my cheeks, I couldn't help but notice his laugh had a certain quality to it.

"Hahaha! Get out of my life, you fuckers! Don't ever darken my rolling tables again! Hahaha! Do I do two point five-kilo bags? Fuck off, do I! Fuck off to all bag sizes! A discount for mentioning my baits? Sponsorship? Fuck the fuck off!" he screamed above the sibilant sound of the released compressed air and the drone of the compressor.

Pup's wand made short work of the ceiling photos and those remaining on the walls. Soon, all that remained was a sparse Magnolia-emulsioned room with Blu-Tack acne. Pup turned off the compressor, dropped the air gun and kicked his way through the photos like a kid through a leaf pile, exited the 18-22mm room and entered the 8-12mm room. Again I followed him, my previous hilarity expired, now replaced by the original creeping disquiet over what was happening inside Pup's head.

I knew in the corner of the 8-12mm room lay Pup's priceless (probably) collection of bait memorabilia. I could remember his reverence towards these bait item artefacts from the time I first met him. However, that reverence was in desperately short supply today. Pup delved into the collection and started to stuff all the old original readymade boilie bags, his anthology of rare flavour bottles, bait books, bait articles and handwritten bait recipes by 'famous' carp anglers into a large black refuse sack. I fleetingly glimpsed the vivid orange-coloured cover of 'Kempastini's Book of Baits', an old black and white ad for Hi-Pro featuring Gerry Savage and some old packaging bags with the words 'Black Majic', 'Duncan's Red' and 'Yellow Slyme' written on them before they all disappeared into the bag's gaping maw. A seemingly endless array of small plastic bottles disappeared as well. I caught sight of one bearing the legend 'Honey Yucatan' and spotted an original bottle of Hutchinson's Scopex.

"Look at that," Pup said, thrusting a piece of scruffy A4 at me. I scanned the five handwritten bait recipes on the page. A few ingredients leapt out at me; 80 Mesh Casien, Chocolate Malt and Whitworth's Semolina to name a few. "Maylin's original list for the book, Fox Pool," Pup decreed. "Don't need it," he said, screwing it up into a ball and dropping it in the sack.

Once Pup had cleared all the bait memorabilia into the black sack, he spun it to make a tube of the top part, tied half a knot in it and chucked it over his shoulder. "Got a lighter?" he asked.

"Those seventy/thirty butane/propane stoves don't light themselves," I truthfully told him

"Excellent. Get an armful of those photos from the other room and meet me on the patio. I need kindling."

Under Pup's instruction, I gathered up as many photos as I could carry off the 18-22mm floor and met him on the patio.

"In there," he said, gesturing towards the metal dustbin-sized brazier he'd placed on the patio's edge furthest from the house. I dropped them in as best I could. "Good," stated Pup, nodding approvingly. "A dash of petrol and away we go!"

Personally speaking, I wouldn't have called it a dash, more a pouring, but it did make a satisfying 'whooomph!' when I ignited it – at arm's length with a lighted photo half, payload delivery into brazier followed by an instantaneous, if undignified, panicked withdrawal.

"Well don't just stand there," Pup told me as the flames licked over the top of the brazier, "get the rest of the photos."

"What all of them?"

"All of them."

"And burn them?"

"Every single one!"

I've done some pretty tenuous things thanks to my obsession with carp fishing, but spending a morning burning thousands of trophy shot photographs certainly adds another one to the list. Once the brazier was really roaring and the heat from it meant it was hard to get close enough to refuel it, Pup took the black sack and lobbed it in. Thick, black, acrid smoke, with, if I'm allowed 5ml of poetic licence, the hint of famous flavours past, billowed upwards; dispersed into the ether by the heat from the flames.

As the pair of us stood soaking up the heat, fascinated by the leaping tongues of flames signalling by fire beacon the end of Pup's old life, I asked him a question.

"Are you sure you *really* want to quit the bait game?" I asked.

Pup nodded without looking at me. "Never been more certain."

The earlier fervour had departed from him and he seemed more relaxed, as if the commencement of clearing out the house of all his bait paraphernalia had exorcised a demon.

"And sell your house?" I said.

"Yep. I just woke up one morning a few weeks ago and knew I couldn't do it anymore. Didn't *want* to do it anymore. To be honest, it's been coming over the last few months." A particularly flammable flavour bottle caused a sudden brief increase in flames and heat. We both edged back a little, a single hand up to shield our faces from the heat. "Do you know," Pup confided in me. "I haven't rolled a single bait for over a week. It's been the most liberating seven days of my life."

I had my answer to the mystery of his gloveless hands. "But what will you do to make a living? And where will you go? What about all your customers?" I asked.

"They can go elsewhere. The world doesn't suffer from a shortage of carp bait companies," Pup replied, truthfully. "I've already begun turning customers away once I'd sold out of the last remaining stock of my various lines of baits. They weren't very happy about it, but that's tough." Pup hitched up his shoulders. "I can always sort a job out a bit later. I've made decent money over the years and have savings put by. Once I've sold the house, I'll be minted. Enough to last me a fair while. If I was really pushed I could sell off some of my recipes, last resort." Pup caught the look of alarm in my eyes. "Not *yours*. I won't sell *yours*, you idiot. Besides, I don't really want to. It would be like selling off my children... Well, how I imagine it would feel selling off my own children, if I had any," Pup quantified.

"Thanks," I ventured with a weak smile.

"Where I'm going is already sorted."

"And that is?" I prompted.

"Italy," Pup replied.

"*Italy?*" I asked confused.

"I'm moving to Italy. That's why I'm selling the house."

"To Italy? What the hell for?"

The pair of us were barking up the tree of madness; up The Magic Faraway Tree to one of the lands at the top, the Land of Living in Italy.

"I've met a woman," Pup answered. "She lives in Italy, so I'm going to live there. Near her. In Italy. Venice, actually. Ideally, I liked to buy a place out there. One where her and I can settle down and live together."

My first thought wasn't about the woman. My first thought was what the sale of Pup's three bedroom bait shrine in oligarch-free East Sussex might allow him to buy or rent in Venice. I wasn't especially au fait with Venetian property prices, but I imagined setting up home in the city known as the 'Queen of the Adriatic' wouldn't come cheap. In fact, I couldn't see his house generating enough cash to afford very much at all. I briefly wondered if there was a gondola version of the houseboat. Then again, perhaps he could permanently bivvy-up on the Rialto Bridge, fishing three rods in the Grand Canal, sneakily hooking food supplies from the delivery boats serving the city.

"How the hell did *you* meet an Italian woman?" I demanded. I *was* thinking of the woman now.

"On the internet," he answered. "But she's not Italian, she's English."

Of course. On the internet. How stupid of me. That's everyone's answer to everything; the fucking internet.

"Are you sure *she's* not a thirty-five-year-old Mafia mobster with a flick knife in his pocket and a motorway overpass footing waiting for a body to be dumped in it before the concrete gets poured?" I asked, sarcastically.

"No," Pup said, defensively. "She's a very nice forty-two-year-old English Foreign Language teacher at a school in Venice."

"And I suppose there aren't enough handsome men in Italy for her, so she went on the internet, joined a dating site, and hooked up with you?" I said, a bit more harshly than I should.

"Oh, she can't stand the Italians," Pup retorted. "She says they're all dark good looks, stylish clothing and sunglasses. She's not so keen on the women, either. For pretty much the same reasons, actually."

"So why's she in Italy?" I queried.

"She loves Venice. Except when it gets too hot, too crowded and the canals start to stink."

"Okay…" I said, somewhat bemused and back-tracked by all the conflicting notions Pup was coming out with. To me, the whole thing had 'disaster' written all over it – in big neon letters in a creepy gothic font. "But don't you think, just to stand back and draw breath for a second, it might be wise to maybe go and see her first and see how you get on?" I offered. "To see if you click, rather than quitting the bait game *and* selling the house before you've even met in the flesh. Perhaps you could rent it out instead of selling it. Maybe tell all your customers you're having an extended holiday. A sort of sabbatical. Keep a few doors open…"

"No." Pup stated, defiantly slamming all doors shut and burning all available bridges while he was at it. "We've worked it all out by email and text. We *have* spoken to each other, you know. We *want* to be together."

"You have seen that TV programme called Catfish?" I asked.

Pup's face hardened. "Yes. And it's not like that at all. Besides, you're not worried about me, *you're* only worried about continuing to get your supply of exclusive, revolutionary, indented, dirty brown bottom bait boilies."

"That's not true!" I exclaimed. "It never even crossed my mind," I said, reiterating my dishonesty. If I was Pinocchio, my nose would have taken one of his eyes out.

"Bloody liar!"

"Look, I'm a friend," I protested. "I don't want to see you get hurt like last time," I added, with a touch more honesty. "And the time before. Like with Melissa… and then with Melloney." Even I shuddered at the recollection of two of the three man-eating Witches of Eastwick.

Pup slowly nodded at my explanation. "Ok. Fair enough. I'm just saying."

"But just out of interest," I said, skirting round the situation. "Now *you've* brought the subject up, how will we continue to get our supply of exclusive, revolutionary, indented, dirty brown bottom bait boilies? Don't forget, it's not all about me and Rambo. The Eye still uses it."

A sly grin spread across Pup's face. "Bloody hell. You carp anglers. You're like an open book. One written by a pathetic, needy author!" Pup laughed, then scratched the back of his head, his manner quickly becoming business-like. "Anyway, now that the matter of bait is out in the open, now we've put our cards on the table, so to speak, *I* have a proposal for *you*." Pup now had a lopsided grin on his mouth, one where I imagined I could make out the sharp and pointy teeth behind his thin lips. "I'll strike a deal with you, if you're so keen to keep using that bait. Interested?"

I nodded. Of course I was interested. How could I not be interested? Rambo and I had been on that bait for over a decade and it was still as brilliant a carp-catcher as ever. It was our constant, our bedrock, the very foundation on which all our carp fishing was built; it was our magnificent starting point, the one allowing us to pour our energies into fitting together the other parts of the jigsaw. To lose it would mean a horrific restart. A bait reboot. An expedition back into the jungle of non-exclusive bait from companies we could never trust as much as Pup. I shuddered and felt sorry for all of Pup's customers who had lost their favourite bait.

Still, fuck them. This was a case of every carp angler for himself.

"What's the deal, then?" I asked.

"I want you to sort out the selling of my house," Pup begun. "I'm not going to use an estate agent, bollocks to them, they've had their chance and blown it. I'll sell it via an internet property site and you can be my contact in the UK, deal with all the viewings, any legal issues with the conveyancing firm and in return I'll give you the recipe for your bait. Even the revolutionary bit. And I'll give you all the contacts you need to source the ingredients. Then you can either roll it yourself or get someone else to do it for you." Pup frowned at me. "Although I definitely *wouldn't* recommend that if you want it to remain exclusive. Plus, as a little bonus sweetener, you can have any of my bait-making equipment you want. You know, to make life easier. I shan't be needing it. How does that sound?"

"Sounds a plan," I said slowly, initially relieved I would still have access to the world's greatest boilie – a feeling soon counterbalanced by what else was entailed.

Bollocks! Did I really want to be showing a host of picky house purchasing punters around Pup's poorly appointed pad? Did I really want to have to go back to rolling my own bait again? In an ideal world, obviously not, on both fronts. About as much as I wanted to walk round with a size two Gardner Mugga hanging from my bottom limp attached to a four-ounce death rig. *And* there was bound to be extra unforeseen admin and aggro involved in flogging Pup's house. On the flip side, bait beggars can't be choosers.

"How soon are you going?" I asked.

"A week Wednesday."

"A week Wednesday! What, in less than a fortnight?" I spluttered.

"Time waits for no one, Matt," Pup said, as if he had just discovered profundity.

"My new life beckons and I can't wait to leave the old one. Now, you *will* do all the house stuff, won't you?"

I knew I was being railroaded, but the exclusive, revolutionary, indented, dirty brown bottom bait boilie was a must have. Rambo would never forgive me if it slipped through our fingers.

"Yes, of course," I said, in what I hoped didn't sound a grudging manner. "I'll sort out the house sale for you."

Pup nodded enthusiastically. "Good. Now, there's just *one* more tiny thing I need you to do for me. And it's a deal breaker."

"Okay," I said warily. "What is it?"

Pup had me over a barrel and I sensed him drawing out his thickest and longest bankstick ready for insertion.

"Unfortunately, I can't take Hobbes with me."

"Why not? His passport expired?" I asked, caustically. "No wait. I know, he gets seasick in a water taxi."

Pup scowled. "Daisy suffers from ailurophobia. Fear of cats. Hobbes will have to stay here in the UK and I want him to be with someone he knows and someone who I can trust to look after him. As you well know, the only person who fits the bill is you."

All joking aside, this was true. Hobbes and Rambo had never got on. Not since Hobbes had tried his Alien facehugger move on Rambo in Boilieeyeboilie's factory. Rambo had peeled the ginger ninja off, along with a lot of facial skin Hobbes had sunk his claws in, and swung him around by his tail before launching him into a bath full of water. Come to think of it, even as a kitten Hobbes had tried to terrorise Rambo. I pulled a face to show my concurrence. It was true. The pair of them were hardly on each other's Christmas card list.

Pup continued. "You'll have to adopt him, Matt. He can move in with you, Sophie and your kids and become your family pet. If I'm quitting the bait game, then so can he. Let him retire to the Williams' household and put his paws up. You can take his basket," Pup added, nodding towards Hobbes. "He likes snuggling up in it and it'll be something familiar to help him settle in."

I curled my top lip and weighed up the implications of getting our first family pet, even if it did come with a free second-hand basket – and then remembered what the consequences were if I refused. So, we were getting a cat. I was sure Amy, and particularly little Adam, would be thrilled, although I might have to work on Sophie and try and bribe my way out of it. A Pandora bracelet, possibly? A new handbag? A weekend city break? Spa weekend? A voucher for one month's worth of me doing the ironing and cooking – a nil compulsory excess insurance policy against melted clothing and burnt-to-a-crisp dinners inclusive?

"Sure. Why not," I said, shaking my head clear. "Hobbes can move in with us. It's a deal. Adam will love him," I said, offering my hand to Pup.

Pup clasped my hand tight and pumped it enthusiastically. He'd got what he wanted. "Thanks, Matt. Do you know, it was the thing worrying me most, getting Hobbes a good home. Forget quitting the bait game and selling the house." Pup's eyes seemed to moisten as he held his mid-distance stare. "You know, I feel really guilty about leaving him, but I mustn't let anything stand in the way of my new life. I've got to break free and go for it. You understand, don't you?"

And I did. Perfectly. He'd gone on the internet and had his head turned by some gold-digging bitch who was going to fleece him of every pound and every penny he had. Or ditto a Mafia mobster with a flick knife in his pocket. Poor deluded Pup. He was prepared to give up everything, literally everything, in the chase for love. In my head, I gave him a generous three months from his arrival in Venice until the day he arrived back home a single, broken, penniless ex-boiliemeister with not so much as a mixing bowl to his name. *If* he got back alive, that is.

"You can always come and visit Hobbes at any time with Daisy... well, she can stay in the car or in the garden," I added, playing along with Pup's fantasy.

"That'd be nice. I'd enjoy that," Pup said, with a dreamy look on his face, no doubt picturing the scene in his mind's eye. "Perhaps I'll ring you at the weekend and arrange a time for you to pick him up after we've had our last few days together. We can sort out the bait-making gear and what I need you to do regards the house at the same time."

I nodded. The sap. Throwing everything away for a woman/Mafia mobster on the internet. Even his bait testing cat. In that instant, I felt a desperate urge to warn him. I wanted to shout at him, tell him he was being duped, to get hold of both his shoulders with manic urgency and shake him into seeing sense. I wanted to let him know it was one big con and he'd be back home, broke and shattered and looking to start rolling bait again just so he could buy himself a fish and chip supper – provided he wasn't enveloped in concrete somewhere in southern Europe. I wanted to spell out how it was going to end in tears. Big time. But then, what can you say to someone whose mind is so set? Not without appearing to be massively negative and effectively calling them a bloody liar and a stupid fool. No, I decided, Pup would have to find out the hard way – and all because I didn't want to lose him as a friend by telling him the unpalatable truth. Especially knowing whatever I said would make no difference. Besides, I didn't *really* think he might end up enveloped in concrete.

I clasped Pup's shoulder and gave him a big hug, thinking it might be the last one he ever got. His track record with women wasn't one to boast about and there was hardly a queue of true friends outside of bait punters.

"Good luck with it all, Pup. I hope it turns out to be everything you want it to be," I said sincerely.

"Peter. My name's Peter. I'm not Pop-up Pete anymore," Pup told me.

# Chapter 2

Arriving at The Lake the following day, I was greeted by the sight of only two cars in the car park – Rambo's and Luke the Christian Carper's. Luke, a long-standing original Lake member, had been suffering a traumatic time going back to the winter of last year. Since that February of last year he had failed to bank a single carp – a period of some fourteen months. This disastrous statistic meant he was exceptionally anxious to get his latest 'new season' campaign off to a successful start. (Both The Lake and The Pit tickets renewed annually on the 15th March.) I was clear on this because Luke and I had discussed the matter at length a few months ago when he had supposedly phoned me up to wish me a Happy New Year. Although I had been vaguely aware of how he had struggled last season, thanks to bumping into him on the bank during my winter sessions on The Lake, conversing with him on that occasion had underlined how low he was. Listening to him talk, craving the answers to questions he no longer even understood, a lack of confidence and stress affecting every word, I had felt for him. As blank had followed blank a wall of bagels, of dots in the book, of no goals scored, had cemented themselves one on top of another to create a towering ego-shrinking mental edifice, a giant banner running across its ramparts stating, 'You Will Not Catch!'

In a long rambling monologue, Luke had explained how belief had been slowly taken from him throughout his blank period; as if he'd become attached to an insatiable credence-sucking parasite intent on leaving its host completely drained of conviction. The niggling doubts on swim choice, bait and rigs had gradually blossomed into a bloated ineptitude, one forming a dark brooding shadow that continued to envelope him. One where every facet of his angling was called into question. Eventually, every trip seemed to take place in a haze of pre-destined, going-through-the-motions, autopilot angling where the inevitable conclusion – catching nothing – was as certain as the sinking of the sun in the west.

There had also been a bitter edge to Luke's voice as he had told me of his carp fishing travails; of his feeling short-changed regards all the money he had spent on the bait and tackle suggested by various bait companies' blurb, tackle firms' videos on YouTube and so-called 'improve your catch rate' carp magazine articles by sponsored anglers.

I guess it's fair to say nearly every carp angler could empathise with his predicament because most had suffered a similar type of drought, if perhaps not so lengthy, at some time or another. I had many years ago, before I had met Rambo and the successful bait we had used in the TWTT – long before I had met Pup and his baits, ones that were even better. Consequently, I could genuinely relate to Luke's suffering. I'm all heart and a Considerate Fishery Owner if nothing else.

Unfortunately for Luke, this empathy didn't stretch to equipping him with five kilos of our exclusive, revolutionary, indented, dirty brown bottom bait boilie or tipping him the wink on The Carper's super trick rig. Despite this, I had truly wanted to help him kick off the new year with a capture. So, I had listened carefully to his desolated, dejected, disheartened and despondent assessment of his hopes of ever catching a carp again, an aspiration plummeting off a cliff faster than a lemming superglued to a lead balloon. Wondering if I had become a call-taker for the carp fishing division of the Samaritans and thinking, 'Here's one needing to be put on suicide watch', I had eased into my bubbliest pep talk in an attempt to nullify his negativity and instil in him some confidence for the new year. I can't remember exactly what I had told him, but I'm pretty sure all the relevant clichés were in there – although, more than likely, as Eric Morecambe famously said to André Previn about the notes he was playing on a piano, 'Not necessarily in the right order'. Yet, it had seemed to work and our conversation had ended with him feeling more positive about his fishing.

Unfortunately, it transpired Luke's uplifted mood was short-lived and his next session had produced a blank. As had the next one. And the one after. When Luke had signalled his desire to renew his Lake membership (still a glutton for punishment) in early March, by email, he had come across as more desperate than ever before. Replying to his message, I had advised him to take a month off, to leave The Lake alone until early April – my thinking had been a half-arsed notion of him recharging his batteries and hopefully getting himself out of the cycle of simply 'going for the sake of it' – and then to phone me the night before he was due to have his 'comeback' session. That phone call had come last night.

I had decided it was time to be more proactive and more specific. Out had gone the generalities and in had come the step-by-step, painting-by-numbers approach. I had suggested he fish a swim called 'Seb's' and had then told him the hot spots within it. Seb's was a reliable early spring open water swim named after another original member who had passed away several years ago. It was a swim where both Rambo and I'd had success in the past at this time of year. Conspiratorially, I had told Luke this and urged him to get to Seb's early and beat Rambo to the swim.

Luke had baulked at this. "Is Rambo fishing tomorrow? I don't want to tread on anyone's toes. Certainly not Rambo's," Luke had said, wisely.

"Don't worry about it," I had said, airily dismissing the problem. "He wears steel-capped bivvy slippers and you're hardly built like a rugby league prop forward."

"What?" Luke had said, missing the joke.

"What I mean is, Rambo would never have a problem with a member beating him to a swim. We don't run our fisheries like that," I had answered.

"Are you sure?"

"Absolutely."

What I didn't tell Luke was I already knew Rambo didn't want to fish Seb's. My little psychological game was purely designed to instil that most elusive of life's enhancers – confidence.

"Thanks, Matt. That really helps."

"No worries. Get in that swim and fish those spots I told you about and I'm sure you'll get one."

The struggling carp angler. There but for the grace of God go I. Actually, this was one subject I hadn't broached when talking to Luke – last night or the time before. I had steered well clear of asking him again, as I had once before, if he had prayed for a run during his year-long blank. Not asking this question had allowed me to avoid an even trickier follow up, should he have answered in the affirmative, Why had his Christian God chosen to ignore a cry for help from such a devoted follower?

Best not to go there, I had decided. Religion is such a touchy subject nowadays.

Much as I had sympathy for Luke's perennial carping conundrum, I can't say his catch rate, or lack of it, were weighing heavily on my mind as I loaded up my barrow. Not even the consequences of my swim/spots recommendations bombing out overly bothered me. No. The most onerous subjects knocking aggressively on my brain's front door were, A) Telling Sophie about taking on Hobbes as the family pet and B) Telling Rambo about Pup quitting the bait game and the inherent ramifications it entailed; primarily the purchasing of all the requisite ingredients and the grim, messy task of mixing and rolling them into finished boilies. As I tensioned the last bungee strap over my hilariously declared 'slimmed down kit' in preparation for the fifteen-minute gutbuster of a push to The Lake, I was still unsure which revelation was going to cause the most angst. I hadn't felt inclined to mention the subject of welcoming Hobbes into Family Williams last night, but Rambo had to be told about Pup today. At least I would soon have a 'going ballistic' yardstick (I couldn't see much genial laughter occurring), one laid down by the Terminator with Tackle to compare with Sophie's eventual thoughts on getting a family pet with the associated litter tray/gross food odours, fur deposits, clawed upholstery, cat-snagged clothing and dead creatures presented on the back doorstep by way of a 'Thank You' note for accommodation provided.

Halfway through the push up the incline to The Lake, with beads of perspiration forming on my brow, my heart thumping in my chest and air rasping in and out of my lungs, I suddenly remembered Sylvester would be with Rambo. Rambo and son. 'Rambo & Son, the work's never done, there's always something new', the line from the old song flitted across my head. I wondered if I had ever seriously imagined that as an actual possibility? Looking back, I guess not. And with Steffi as the mother? Definitely not. An ex-porn star and now a mother? Not so incredulous, I suppose, yet, to my mind, an unlikely and somehow incompatible combination, particularly when you threw a character like Rambo into the mix. Mind you, if big budget mainstream TV like Game of Thrones was riddled with porn stars, why not the odd one at the local primary school drop off zone? It was simply a case of quantifying motherly chores alongside 'stuff' leading ladies in porn have done. I stopped and mopped my brow. Briefly, my mind pondered on a future Sylvester's career options, one tilted by genetic inheritance and parental stereotyping.

Hmmm.

"Just concentrate on pushing the barrow, Williams," I muttered to myself.

For once, I did as I told myself and closed down the window in my head.

After another five minutes or so, the terrain eventually levelled out and to the relief of my tiring body an expanse of water became visible. I had made it to the bottom bay of The Lake where the path from the car park emerged adjacent. I stopped walking and straightened upright, my hands releasing the barrow's handles. As I stood unencumbered by my kit, I curved my spine the opposite way to its most recent posture, thrusting my stomach forward to try and ease the nagging pain in my lower back. Then, I rolled my head from side to side easing the stiffness in my neck and shoulder muscles. Finally, my Pilates session now completed, I wiped my brow with the heel of my hand and took in the view.

The dense broad-leaved trees surrounding The Lake were just starting to hint at the colour green as nature began her yearly cycle of renewal. In contrast to this, the track around The Lake was rutted and brown, made so by the constant passage of anglers to swims over winter months. The recent lack of rain meant the ground wasn't muddy, but it remained soft. The lack of sunlight on the banks, forever in the partial shade of the well-established trees, meant the ground never really got the chance to fully dry out. The bark chippings in the swims I could see from where I was standing, if I was being critical, could have done with topping up. Another job to do, I noted.

The Lake itself, serene and silent, barely a ripple on its surface, was not only devoid of movement but also aquatic vegetation – it was far too early for the five sets of pads to be up in the water. These most iconic plants, forever linked with carp and carp fishing, were sadly nearly always absent during my sessions on The Lake. By the time they were in their pomp and glory I had moved on to fishing The Pit and by my return in early winter they had almost always inevitably died off. A shame, but it was the way it was meant to be. The Lake was for the winter and The Pit for the rest of the year. It was always intended thus.

The years had flown by since Rambo and I had opened The Lake, after stocking it with Mr Kane's carp – the ones with the inherent genetic predisposition to feed heavily during the winter. Hamworthy Fisheries, (venue plurality – Michael Brown's origin concept), had gone from strength to strength over that time. The Pit had continued its dominance to remain, head and shoulders above the rest, the finest carp fishery in the UK, while The Lake had thrived beyond even my and Rambo's hopes and aspirations. The Pit, currently holding the country's largest carp by some distance and complemented by many backup fish around the sixty and fifty pound mark, plus a fantastic head of forties and thirties, was an incredible water. Equally, The Lake had also become something quite special. Much smaller than The Pit, at around four acres, and originally stocked with fifty-eight fish, this estate lake had morphed somewhat from the initial idea. Originally, Rambo and I had set it up as a winter runs water, somewhere to spend a cold day with a great chance of having your rod bent by a good sized fish. However, over the years it had gradually changed into something much more fascinating.

Over ten years of pressure, coupled with the restriction on space – every square inch of the water was there to be easily cast at – had created a venue where stealth, watercraft, cute tactics and intimate understanding had become the watchwords for success. This was as true a statement in the summer as in the winter because, thanks to our original stocking policy, the fish were almost as catchable in the short, cold days as they were in the long, hot ones. Fish well, at any time of year, and you would be rewarded. Get it wrong, your location not right for the day, fish heavy-handed and with no real class, use ill-considered bait application and you would struggle. To summarise; The Lake afforded its anglers with rewards parable to that of their individual technique and approach. The carp were catchable, all year round, if you got it right, and the balance of success to effort – applied thoughtful effort, not grinding just-putting-in-the-hours effort – was virtually perfect. In a nutshell, the fish were up for it if your angling skills were up to it.

Casting my gaze over to The Far Side (see Gary Larson), pretty much central to the four acre body of water, I saw Luke's bivvy pitched in Seb's. No doubt with him ensconced inside, perched on a bedchair, endlessly toying with a monofilament string of helicopter beads acting as angling Rosary beads. Up to my left, on the near side of The Lake, stood a two-man bivvy. Standing alongside it, arms folded and legs astride, I spotted the unmistakable figure of a huge man in camouflage clothing scanning the water. A man, should you have no clue as to who the individual was, whose whole demeanour somehow screamed out a warning. One like, 'Don't fuck with me if you want your head to remain attached to your neck'. Even from a distance of ninety yards (or twenty-two point five wraps (yawn) if you use twelve footers and you're into that kind of thing) the aura and power emanating from his being was disconcerting. Eyeing my long-time buddy, fishing and business partner, I briefly tried to analyse exactly what it was about Rambo's body language and posture that was so intimidating. Yeah, sure he was big fucker and sported an aggressive haircut, if there is such a thing, but that alone couldn't account for it. I shrugged. Whatever. He was on my side and that was the most important thing. I took hold of my barrow and started off towards him.

A gentle lob cast away, Rambo spotted me in his peripheral vision, or perhaps heard me, and turned in my direction.

"All right, boy?" he called out jovially. "Survived the push, I see."

To the unwitting, this might have seemed an innocuous comment. To all the original and subsequent members of The Lake it had a hidden meaning, one concerning another tiny piece of the ever-growing history of The Lake. Seb the Slaughterer, abattoir worker and prolific red meat eater, had collapsed and died from a massive coronary on the push. On the way back. Going downhill. After fishing a forty-eight hour session in the swim Luke was in. I suppose it's easy to be wise in hindsight, but Seb really should have rationed his intake of rashers, slowed down his consumption of sausages, cut out the cutlets and most definitely forgone the fillets. However, he hadn't and instead it had been a culinary case of Carry On Carnivore. Bucketfuls of bad cholesterol had gradually built up and run their course around his body – or rather, to be accurate, they hadn't. What they *had* done was choke his blood supply, like vehicles in a multiple pile-up where a four-lane arterial motorway had suddenly and unexpectedly converged into a single lane tunnel – at night, in thick fog – just to the south of his heart.

As a consequence, the ambulance crew in attendance had done their own medicinal version of the push – not that they had bothered with any of Seb's gear. Rambo and I were left to deal with it. In a way, there was precious little difference between what the paramedics had moved and what we had moved. Sadly, both Seb and his gear were inanimate, lifeless objects by the time they had been taken away.

I can't pretend the episode of Seb's passing was particularly edifying; death and fishing have never been mutually exclusive in my and Rambo's world. But at least we had dealt with it from the standpoint of having experienced it before. For all the other members it had been a far different matter and in the immediate aftermath of Seb's death the incident became *the* topic of conversation, usurping fish captures, 'going baits' and the usual membership gossip. Some had seen it as a terrible tragedy, others had philosophised dying whilst partaking in your life's passion wasn't such a bad way to go. Personally speaking, I felt as if Seb had needed a fair few more miles on the clock for me to be able to concur with the latter sentiment.

Naturally enough, human nature being as it is, once Seb had been laid to rest, The Lake membership had soon returned to normal. Within weeks, his demise had faded from minds, and therefore from conversation, and stopped being the topic on everyone's lips when on the bank. Even so, every now and then a member had repeated an anecdote involving him, or retold one of his horrendously non-PC jokes and this had brought him back into our memories, if only for a fleeting time. Just long enough to make him a part of present day happenstance. It had been on one of these occasions when I'd had the notion to name a swim after our lost member – the last one he ever fished. To a man, The Lake members had agreed and Seb's Swim had been born as a fitting tribute to the deceased abattoir operative. I would like to think, if Seb is watching down on us (the ghost on The Pit? Remember? Everything, it seems, is possible), that he appreciates the gesture.

And what to make of it all in retrospect? That, at least, was patently clear. One man's meat is another man's access into a top fishery. Well, it definitely was for Eccentric Ed anyway – the angler who replaced Seb. Dead man's shoes and all that.

"Just about," I said, answering Rambo's question. "Doesn't get any easier, though. No matter how many times I do it."

"You're letting yourself go, boy," Rambo admonished.

I rolled my eyes and grinned ruefully. There may have been a small element (a large element, if I'm honest) of truth in Rambo's words. I hadn't been to the gym/for a jog/taken part in any exercise for years. And my trousers were getting tighter. And not because Sophie had put them on too hot a wash.

"Not me, mate. I'm getting younger and fitter by the day," I said, parking the barrow's front wheel a few feet from Rambo's combat boots.

Rambo smiled. "That'd be a neat trick to pull off."

At that moment, a young boy's head popped out of the large bivvy's opening. A pair of bright blue eyes set beneath a shock of spiky blond hair spotted me and his mouth turned into a smile.

"Guten Morgen, Onkle Matt. Fischen Sie heute?"

"You're not talking to Mum, Sylvester. English, please," Rambo told him.

"Good morning, Uncle Matt. Are you fishing today?" Sylvester repeated.

Whatever language Sylvester was using didn't matter. My heart melted and I smiled at the boy. A father and son going fishing. It would only be a matter of time before I too could replicate this desirable concept. In a few short years, Adam would be old enough to accompany me to The Lake. In my mind's eye, I pictured the years spreading out before the pair of us, ones where he gradually learnt from me as we fished together and, as he grew in stature – physically and in terms of his fishing prowess – how he would eventually surpass me. I pictured a more distant future, one with him now guiding me, coming up with new ideas and tactics, a better angler than myself – the pupil now the teacher. I saw him waiting patiently for me to catch up as we pushed our gear to The Lake, him in his physical prime, myself older, greyer and slower. 'Come on, Dad! We can't keep those carp waiting for us to catch them!' And then, much more in the future, there was Adam's son – me a grandfather! – and I was showing the young boy, who looked a bit like me, all my old capture photos, both digital and hard copy. 'Wow, Grandad! They're massive! You've caught loads of big ones!' Tilting my head, I modestly replied, 'Well, I guess I've caught my fair share.'

Back in the here and now, Sylvester glanced up at his dad as if considering his next move and, throwing the paperback he had in his hand to the floor, suddenly launched himself out of the bivvy and started to run full pelt towards me.

"Attack!" he screamed, and my dream bubble instantly popped.

Now, I am no stranger to Sylvester's boisterous nature and his love of play fighting. Unfortunately, neither are my testicles. My delicate bits have been at a seemingly optimum height for some time now to be regularly caught by flailing haymakers during his unheralded spontaneous assaults. And believe me, regular occurrence and physical familiarity do nothing to help overcome or lessen the sickening pain. What does help is protection – in the form of padding, rather than hired hoodlums. With the distance between us now halved and it being apparent I had been somewhat negligent in opting out of fishing a two-day session wearing a cricket box, I quickly tore my packed-away sleeping bag off my barrow and cuddled it tightly across my midriff and reproductive organs. Managing to get to a state of

'Shields up, Captain' within the required timescale, Sylvester thudded harmlessly into my padded wall. For an instant, I felt the warm glow of self-satisfaction as his wild onslaught was easily absorbed by my five season bag.

My smugness was short lived. What I hadn't banked on was the high kinetic energy of Sylvester's attack. I had stupidly forgotten what a big and powerful boy he was for his age. The impact knocked me backwards and pushed the backs of my knees into one of the barrow handles, causing my knees to bend as nature intended. Off balance and past the point of no return, I had no option other than to collapsed backwards over the two handles. With angular metal digging into my lower back and side, I twisted and rolled off the listing barrow, dropping my sleeping bag as I instinctively put out my hands to protect myself as I hit the ground face down. Almost immediately, Sylvester jumped on my back. With his knees astride my torso, full weight on my middle back, I suddenly felt a cold pressure on my right temple.

"Go ahead, make my day, Uncle Matt," Sylvester threatened.

Trying not to panic as I attempted to rationalise my concern Sylvester might have a shooter in his hand, and desperately forcing myself to remember that I was the adult, I asked in a voice as calm as I could muster, "Is that a gun you're holding against my head, Sylvester?"

Sylvester rolled off my back and showed me, waving a lurid orange-coloured weapon in front of my face. "Look!" he exclaimed. "It's a Glock! A Glock 17! Cool, eh? Dad got it as an early tenth birthday present so I could get used to carrying a gun all the time."

Rambo, who had been standing and chuckling at the whole event, must have noted the earlier look of terror on my face.

"Calm down, Matt. It's only a spring BB gun. You couldn't kill a mouse with it, not unless you clubbed it to death with the handle."

"I knew that," I lied, standing up and dusting myself down. There'd be bruises later, I could tell. "Anyway, what's the book you're reading, Sylvester?" I enquired, keen to move off the subject of firearms.

Sylvester tucked his gun into his trousers and ran back towards the discarded paperback, picked it up and returned to my side.

"It's really good," he enthused. "I've read fifty pages since we've been here."

I flicked a glance at Rambo. "I bet your Dad has told you off for not watching the water," I commented, tongue in cheek.

"There's not much to watch," Sylvester said, his nose wrinkling. "It's just water. My book's more interesting."

Ignoring the young boy's best practice carp fishing heresy, I took the brand new paperback from him and scanned the front and back cover. The novel, 'Night Bites', seemed to be based around the otherworldly events occurring in a posh home counties boarding school – one exclusively catering for teenage vampires, werewolves and zombies.

"Cool," I said, slipping into Sylvester's vernacular and handing him the book back. "So, which rod is yours?" I asked, nodding towards the pair in front of the bivvy.

"The one that gets the first bite! Dad said we should take it in turns. I shotgunned the first take," Sylvester answered, a big grin on his face.

"Good call!" I remarked, giving Sylvester an exaggerated thumbs-up. "Just got to get one, that's all."

Sylvester hunched his shoulders. "Dad said we would." A few seconds of silence held sway as the young boy lapsed into a contemplative mood. "See ya!" he pronounced and I watched him disappear back into the bivvy.

I turned to Rambo. "It could be the new game he's downloaded on to his iPad," he told me, by way of an explanation for Sylvester's actions. "Or he wants to get back to the book. He's a good little angler, but he can't just sit and doing nothing. He's always got to have something on the go to entertain him."

"Him and every other kid in the country," I observed. "So, what time did you get here?"

"Just after nine this morning."

"Was Luke already here?"

"Yeah."

I nodded and paused, knowing our conversational small talk was over. I couldn't be bothered to tell Rambo about Luke's problems seeing as we had one of our own he needed to know about.

"I'm afraid I've got some news to tell you," I started.

Rambo rotated his head towards me. "Bad?" he asked.

I wobbled my head from side to side to indicate I was weighing up the situation. "Surprising, certainly. More majorly inconvenient than bad."

Rambo puffed out his cheeks with an air of resignation. "Come on then, boy. Let's hear it."

I took a deep breath. "You're not going to believe this, and this is one hundred per cent genuine and not a wind up, Pup's selling up and quitting the bait game," I told him.

Rambo afforded me a prolonged and overstated blink and a sharp backwards movement of his head. "Wow! I wasn't expecting you to say that."

"That's exactly what *I* said to him when he told me!" I replied, with a hint of incredulity. "Want to know why?" I asked, my tone changing. "And what the deal is?"

"The *deal*?" Rambo queried.

"The deal giving us continued access to our exclusive, revolutionary, indented, dirty brown bottom bait boilie."

"Is this the 'majorly inconvenient' bit?"

"Yeah. Though more for me than you, I think it'd be fair to say."

Rambo's mood suddenly seemed to lighten. "Okay," he said, chirpily. "Tell me all about it. If I start to doze off, prod me with my landing net handle."

21

"Any particular place?" I asked, sarcastically.

"Not the bollocks," Rambo replied looking down and indicating his nether regions with a circling index finger. "Apparently, it hurts like hell when you get hit down there. Do you know, I've actually seen a five-year-old kid bring down a full-grown man with just *one* playful punch to the gonads."

"Well, perhaps in that instance the five-year-old kid should have been more adequately supervised by his father," I responded, pointedly.

Rambo laughed. He didn't exactly say, 'That's my boy!' like Spike the bulldog used to say to Tyke in the Tom and Jerry cartoons, but it was implicit.

"Sorry, Matt. I promise to tell him to go easy on you in the future. I'll tell him his favourite uncle is getting a bit long in the tooth for rough and tumble."

"Thank you very much. You're all heart," I said, trying to maintain my caustic attitude. "And I can see how much you had that sentiment in mind by how helpful you were earlier."

"That's not fair," Rambo answered, earnestly. "I would have stepped in if I'd thought he was going to pull the trigger."

"*Really?*"

Rambo's gaze shifted self-consciously to the pair of rods a few yards away. "Pup," he said. "Tell me about Pup."

So I told him about Pup. By the time I had finished, Rambo's chirpiness had dissipated quicker than a PVA bag lobbed into a hot bath.

"Bollocks! What is it with him and bloody women?"

Although this was evidently a rhetorical question, I took it upon myself not to answer it and indicated as such through the medium of body language. Rambo acknowledged my paucity of input with a twitch of his head, and pressed on to other matters.

"I'll tell you what, boy, the idea of having to roll bait again doesn't sit too well. Not one bit!" Rambo shook his head in disbelief and lapsed into bitter self-recrimination. One which I couldn't help but notice included myself. "Why the fucking hell couldn't we have had the foresight to have kept our stock levels higher?" he asked. "How come we never thought to prepare for eventualities like this? Say, like having five or six hundred kilos of the stuff all ready rolled and stashed away in a shit load of freezers somewhere."

I didn't have much of an answer to that question either, seeing as what Rambo was suggesting was easier said than done – even if we had thought of it in the first place. Where on earth do you keep a shit load of freezers stuffed full with hundreds of kilos of our exclusive bait, for a start? *Not* in the functional wooden clubhouse at The Pit, that's for sure. Not where all the other members could see our bait, help themselves to a few handfuls, smell them, taste them, have them chemically and nutritionally analysed, subsequently duplicated and finally fish with them. (Nickedbaitphobia can be a terribly debilitating thing.) Instead, what I did mention was however much bait the hypothetically well-prepared Matt and Rambo might

22

have put into stock, should they have found an adequate storage facility, it would have still only delayed the inevitable.

"But he might have been back and making it by the time that lot of bait had run out!" Rambo countered. "Do you really think this school teacher and him are going to hit it off? That it'll last?" Rambo saw the look of doubt on my face. "Exactly!"

"I know, but the thing is," I began to explain, "I got the distinct impression he'd had enough of making bait full stop. Forget whether it pans out with her. I honestly think he's completely and utterly sick to death of rolling bait. I'm pretty convinced he'll never make up another ten-kilo bait mix in his life." I put on my most harrowing face. "He *actually* insisted on me calling him Pete, for God's sake. He said his name wasn't Pup anymore."

"What's in a name, though?" Rambo asked.

"Well, Mr Shakespeare, you know the answer already." I shrugged, "If he's not making them, he's not fucking making them. Whatever his moniker."

# Chapter 3

My rods were out and baited up, with both of them – I thought it fair to say – bang on the money. One, a bottom bait (you know the one) surrounded by a couple of pouchfuls of 10mm boilies (you know the ones), margin fished under an overhanging branch. The other, a single pop-up (Pete's, Pup's, whatever) fished an inch off the deck at around thirty yards on a line I knew was a patrol route. Dry side, my bivvy was up; bedchair with sleeping bag atop plus additional but unspecified kit precisely located within – and the kettle was on. Game on! Let the session begin! May the cursed Gods of Blanking be cast into the Dungeon of No Escape; May the Fairy Carpmother bring forth her cornucopia of concentrated Rundust and sprinkle it liberally on my noble Delkims; Let their shrill call be heard across land and water.

Or something like that.

It was mid-morning and the buzz of anticipation was coursing through my body. The buzz of the anticipation of catching a carp; the buzz that never gets old. Unlike myself, despite my earlier contradictory declaration to Rambo. From my side-saddle seating position on my bedchair, I leant forward and lifted the whistling kettle off my stove. Pouring out the boiling water, for some reason, I wondered how many mugs of tea I had drunk while fishing and what my catch rate to teas drunk ratio might be. Intriguingly, I considered what if, by some strange unfathomable and inexplicable law of universal causality, that number was a relatively fixed ratio. If so, by definition, that would mean I could improve my catch rate simply by drinking more tea. I might have to get up for a piss six times a night, but I would be hauling! Sod the extra milk/tea bag/fuel costs, check out these capture photos! I laughed to myself. Capture shots. Pup really should have got all his scanned on to a hard drive, then he wouldn't have had to have gone to the trouble of blasting them off his walls and ceilings and incinerating them. True, Blue Tack shares would have slumped as a by-product, but then again digitalisation was killing off many an industry.

I lifted my mug, tea now made, took a first sip and grimaced. My back and side were sore and tender from my unexpected piss-poor Fosbury Flop over the barrow's handles, let alone from the physical expenditure of the push. Despite this, thinking back over recent physical ailments, Sylvester was easily outstripping aging regards to damaging my body. I knew the lad wasn't doing it on purpose as such, it was… well, what was it? He was son of Rambo. That's what it was. That was the answer. How could I expect anything else? Like father like son is the maxim and with Sylvester it appeared to be a maxim set on maximum. Christ knows what he'd be like when the testosterone kicked in. I envisioned a sixteen-year-old Sylvester kicking off alongside a fifty something Rambo, the pair of them dispensing physical violence upon some hapless fool who had somewhere crossed a line. Something to look forward to in the future, I suppose.

I glanced out through the rising steam from my mug at the two rods reclining upon my trusty Chris Brown rod rests. I was using my old Ballista Slims again, the burgundy dipped ones, I had used on The Pit years ago. Now somewhat softened from their original 2¾lb test curve rating, they were ideal for a smaller water like The Lake where casting was limited to around eighty yards at an absolute maximum. They still possessed enough power to deal with the large carp present, but the real joy of their employment lay in their fish-playing qualities. Soft and designed to bend right through to the butt, they were a delight to play a carp on. Every surge of a hooked fish was there to be felt via the tangible feedback of a bending rod. A tippy broomstick they most definitely were not. Every lunge while playing a fish was counterbalanced by an accommodating gradually increasing arc of low diameter carbon fibre tubing. The rods had played a small part in my own personal carping journey over the years and it was great to continue using them in an environment where they could still shine brightly.

I had decided to couple the rods with a brand new pair of Shimano X-Aero 8000 Baitrunners, the ones sporting a single handle, from last season. These relatively small reels were a perfect partnership for such a slim, light rod and I loved using them for the close in/margin fishing style required on The Lake. I had wondered why a few of the members, especially the younger ones, employed heavy Big Pit style reels and 3lb+ test curve rods on a venue like The Lake. When I had mentioned it in passing to Rambo, he had pointed out if someone could only afford one set-up then the beefed up route would always take precedence. An angler could 'get away' with a more powerful kit on venues similar to The Lake, yet still be well prepared for bigger venues.

Rambo was right, of course, but I had still felt carp fashion and carping trends had something to do with it. I had told him you only had to go back to the 1980s when entry level carp rods were typically rated at, by today's standard, a piffling 1¾lb test curve. 'Easy, Grandad. I know nostalgia isn't what it used to be, but that *is* over thirty years ago!' he had replied with condescension. It had shut me up. I mean, who wants to turn into a carp fishing version of their dad? Always banging on about how things used to be in the past, and how the kids of today don't know they're born. I didn't admit it to Rambo at the time, because it contradicted my argument, but I would feel undergunned using the slims on The Pit.

On the subject of The Pit, Pup's imminent departure to Venice meant there was shortly to be a space on that water. Filling it wouldn't be an issue, other than the usual dilemma of finding a suitable angler. Over recent years we had 'promoted', for want of a better word, several anglers from The Lake on to The Pit when members had left what Rambo and I considered the premier water of the two. The policy had worked out well and everybody who had been promoted had turned out fine – despite Rambo's original mentalist credentials for The Lake's membership. A policy he had continued to employ when we had interviewed for the vacated places of those promoted.

On the whole, membership of both venues had been relatively stable over the years they had been up and running. Few wanted out once they were in, but inevitably there was a gradual changing of the guard, so to speak, as the years crept by. Seb's death specifically and more general issues such as financial pressure, vocational pressure, partner/home life pressure and carp catching pressure had all contributed to personnel changes. For example, how much longer would Luke stomach it if he didn't land a carp soon? How long *do* you bang your head against a brick wall, and pay good money for the privilege of doing so, before deciding, 'Fuck this for a game of soldiers!' and sloping off with your tail between your legs? If memory serves me correctly, I think there have been around half a dozen members who have left because of a poor success rate – although none were brave enough to admit it at the time, all citing other bogus issues!

The other big change to come about over recent years was the now far more widespread knowledge of Hamworthy Fisheries as compared to in the past. Although Rambo and I had never admitted a 'name' into either of our fisheries – and believe me there was no shortage of them knocking on the door, desperate to catch our fish and tell the world about it – and an outright publicity ban regards to magazine articles or features still being in place, it had proved impossible to keep things low key. Social media; Facebook, YouTube, Snapchat, Twitter, WhatsApp, Instagram, Vimeo and CarpPorn, to name but a few, were all now well-established outlets for the word to get out. Ones virtually impossible for us to keep tabs on, let alone control. All it needed was a single member to send a picture of a huge fish he had caught to a friend and then, thanks to everyone being connected to virtually everyone else, it would go 'carp fishing viral'.

The Pit in particular, now received far more publicity than Rambo and I cared for. The internet plus smartphones and all their apps, plus 4G coverage, had shifted the goalposts well beyond their original position. Short of entering into an annual contract with Cheltenham GCHQ and getting them to trace words like 'pit', 'seventy', 'sixty', 'whacker' and 'lump' – instead of their usual terrorist activity markers – and once having pinpointed the individual responsible paying a hitman to take them out, there didn't seem much else we could do. (No doubt costs would be prohibitive regards utilising the aforementioned services. And that's before considering the legality of the crime of Pit-caught-carp-publicised-by-social-media being punishable by death). Asking members not to post capture shots on Facebook or Twitter? Insisting on being in their WhatsApp group so we could monitor them? It was never going to happen.

No, the genie was well and truly out of the bottle and nothing could put it back. Rambo and I had soon learnt the lesson that in a free society it's pretty nigh impossible to control what people want to say or do on the web and on their phones. Consequently, word got out. Big time. To Rambo, the ultimate man of action, all of social media was an anathema and despite him appreciating its power, he had no time for it – as either a user or as an observer. I kept him up to date on the situation and, as Supreme Fishery Leader, the constant whine of wannabe members keen to get in on the action incessantly bombarded my eardrums rather than his.

A typical verbal membership application from someone about whom I had no prior knowledge, a membership application 'cold call' if you like, might go something like this. Firstly, I would hear a preliminary waffling introduction from the punter where he told me his carping life story, how experienced he was at handling big carp and how good he was at casting, watercraft, bait application and tying up a hinged stiff rig. Listening until I had a chance to slide a word in edgeways, I would inform him, despite now being fully cognisant of his carping attributes, it still made no difference with regard to what I was going to tell him.

'And what is it you're going to tell me?'

'That we're full up. There are no spaces.'

'No spaces at all?'

'None at the moment.'

'So...' Sound of brain grinding. 'Are there likely to be any spaces in the future?'

'Well, obviously spaces do crop up from time to time. Although very, very rarely.'

'Is there a waiting list, then?'

'There is a waiting list. An extremely *lengthy* one.'

'Ok, I appreciate that, but if possible I really *would* like to go on it if I can.'

'You can go on the list if you want. Don't expect any quick results, though.'

'What, you mean I might not get in, in the next couple of years?'

'I can categorically state you *definitely* won't get in, in the next couple of years.'

'How about if I slip you an extra ton as a sweetener, for when a space comes up?'

'Wouldn't make any difference.'

'*Really?*'

'Really.'

'Right... It'd be in cash...'

'Cash, cheque, Postal Order, bank transfer or gold doubloons, it won't make any odds. We don't operate on those sort of terms.'

'Fair play, no, that's good. No worries. Sorry if I've offended. I can still go on the list, though? Shall I give you my details? As I said, my name is...'

'*If* you could email them, that'd be best.'

'Ok. Sure. What's the address?'

'matt.williams487@gmail.com.'

Painstakingly slow regurgitation of email address needing my confirmation.

'Okay. Thanks. I'll email my details over straightaway.'

And he would.

And then I would delete them.

That conversation was typical of one when I was in a good mood. Often I would hear the oh-so-familiar opener and just say, 'Sorry. We're full and so is the waiting list' and disconnect them.

I do genuinely have a waiting list. It's got about twenty names on it. What's the point of having any more?

Three years ago, in an attempt to stop the onslaught, I changed my mobile phone number and email address and told members not to pass them on to anyone who wasn't a member. Rambo did the same for his mobile. It helped for a while. Until the cold calls gradually started over again. Members had leaked them to friends, no doubt when put under pressure, who in turn had leaked them to other friends.

It proved what I had known for some time and the undeniable truth was evident; it was now impossible to control the pulling power of the carp in The Pit, and to a lesser extent, The Lake. The Pit carp had reached the point of critical mass where they were simply too big for carp anglers to ignore. Their magnetic force was too strong and every iron filing of a carp angler seemed remorselessly drawn to them – like a moth to a brazier of burning carp trophy shots, or like bees around a six-yard skip full of honey. Those who had seen pictures or videos of them on their phone or PC, thanks to a mate of a buddy of a pal of a mucker who knew someone who was best friends with the guy holding the chunk, were intoxicated by their size and beauty. There were now eight fish in The Pit capable of smashing the UK carp record, should anyone dare claim it, possibly a dozen depending on the time of year they got caught. In days gone by, the carp fishing grapevine was an efficient enough tool in itself. Now, spliced with modern day communications, it was a mind blowing tour de force. Word was out. See that blue speck on the map? There be monsters!

Perhaps one method of managing the rush would be to up the annual membership fee to a ridiculous amount of money. One so high it effectively put The Pit out of financial reach for ninety-nine per cent of all carp anglers. It was a route I felt, as the owner, strongly against taking and Rambo, as my trusted lieutenant, fully agreed. For a start, if the money rose to such an exorbitant level we were sure we would lose all the existing members. Decent members, some of whom had been involved more or less right from the start – from the Michael Brown days, before even Rambo and I had appeared on the scene. This wouldn't have been fair on them because they had all proved to be good members, so far. (Rambo and I had weeded out the bad ones years ago.) Another reason against such a policy was the abhorrent idea of it creating a membership based purely on financial elitism, one leading to a narrow, less diverse group of anglers fishing The Pit.

Besides, the likelihood of upping fees being a complete panacea seemed unlikely knowing what carp anglers were like. You would still get people phoning up, the deluded ones, the ones convinced they might win the lottery or get left a sizeable inheritance. You would still get pestered by the ones prepared to sell the family home, pimp their girlfriend/wife and the ones supposedly on the cusp of untold riches because they had cracked cold fusion, perpetual motion, an elixir for eternal youth or the next must-have killer app. And there would still be those wanting to go on the list in case 'something crops up and I can suddenly afford it'. Maybe the answer was to charge a couple of grand to go on the list. That might sort out the tyre kickers.

Nevertheless, it wasn't our way and I could never imagine it becoming so. Membership for The Pit was still expensive, but not massively excessive. I was happy with what I was making out of it regards to remuneration, as was the case for both of us with our cheaper second water, The Lake. Over the years, we had allowed membership fees to rise by inflation. Income was sufficient to convince our other halves we were earning enough out of it for it to be classed as a vague form of 'work', whereas the truth was we were more concerned with it funding our fishing lifestyle. All in all, we were in a great place and it was a place Rambo and I were determined to protect. To protect our incredible stock of fish, to protect our waters, to protect our financial interests and to protect our fishing. Maintaining it, in the burning beam of limelight we now found ourselves by virtue of becoming victims of our own success, somehow now felt more tenuous. As if by our very success we were vulnerable. Mind you, I could hardly complain about my carp being too big, now could I? If it was a problem, then as the saying goes, it was a nice problem to have.

My ears pricked up. The distant sound of a buzzer! I looked out of my bivvy and to my delight, across The Lake, I saw Luke scuttling towards his rods to hit the take. Disappointingly, I noticed he never made the sign of the cross over his chest like a Premiership footballer coming on as a sub. Instead, he hit the take with all the calm and poise of a cocaine-addled learner driver trying to powerslide a Porsche 911 around a gravel-strewn hairpin. First, he slipped and nearly fell arse over head as he lunged for his rod and second, having managed to get upright and his legs under some semblance of control, he committed the all-time classic carping misdemeanour – striking without tightening the clutch. Leaning forward on my bedchair, soaking up the drama from across the water, I could almost smell the panic in the air.

Frantically, with a boxing glove-clad hand, the Christian Carper tightened the clutch – only by too much. His rod was yanked forward from something way past vertical to a warning light flashing, siren alarm screaming, dangerously near horizontal orientation. (It's called getting 'flat-rodded' in the trade and is synonymous with hooking a mahoosive carp!) More front of reel fumbling finally returned the clutch to a half sensible tension. I nodded my approval as his rod returned to a proper fish-playing position, a wry smile on my face. I could understand the stress he was under. Over a year to get this one take. Who wouldn't be bricking it?

Luke now appeared to have things under control, only for me to realise, a few seconds later and much to my bemusement, nothing could be further from the truth. The earlier elementary mistakes hadn't been eradicated and were still continuing. As the playing of the fish progressed, it became clear indecision was haunting Luke's every physical move. This indecision, undoubtedly caused by the paranoia of losing a long-awaited fish, was playing havoc with his thought process and creating a huge uncertainty of purpose. Twice Luke shuffled down the bank in order to get closer to the hooked fish and twice he thought it a bad idea and shuffled back. When he did eventually gain on the fish and succeeded in getting it in much closer, he then backed off the clutch. This in itself wasn't unreasonable thinking, he was no doubt concerned at the increased chance of a hook pull now there was less line stretch to help buffer the fish's powerful runs. The trouble lay in his slackening it off too much. This action permitted the fish to get up a head of steam and take line from him time and time again. Watching him was so frustrating I actually swore under my breath for Luke to 'Fucking sort it!' Eventually, after several in, out, shake it all about escapades, Luke got it right. The fish only gained a few yards on each run and stayed closer in, boiling on the surface five or so yards out.

"Finally!" I exclaimed to myself in agitation.

Luke was now in the driving seat – the unresolved problem being he was still a cocaine-addled learner driver trying to powerslide a Porsche 911 around a gravel-strewn hairpin. The final minor obstacle lay in the fact it was his right-hand rod that had gone off. Luke was also playing the fish to the right of his pod, but his landing net was to the left of his left-hand rod, still in its original set-up position. I counted three aborted attempts to pick up the landing net, each one halted by the carp's lunges draining Luke's paranoia-depleted CPU capacity.

I imagined him thinking: 'Ok, better get my landing net ready. Just bend over and... Nope. No! Carp's getting a move on! Forget the net! Forget the net! Oh, God! Please don't come off. Please don't come off. All right. Okay. Back under control. Under control now. That's better. I can get the net now. Just move over a bit and get the net... No. No! Leave the net! Leave the net! Don't let the fish come off. Concentrate on not letting the fish get off. You *have* to land this fish! Easy. Easy. That's fine. Everything's okay. Can't land the fish without the net, though. Get the net. Need the net to net the fish. Just have to get over there and carefully pick up the net... Look out! It's running! It's running again...'

To be honest, it was getting a bit embarrassing watching Luke's horror show of carping ineptitude and my original empathy had by now eroded to irritation by his lack of application. I watched with an ever-growing sense of detachment as he finally managed to get hold of his net, slid it into the water, eased the now surface-wallowing carp back towards it only for his rod to ping back violently as the hook pulled out. Luke's whole body slumped, his rod dropped to the floor and he pulled his head back to stare into the afternoon sky. I couldn't be bothered to watch anymore and swung my legs up on to my bedchair to stare at the inside of my bivvy. It was no good Luke looking to God for salvation. Sometimes you have to look to yourself. Christ, I had tipped him the swim and the spots. What more did he want? Me to go round and land it for him?

Surprised at how grumpy I had got at Luke for cocking it up, I was only too pleased to watch someone else have a go at landing a carp. Not *as* pleased as if it had been me playing one, obviously, but less than one hour after Luke's debacle I felt relieved to see Sylvester scramble out to a take on Rambo's left-hand rod. Keen to observe the budding young carper at closer quarters, I popped my Delkim receiver into the leg pocket of my cargo pants and sauntered down to the action.

With the reel seemingly buried in his groin and the butt section of the rod reaching down to his knees, I found Sylvester leaning his whole body back on his heels as he grappled with what was evidently a good fish. With his right hand up towards the butt ring and his left tenaciously gripping the reel handle, Sylvester's attitude and body language was the antithesis of Luke's. Positive, aggressive and sure, everything about the young man screamed assurance.

"Looks a good one, Sylvester!" I proclaimed as I approached.

"Yeah. Think so, Uncle Matt," the young boy answered, without taking his eyes off where his line entered the water.

"Keep the tip up, Sylvester. Remember what I told you when we watched the other man," Rambo advised his son.

I made my way to stand alongside Rambo. "You clocked all the nonsense, then?" I asked, quietly.

Rambo nodded. "Not a pretty sight."

"He hasn't had a fish since the season before last."

"I'm not surprised if he plays them all like that."

"Let me rephrase. Not had a *take* since the season before last."

"Ouch!" Rambo answered, wincing.

The pair of us lapsed into silence as Rambo watched his son play the fish. I alternated between watching Rambo watch his son play the fish and watching it for myself. What was it I could detect in the camouflage-clad warrior by my side, as his son took several more progressive steps along the path of his father's obsession? Pride? Certainly. Love? Definitely. But what else was it? To begin with I couldn't put my finger on it – and then I saw it. Saw it in the memory of my own reaction to Luke. There! The merest hint of annoyance, fleetingly drawn across Rambo's face; a transient dissatisfaction, appearing for the briefest time span when Sylvester did something his father perceived as slightly inapposite. Of course! Rambo the hard man, Rambo the hard taskmaster! Sylvester had a lot to live up to when under the burning gaze of his father. I shifted uneasily from one foot to another, pondering on whether the pressure Luke had recently been under might prove nothing compared to the burden of expectation Sylvester was likely to experience while growing up.

What psychological pressure Rambo may or may not have been exerting on his son, the youngster seemed unfazed by it. In ten minutes of no nonsense action the fight was over and Sylvester had done his father proud. Apart from Rambo netting the fish and giving him the odd snippet of sage advice, Sylvester had landed the fish completely unaided. Advanced for his age in both technique and application, let alone physicality, the young boy was well on the way to becoming an excellent angler. Once the ritual of unhooking the fish and placing it safely into a weigh sling had been accomplished, Rambo held it up for me to shout out the one bold statistic that mattered. The needle never wavered as I peered at it. Rambo's arms were as strong as ever.

"Thirty-six eight!" I declared, reading off the Reuben Heaton scales. "That's a PB, isn't it?"

Sylvester nodded, a huge grin splitting his face.

"Well done, Sylvester! Let's get some photos," Rambo said, putting the weigh sling back on to his unhooking mat and handing me the scales. "It's a big fish. You'll be okay lifting it, won't you." It came out as a statement, not a question.

"I think so," Sylvester answered.

"I think so, too. You've been really pushing on with your weight training lately."

Rambo awkwardly flicked his eyes at me when he said this. I hoped he wasn't psychic [Hold on a minute, *I'm* the one who's meant to be psychic. Or least I used to be. Those days seem to be long gone.] because inside my head I was thinking, 'Weight training! At nine! Bloody hell!'

"Remember what I told you," Rambo continued. "If it feels like the fish is going to flap, tilt it back towards your body and hang on to it tight. Whatever you do, don't drop it. And don't worry about your clothes getting slimed up, Mum can always wash them."

Not wishing to speculate, verbally or mentally, on Steffi's apparent descent into humdrum domesticity, I put the Reuben's back in their pouch. Rambo in turn grabbed his camera from his bivvy, leaving Sylvester to care for the fish. Once the Terminator with Tackle was set and happy with the framing of the photo, he told Sylvester to get the fish out of the sling and hold it up. The young boy did as he was told, diligently clearing the sling away from the fish – no tweaked pectoral fins – and lifting it up with careful precision. Whatever exercise regime Rambo was putting his son through was paying dividends because the physical process all looked fairly effortless. Squatting on his haunches, forearms locked on top of his thighs to ease the holding of the fish's mass, Sylvester looked as if he could attain YouTube junior carp stardom at a stroke. All that was lacking, the one precious detail in our commercial era, if I was being cynical, was the atrocious lack of a tackle/bait manufacturer's hoodie or beanie hat.

I decided there and then if I ever became the proprietor of any carp kit/bait manufacturer, all my beanie hats would have a little propeller on the top; one that would spin round in the wind and power my firm's flashing LED brand logo. Not with a gross ostentatious vibe, certainly, more a knowing ironic one. And yes, you *would* be able to tell the difference.

"A bit more upright, it's leaning back to you too much," Rambo instructed. "That's better. Hold it there. Nice." The SLR fired off a fusillade of shots. "Okay, now the other side..." Once Sylvester had flipped the fish, more shutter action ensued. "Good. Yep. Okay, just let me check them... Yeah, they're fine, Sylvester. You can put her down."

With the ritual almost complete, I spoke to Rambo. "I'm going to head back to my swim now. Well done, Sylvester. Cracking fish."

"Thanks, Uncle Matt."

"Okay, boy," Rambo acknowledged. "I'll catch up with you later. Maybe tomorrow sometime I'll wander up and we can have a chat about all things Pup."

I nodded, turned and headed back up the bank to my swim. As soon as I had left their company, I couldn't help but think I was the only one on the water who hadn't had a take yet.

# Chapter 4

My lack of contribution in the runs department ended just before dark. My margin rod [*1. Torn apart whilst financially cheated (6,3)*] and after a [*2. – Encounter. Film 1945 (5)*] tussle, I landed a lovely mid-twenty [*3. Universal; Ordinary (6)*]. To say I was [*4. Dleespa Anag (7)*] to have avoided a [*5. Second of a two-worded title for a shit TV game show hosted by Terry Wogan and Les Dawson amongst others (5)*] was an understatement.

Having taken a couple of self-take photos, recast, baited up and hung out my weigh sling and retaining sack to dry on a nearby tree in the gathering darkness, I got back in my bivvy. Feeling peckish after my fish-catching exertions, I cooked some grub – a tin of Marks and Spencer chicken casserole followed by custard with fruit, a cuppa and a few Rich Tea biscuits – and settled in for the night. Inside my toasty bag, I also benefitted from a cosy internal warmth. The relief experienced in getting the session off the mark might be yet another carp fishing cliché to add to the day's collection, but was a welcome one nevertheless. I phoned Sophie to check everything was okay at home and said night-night to little Adam. Amy was too busy doing revision for her upcoming A2 exams to do more than shout 'Hi, Dad' from a distance (well, that's what she said anyway), so I had little choice other than to accept what I was offered.

The time when I had been the most important male figure in her life had long passed. I had recognised some years back it was fast approaching – like an incoming cracked-off four ounce lead cast by a directly-opposite far-margin freak – and at the time its arrival had hurt. Nowadays, there was only acceptance, the pain long having faded as my understanding of the situation increased. On hearing her voice, all one second's worth, it was hard to believe the day she was born, over eighteen years ago, was the same one as when Mr Furlington had read out Michael Brown's will to the entire membership. The will in which he had left Hamworthy Fisheries to me – much to the disgust of some of the membership. Ah, happy, if not violent and traumatic days.

With my hands clasped behind my head and staring into the blackness of my bivvy's ceiling, I returned to the present. It was a Friday night and I was a little nonplussed at the lack of anglers on The Lake. Typically, I would have expected at least a couple more to have turned up after their week's work was done. Maybe they were all at home watching high-quality US television dramas – either that or yet another cooking programme. In retrospect, I decided nobody watched television if they had something better to do because there was no need. The country only gathered around the 'box' (envelope? curve?) en masse for the odd major sporting event. Only then did the idea of watching something 'live' seem important. The rest of the time it was a case of get it when you want it. Other than that, what else it could be waylaying The Lake's membership, I had little inkling. Life, I supposed. It had a knack of inhibiting even the keenest of anglers.

Regardless of the number of anglers on The Lake and the reasons behind it, my current session was most likely to be my last before next winter. I would soon be moving on to The Pit. I suspected Rambo would too. We were now into April and it wouldn't be long before The Pit's fish began waking up. Dreaming of how it might do its first ever eighty this season, and how I might be the angler fortunate enough to catch it, I soon drifted off into the land of nod.

Some hours later, I jolted awake from my sleep. "What the f...?"

The cold, hard object that had been jammed in my temple, the one rousing me, lifted off my skin. Instantly, I recognised it as something I had experienced before.

"You're dead, Uncle Matt," the voice whispered quietly. "It's mission accomplished."

My heart was hammering into my ribcage and I felt a deep unease caused by the intrusion into my angling home – even if undertaken by a certain nine-year-old. This was somehow so very different from being yanked from behind the wall of sleep by a take.

"Fuck me, Sylvester! You frightened the life out of me! What is it with you and jamming that BB gun of yours into my temple?" I hissed into the dark, pulling myself up on to my elbows, unable to control my language due to the shock of what had just occurred.

A small, dark silhouette was kneeling down right by the side of my bedchair. He was there, right in my bivvy! Within inches of me and I hadn't heard him come in at all. He could have been doing anything in there; like stealing my gear, my bait or one of my rigs – or killing me.

"And what the hell are you doing up at this hour? It's... three in the bloody morning!" I declared, after checking my phone.

"What? Oh... Just practising."

"Practising what?"

"A night time assassination."

"*Seriously?*" I demanded, incredulously. "Shouldn't you be tucked up in your bag looking at pornography on your phone like a normal nine-year-old?" I asked, caustically, before firing off a more searching question. "Does your Dad know you're doing this?"

"No," came the sheepish reply.

"Then what the hell are you up to?"

"Dad told me a bedtime story about how he had to go and kill some nasty man when he was in the army. Behind enemy lines."

"A bedtime story?"

"Yeah. Dad tells me lots of bedtime stories about his time in the army."

"*Does* he?"

My sarcasm went over Sylvester's head and the young boy continued with his reasoning. "I wanted to pretend I was Dad. I wanted to practise," he added.

"What, practise for when you really *do* want to sneak into a carp angler's bivvy and kill him?" I enquired, thinking there were quite a few times over the years, given the requisite skill set, I might have given it a go.

"No. Practise for being a soldier. I want to be a soldier when I grow up. Just like Dad. He was a really good one, you know."

"I know he was, Sylvester. One of the very best." My annoyance with Sylvester had waned somewhat and was replaced by interest. "So, does your Dad want you to be a soldier?" I enquired, thinking the weight training reveal now made some sort of sense.

"Dad said he would never stop me from being one if I really wanted to. He said I should try for the SAS if I did decide to become one."

"And what does Mum say?"

"She says nothing was ever solved by one lot of people killing another lot of people. Dad just laughs at that. They argue about it a lot. Mum thinks I should do something else. That's why she buys me books and bought me a guitar. She pays for my guitar lessons. Dad told her being able to play guitar was usually a sign of a life lived in poverty. He said you only had to go down the town centre on a Saturday morning to see it. Mum said it was better to have a full life of poverty than to wind up dead on a battlefield fighting old men's wars."

"What about a job connected to carp fishing?" I asked, intrigued at the picture Sylvester was painting of his life and the way his parents were squabbling over its direction.

"Dad said it probably wasn't the best idea. Something about losing the reason for going in the first place. He said what you and him do couldn't ever be considered real work, even if you do make money out of it. Huh! He never says that in front of Mum," Sylvester said in a huff. "When he tells her he's going fishing, he always says he's 'off to work'."

I laughed at this. "I guess everything your Dad and I do is pretty much on our own terms. We don't have to answer to anyone else but ourselves," I explained. "We're very lucky." A silence fell over the pair of us and I have to admit my heartstrings were tugged by the young boy next me. "I'll say one thing, Sylvester, as your uncle and for what it's worth. If you do become a soldier, make sure the reason is because it's *you* who really wants to become one. It's a dangerous business, not one to go into without a very good reason."

"Oh, don't worry. I won't get hurt, Uncle Matt," Sylvester replied, earnestly. "Dad never got hurt. He'll teach me how to never get hurt."

On hearing this, my mind went into flashback as I emptied the Glock into the man about to shoot Rambo. Good as he was, Rambo wasn't Captain Scarlet and wasn't indestructible. Without me intervening, history would have noted the fact.

In the moment of the flashback, I dearly wanted to ask Sylvester if his father had ever told him how I had once saved him from certain death. Instead, something inside held me back and I couldn't bring myself to say it, as much as I wanted him to know of the daring rescue his uncle had performed. Somehow it didn't seem right to burden the young boy with a story that unpicked his father's infallibility.

"I guess what your Dad doesn't know about being a soldier isn't worth knowing," I said as an alternative. I waited a little. "I do think it's best you get back to bed, though. Now you've managed to complete your mission and bump me off. Remember, one more bite and it's your turn to strike again!"

There was a barely perceptible pause before Sylvester said, "See ya!" and shot off out of my bivvy and into the dark.

I snuggled back down into my bag, hoping Sylvester's desire to emulate his father didn't come back and bite him in the arse when he was older. Then again, maybe Steffi might win the argument and against all the odds the lad might become a pop star or an academic. I smiled to myself. Like she was ever going to win.

I had been awake, with no further action on the carp front and no further action on the Sylvester mock-murdering me in my sleep front, for around fifteen minutes when I heard the thunderous voice of Eccentric Ed outside my bivvy – carp angling's answer to Brian Blessed, vocally speaking. Eccentric Ed was the only person other than myself and Rambo who held a ticket for both The Lake and The Pit. Replacing Seb, he'd been promoted several years later and had wanted to keep his original Lake membership running in tandem. He could easily afford both tickets and we had decided he could have them. In his mid-fifties and an OTT mentalist with mullah – an entrepreneur with a portfolio of several small and very successful businesses – he had ticked Rambo's Lake membership criteria and had proved himself sufficiently to be offered a place on The Pit when one came up.

"Morning, Matthew!" he boomed. "Been hanging out the black rags of success, I see! Any good?"

I looked out to see he was nodding towards my retaining sack and weigh sling up on the tree.

"Low twenty common," I replied, getting out of my bag and popping on my loosely laced, ready-for-a-run-in-the-middle-of-the-night trainers and walking out to where he was standing. "Had it last night, just before dark."

As I stood beside Eccentric Ed, I felt a coldness in the air that hadn't been there last night. The wind had picked up and turned easterly, making its keen presence felt despite the cover offered by the trees surrounding The Lake. If the wind stayed like this bites would be harder to come by. A cold easterly wind was the one weather scenario to significantly slow The Lake carp's appetite.

"I hear Sir Rambo's young lad captured a good one," Eccentric Ed remarked. I nodded my concurrence at the truth of this statement. "Well done, Master Ramsbottom, I say! Shame Unlucky Lukie lost one." Eccentric Ed nudged me conspiratorially. "That's what I've started calling him," he said in hushed tones.

"Unlucky Lukie! Oh dear! The poor chap, a whole year without a fish! It's as if God himself has sent a pestilence upon his fishing! Perhaps He's testing him!"

Eccentric Ed guffawed at his own comment, his body shaking with mirth. He had both hands jammed in his front trouser pockets and his omnipresent 'fuck off' watch – all titanium case, unidirectional bezel and Helium escape valve, its face the size of a saucer – hung loosely from his left wrist. If past form was anything to go by, his powered barrow, piled high with top quality gear, would have been left by the end of the path down by the bottom bay. At the other end of the path, in the car park, would be his new plate Audi Q7. Not unless he'd chopped it in and bought another top end car in the last week – something that was always a distinct possibility.

"Matthew," Eccentric Ed continued, his voice taking on a pained tone, "have you heard Pup's stopped making bait?" I replied that I had. "A right pain in the rear end department, if you ask me. I can't believe he's giving it all up. Such quality products. The last three baits he brought out were all delightful, great fish catchers, brilliant even by his standards. I've been using his PhD mix for the last two years and my catch rates improved greatly. It's an *awful* shame I'll no longer be able to purchase it. As soon as I found out," Eccentric Ed informed me, laying an ex-pocketed hand on my forearm, "I went straight round to see Pup and offered to buy all the stock he had left, and all his recipes." Eccentric Ed shook a sorry head and put his hand back into its warm pouch. "Sadly, the house was bereft. There wasn't so much as a single boilie left. The place looked a pale and empty imitation of its former glory without any bait or photos. And, do you know, he wouldn't contemplate selling me a single one of his recipes? Didn't offer me the time of day. Virtually manhandled me out the door despite me being a loyal customer. Between me and you and those cheap old rods of yours, I offered him a considerable sum of money for those recipes."

Ignoring Eccentric Ed's cheeky jibe at my Slims, I merely smiled. His news pleased me. I wouldn't have wanted Eccentric Ed to buy the remnants of Pup's bait empire. Much better Pup kept all his secrets under his hat; all hidden and snug, tucked up and protected like a hamster in a safety deposit box filled with straw. All except for one secret; the one living rent-free under both my and Rambo's headwear for as long as we wanted. I also concluded the other positive, Pup's disinclination to sell any recipes, might hint at a certain pragmatism on the ex-boiliemeister's behalf. Perhaps he was holding on to his most valuable assets in case things did go desperately downhill with Daisy. Maybe Pup had had second thoughts after our chat and now wasn't so completely blinded by all things Daisy.

Eccentric Ed carried on talking. "If he had allowed me to purchase his recipes, I intended to set up my own bait company on the back of them. I would have acquired a small industrial unit, employed a few keen young bucks to help and got the thing on its feet. It would have been a nice little business to add to my others. Unfortunately, he was adamant he wouldn't sell, so much so, in fact, it made me speculate he may have already sold out to somebody else. When I indicated this was my impression, he simply scowled and wouldn't give me an answer." My face remained neutral and I said nothing. "Come, come, Matthew! Don't give me all that!" Eccentric Ed said, rounding on me and upping the decibel level even higher. "I *know* you and Sir Rambo use his bait. And might I say a bit of a special one, too, I reckon. Not for the likes of us mere mortals." Eccentric Ed's eyes gleamed. "You two are as thick as the proverbial thieves with our Pup, aren't you? I reckon his retirement from the bait business will impact less upon your good selves than us outsiders."

"You don't know what you're talking about," I said dismissively, inwardly cursing Eccentric Ed's perceptiveness. "However, I will set you straight on one thing. There's no way Rambo and I would want to set up a bait company. Running Hamworthy Fisheries is more than enough to keep us occupied."

Eccentric Ed gave me a theatrical bow and moved on. "Indeed... Now. Do you have any information regards knowing what exactly it is Pup is going to do? I'm curious, that's all. I could only determine from him he was relocating abroad. You see," Eccentric Ed's face crinkled and pulled into a scowl. "He doesn't *exactly* strike me as someone who's especially cosmopolitan."

You're not fucking kidding, I thought, suddenly wondering if Pup had a passport, let alone knew how to book on easyJet.

"No idea," I lied. "I got the impression it's done his head in, rolling so much bait over the years. I think he wants out and a change of scenery. Not exactly a fun job, is it? Not doing everything all on your own. Can you imagine it?"

Eccentric Ed pulled another face and nodded his agreement. "Nevertheless, the fundamental problem remains. If I accept you and Sir Rambo are aboard the same vessel as myself, and that we haven't got a means of propulsion between us, what are we to do? Have you got another company's bait in mind? I've been recommended a couple, but it's still going to be a *huge* leap of faith."

I knew where Eccentric Ed was coming from. Having full confidence in a bait was the great starting off point for any angler. It meant you could fully concentrate on other matters, rather than bait, and not end up with underwear looking as if a conger eel had been spinning on the crotch for a couple of hours.

"I don't know yet. We've got a fair bit of Pup's bait left. We'll use it up and then cross the replacement bridge when we come to it," I answered, trying to gloss over the subject.

Eccentric Ed nodded. "Still, him selling up and going abroad creates a vacancy on The Pit, doesn't it? *Someone's* going to get very lucky. I wonder *who* that someone might be?" I didn't bite on the floater Eccentric Ed had cast under my nose. Consequently, he had to reel it back, prop the rod on the side of his bivvy and stare wistfully at me swimming on by. "I understand," Eccentric Ed said, smiling and spreading both his ex-pocketed and pre-warmed hands.

I couldn't help but be momentarily transfixed by the movement of Eccentric Ed's watch and saw a fleeting recognition of the fact appear on his face. The silly fucker. What he didn't realise was my watch knowledge was so scant I didn't recognise the make, or have any idea *how* expensive it was, other than it was just expensive. This surely had to be the sole point of wearing such an unusual timepiece. Why else would you pay thousands for a watch capable of telling the time umpteen fathoms under the sea, on *dry* land, if not to impress other aficionados?

"It's none of my business," Eccentric Ed continued. "I'll leave you in peace. I'm going to have a wander and see if I can spot any of our quarry. I might drop by and give Unlucky Lukie a pep talk while I'm passing. The poor fellow has to get one today or he'll have drawn another blank. His good book doesn't permit him to fish Sundays! Good day to you, Matthew and *bonne chance!*"

As Eccentric Ed moved up towards the top end of The Lake, I shivered involuntarily and not because of his awkward questions about Pup. Christ, it really was quite chilly. I went back to my bivvy, popped on a coat, a woolly hat, changed my trainers for boots and came back out to stand and peruse the water. Its surface was being pushed up from the bottom bay, past where Rambo and Sylvester were fishing, to the top end of The Lake by the keen easterly wind. As I stood and watched, I felt confidence slowly ebb from me. My initial euphoria from the start of the session, when I felt as if I had everything spot on, had now gone. Conditions had deteriorated and not even a move to the bottom bay to try and fish on the back of the cold wind was likely to help.

I decided to consult the weather app I had on my phone. It indicated a swirling clockwise high pressure was now pulling in air from Siberia for the next eighteen or so hours. Once it had moved off northwards, a warm front was coming in off the Atlantic, bringing in a light south-westerly by tomorrow morning. Decision made. Fuck it. Sit tight and hope to winkle another one out tomorrow before my mid-afternoon pack up time. I looked over to Luke's bivvy and doubted he would get another chance today to set right the horrors of yesterday's debacle.

Fishing when you know you're not in with much of a shout is something every carp angler has to put up with. Even on a water specifically stocked to eradicate that scenario. The Pit, for example, had a five-month period each year when it felt as if you might as well be fishing a puddle by the side of it. Other waters had very precise bite times, where the periods in between were merely stretches of time available to get everything set and ready for the witching hours. Others, the rock hard low-density-of-stock big pits were fished in a perpetual mode of virtually no hope. The fascination of that peculiar type of challenge lying in the knowledge any second of any session might be *the* second of *the* session to produce a bite. Naturally, very difficult waters were only for the small minority of anglers, the select few who were the most strong willed. Me having to sit out the best part of a day with little hope of a take was nothing in comparison. Laughable almost. Yet, on the other extreme, to those fishing commercial puddles, a day without a bite was as unthinkable as a fourteen-year-old Japanese girl never having taken a selfie.

Each to their own and best not to judge on such matters, I told myself. So long as each individual enjoyed their style of carping and went home happy was all that mattered. The one major flaw in that argument was anglers don't always go home happy. More often than not they go home frustrated, gutted and totally pissed off. Perhaps it's what makes us come back for more. It's what gives our sport its masochistic trait, its 'gluttons for punishment' truism and its 'I'll be glad when I've had enough of this!' quotation. Toughing it out through a bite-free period was all part and parcel of the game.

Rambo clearly had similar thoughts to myself because he came up to see me early afternoon.

"I've left Sylvester in charge," he explained. "I said he could hit the next take if there was one before I got back."

"Very generous of you," I said, tongue in cheek.

"Yeah. Not looking good, is it? Tomorrow should be better. Hopefully." Rambo wiped his nose with a sausage finger. "You didn't by any chance hear or see Sylvester about last night, did you?"

"Well, funny you should ask, because he did actually pop by. At *three* in the morning. Just to say 'hello', like you do," I answered.

"Hmm, I thought so. I haven't let on I know yet, but he woke me up last night when he took *my* Glock. I pretended to be fast asleep, let him take it and when he returned to put it back, some thirty minutes later, I let him do it without saying anything."

I felt my knees weaken at this latest revelation. "Was it loaded?"

Rambo looked at me with disdain. "Of course it was loaded, boy. What's the point of having a fucking gun if it's not loaded?"

"Okay," I squeaked, weakly. "Just wondered."

Rambo surveyed my face. "Are you all right, boy? You look a bit peaky."

"He put it against my temple. Like he did his BB gun. He said he was practising a night-time assassination. He told me I was dead," I mumbled in a state of shock, considering an itchy trigger finger and a worst case scenario of blood and brains all over the sleeping bag. You would never get it out, not even using Vanish.

Rambo seemed tickled by my explanation and chortled at his son's action.

"That was because I told him a story about one of my army escapades, I expect."

"You think?" I asked, barely managing to muster a smattering of indignation in my words.

"Oh, don't make such a fuss," Rambo reprimanded. "You were in no danger. The boy knows his way around a gun. He would have had the safety on. I've been taking him to fire his own Glock in the old wood by The Pit since he was six. The BB gun is only a toy I bought him to help get used to discreetly carrying a gun about his person."

"Does Steffi know all this?" I asked.

"Fuck me, no!" Rambo replied with alarm. "The Glock he fires in the old wood was her gun. The one I gave her shortly after we first met when there was still a threat of trouble. She thinks we go to the library when we go shooting. We both take a change of clothes and everything. One of Sylvester's school friends gets the books out for us. It's our secret father/son/Glock bonding time."

"Christ!" I exclaimed, genuinely taken aback.

It was Rambo's turn to be indignant. "Look, he's got to learn how to take care of himself. I make no apologies for teaching my son how to do that, boy. It can be a violent world out there and no boy of mine is going to be an easy target."

"I think you'll find *I'm* the easy target," I answered.

Rambo gave me a playful slap, one nearly knocking me over. "You're his favourite uncle! He's not going to kill you, now is he? Not by accident or by design. Come on, let's both get ourselves into that bivvy of yours and out of this wind and sort out what were going to do about Pup's bait-making gear. I've got a few suggestions to run past you."

We did as Rambo suggested – you kind of do – and we both shoehorned ourselves inside and sat down on my bedchair; me up the foot end tucked tight against the bivvy's inner lining, Rambo lording it over the middle section. Crammed into such a small space, sitting directly alongside Rambo's jack-knifed body, only emphasised what a big son of a bitch he was. Time seemed to have made little impact on him and to my eyes he looked pretty much exactly the same as when I first met him. Maybe there were a few more lines on his face and a tinge of greyness to his close cropped hair, but otherwise, physically speaking, he looked and moved as he always had done. One thing was for certain, and it was emphasised by his attitude towards Sylvester and live firearms, mentally he hadn't mellowed one iota.

"I think we'll move all Pup's stuff into my garage and make our bait there. There's no point us bitching about it, we'll just have to get on with it and do it."

"The circle closes and we're back to where we came in," I remarked.

Rambo snorted. "Fucking hell. Do you remember my old flat?"

"When I went there to help you make bait for our TWTT campaign, when I stood outside and rang the doorbell, I changed my mind from thinking you were going to bugger me to thinking you were going to cut me up and slip me in a bath of lime!" I admitted.

Rambo chuckled. "When *I* answered the door, I remember thinking I'd made a big mistake by offering you a chance to come in on bait with me. I thought you might bottle it and go behind my back and tell Watt about our plans to prebait."

"Yet here we are. Still going strong."

Rambo nodded. "Yes, Matt. Still going strong."

I felt a huge wave of nostalgic warmth towards my best friend, even if he was a bit lax controlling his son with a gun. If the pair of them lived in the States, they could have been poster boys for the NRA.

"Do you remember the time you had that fight with Spunker at Lac Fumant? When you chinned him with a left uppercut during the thunderstorm?"

"Not as much as the time you killed the bastard who took Charlie out and was about to take *me* out!" Rambo responded.

"My finest hour," I said with no exaggeration.

"Certainly was from my point of view, boy." Rambo turned towards me. "One day I'm going tell that little story to Sylvester. When the time's right. When he's a bit older."

"Steffi's never told Sylvester, then?" I asked, relieved I hadn't blown it by mentioning it myself and quickly realising how much cooler I would appear to Sylvester with it coming directly from Rambo. It was a situation I found so overwhelmingly appealing, I was actually surprised by it.

"Nah. She'll never tell him. In her mind it would only glamorise firearms. Never mind without a gun you could never have saved my life. The only thing left still of interest to her is the foresight vision aspect of it. How you saw it happening beforehand." Rambo's head hung down as he continued speaking. "It's funny how she's changed. She had it real tough growing up and she did what she had to do to survive. It was partly why I was attracted to her, because she had been through the mill like I had and successfully come out the other side. She was a fighter. Literally, a fighter. A black belt in karate, and I admired her for it. Respected her. Remember how she sorted out those blokes shortly after we first met her?"

"Yeah, I do," I quietly replied.

"She's not the same woman now. It's like she's forgotten her past now she has her safe comfortable lifestyle. I don't know, boy, perhaps she *wants* to forget her past. Perhaps that's why she tries to shield Sylvester from everything nasty because she doesn't want him having to go through what we both had to go through when we were growing up."

I moved my head up and down slowly. "How are you and her…?" I felt too awkward to say any more.

Rambo shrugged. "We argue over Sylvester a lot. A hell of a lot. And we argue over the amount of time we spend together. She wants us to spend more time together and I don't, especially if it cuts across my fishing. I mean, what the fuck are we going to do together? Go shopping? Go and have a coffee and talk about what books Sylvester ought to have read? No thanks. The sex isn't what it used to be, either. The fire's been gradually burning lower and lower over the years. We still have our moments, but it's never going back to what it was like in the beginning." Rambo looked me in the eye. "And before you ask, Hollywood's two stunning looking, lap dancing, ex-international gymnasts, who were also bisexual nymphomaniacs are long gone."

"That's a shame," I said, flatly.

"Tell me about it," Rambo retorted, before going quiet and getting lost in the moment. "Okay," he said eventually, with a quick shake of his head. "As I said. We pick up Pup's bait-making gear, fuck it all in the back of your van and set it up in my garage…"

By the time Rambo had left and returned to Sylvester, we had mapped out our game plan for a life without Pup – in terms of bait and his place on The Pit. It felt good to have chewed it over and got something definite in place. The final deed, and Rambo had made the point of it being a must-happen, was me telling Sophie that Hobbes and his blanket-lined wicker basket were moving into our house.

"I hope she doesn't mind about the old basket," I had said, musing out loud. "Pup's sure it'll help Hobbes settle in, only it is a bit gross and grubby."

"Just you remind her it's only a fucking wicker basket, boy," Rambo had retorted with scorn. "It's not a nuclear bomb, or a fucking specially adapted cat-friendly drum kit Hobbes is going to be playing at two in the morning."

Late afternoon I reset my traps, putting both rods back on their original spots and in their original configuration. Bottom bait, pop-up; pop-up, bottom bait. Aha-ha-ha! Just like that! As I was doing so, I saw Luke mooch down to his rods, utter dejection spray-coated to every movement and gesture he made. If I had been in possession of one of Rambo's Glocks and had managed to put a bullet in his head from across The Lake, I could have probably successfully claimed the mitigating circumstances of it being a mercy killing. To be honest, I fully expected him to reel in, or just walk off home leaving all his tackle behind, but instead, to my surprise, he recast and rebaited both rods before skulking back inside his bivvy. I assumed this meant he would fish on until late at night and then pack up last knockings, in the pitch black, so he could follow the written word of the Bible and make the seventh day one of rest. Fair play to him for sticking it out to the bitter end, though, I thought.

When I flew out of my bag early the following Sunday morning to a belter on my right-hand rod, I saw I had been wrong. To my amazement Luke was still there, defying his faith and apparently a lifetime of previous religious commitment. Consciously dismissing the Luke conundrum from my mind, I refocused on landing the fish that had so obligingly gobbled my single pop-up. To my gratification, all went sweetly and a lovely big-scaled lower thirty was carefully photographed after landing and weighing her.

From then on, things in general turned a bit manic. The weather app had been spot on and the low pressure and warmer south-westerly had undoubtedly kick-started The Lake's carp into feeding. I spotted Rambo, and then Sylvester, share a quick brace of takes, with both rods going off within forty-five minutes of each other, not long after my first-of-the-morning take. On both occasions, I never once considered going down to their swim to play rent-a-crowd and view the spectacle at close hand as I had the day before. No way. We had all made it through the dark period of no hope and entered into a sunlit opening – one where the little wooden sign hammered into the lush grass didn't read 'Keep Off!' but 'Bite Time!' The place to be was close to your rods, ever vigilant and staring at your indicators, willing them ever upwards, knowing at any time soon there was a very good chance you could convince yourself you had the power of telekinesis.

To prove the point, just a couple of hours after recasting my right-hand rod and offering much mental indicator inducement, I was in again. A real fast blur of a take that turned out to be caused by a thirty-one six common. The fish, a fantastic long, dark slab of perfection, fought hard. I, the middle-aged man, a bit fatter than I used to be and not as fit, fought back – and remarkably, given the apparent physical mismatch, it was I who won. Thrilled with the upturn in my fortunes, I carefully returned her to The Lake's waters after the compulsory photo shoot and watched beguiled as she swam off strongly. Brilliant. This was more like it. This was The Lake coming up with the goods.

Keen to give myself the chance of another fish ASAP I went to rebait with a fresh pop-up – the previous one had been partially torn off the hair during the fight – only to find the hook point was dinked. The old favourite test-on-the-back-of-a-thumbnail, which was a ritual before *every* cast (it's about the only proper angling tip you're going to get out of all this, so make the most of it), had revealed fatal 'hook point skid' and a change of component was the only remedy. Feeling a little flustered at the delay, I set about retying the rig because my Blue Peter 'one I prepared earlier' vibe had been hideously lacking and no replacement was readily available in my rig box. It was then, as I salvaged the tiny ring and hair from the D rig while berating myself for my laziness, I heard the staccato call indicating Luke's second take of his session.

Standing by my bivvy, I watched it all unfold; the initial thrill, the agony and angst of possible failure, the mechanics of physical movement attempting to overcome a massive mental block and when, incredibly, as the fish finally hit the back of the Christian Carper's landing net, the celebration. Now, as someone who has watched an awful lot of football on TV, I would say Luke's initial celebration, the twenty-yard run down the bank with a single vertical outstretched arm and finger, was very Alan Shearer. The knee slide taking him down to within inches of the water, in the next swim, was more Didier Drogba 2012 Champions League equaliser. The aggressive 'sticking two fingers up' sign towards the heavens, I felt, was much more personal.

"Uncle Matt!" It was Sylvester, who must have taken off his Invisibility Cloak (also ™ J K Rowling), such was my complete surprise at his unexpected emergence by my side. "Sehen Sie dieses sich an!" he gabbled excitedly.

"What?"

"Look at this! I found it on the ground by that man's bivvy last night," he said, indicating over towards Luke.

Sylvester handed me a rectangular piece of thick material no bigger than three inches by two. I looked at it and saw it was a sew-on badge of some kind. Something that could adorn a T-shirt, a beanie hat, or perhaps a piece of kit, say a rucksack or rod holdall. The badge was of simple design; a white background with thin black edging. Centralised in an Old English style of font, were the three letters **BℜC**

# Chapter 5

Little Adam tottered down the hallway with Hobbes flung over his shoulder, like he was giving the cat a fireman's carry, and disappeared into the kitchen. To my relief, the ginger ninja seemed to be taking all the extra attention and physical assaults from my four-year-old son with a calm benevolence. As predicted, Adam had been overjoyed at having his very own 'tiger' come to tea with him. So far, the cat had dominated his attention to the point of the absolute exclusion of all his toys. Hobbes had moved in with us four days ago and to date he hadn't clawed a single person's eye out or ruined any soft furnishings, which was nice. He had dropped a turd on our kitchen floor during his first night, but we had all put it down to nerves and a lack of familiarity regards litter tray location rather than it being a dirty protest of any sort. (I'm a Celebrity Feline Bait Tester… Get Me Out of Here!)

Pleasingly, Sophie had been very understanding about Hobbes' little accident. Not *so* understanding she hadn't insisted on making me clear it up and wash the entire kitchen floor – 'He's only done it on that little bit!' I had protested. 'Why have I got to wash *all* the bloody floor?' – but understanding nonetheless.

After issuing the floor washing decree, she had taken me to one side and underlined the situation as she saw it.

"Listen, Matt. These little accidents happen, no problem, and I've accepted the reasons why we now have to have a family pet, one previously belonging to one of your friends. The thing is, *you* invited pussy into the house, so *you* will have to look after pussy. *You* have to clear up any mess pussy makes, buy its food, take it to the vet if needs be, clip its claws, de-flea it, whatever is required. I've enough to do cooking, cleaning and looking after the house, Adam, Amy and you. Especially when you're out fishing as much as you are." She had stared me in the eye and, clearly seeing a lack of commitment on my behalf, had added the rider, "If you *don't* do what I've asked you to do, you won't ever get to see another type of pussy again. Understand?"

Despite the words, 'I don't get to see much of *that* particular feline, in any case,' forming on my lips, I had wisely kept my mouth shut and nodded my acquiescence.

"Good," she had said, her manner softening. To my surprise, pouting and leaning into me so she could whisper in my ear, she had added, "If you play your cards right and behave, I've got an idea you might be interested in. After what you said about Rambo and Steffi, I started thinking. Both of them, and, I admit, us too, have fallen into the same predicament thousands of long-term couples find themselves. It just sort of happens. It creeps up on you almost without you realising it, what with everything else going on. There's just so many other demands on everyone's time and as a consequence everyone gets tired and stressed." Sophie had rolled her eyes at this point. "Not that you and the lummox have got much going on to get stressed about. Anyway, putting that to one side, what I'm trying to say is we are *not* old yet. The only answer is to set aside a special time when the effort can be made to climb out of the hole we've dug... And I've got an idea what the ladder can be. I'll tell you later tonight."

And she had. And I had thought it was a really, really good ladder – an aluminium Youngman Trade 200, at least.

Pup was now supposedly safely in Venice with Daisy. I say 'supposedly' because I had no hard physical evidence to substantiate this, only an email from 'Peter' telling me so. He had met up with Daisy, found accommodation and the pair were spending time getting to know each other better. Apparently, all was going swimmingly – which I took to be a good omen for a couple living in a city where there was so much water.

Pup's bait-making gear, I could more definitely state, was safe in Rambo's garage. Put there, lock, stock and barrel when Rambo and I had become 'men with ven', as Super Hans would say. We had shifted it, like a couple of furtive, doing-it-cash-in-hand, no-VAT-luv removal men from Pup's house to Rambo's garage in one go, at night-time, so we were less likely to be spotted by someone who knew us. Equally, the recipe for our exclusive, revolutionary, indented, dirty brown bottom bait boilie was also hopefully as safe. At least as safe as anything can be on a couple of computer hard drives. The day I had transferred the recipe from the handwritten piece of A4 paper into a Microsoft Word file via my two-fingered typing, had also been the same day I had previously purchased additional internet spyware, malware and firewall protection.

"Don't save it in a file called 'Boilie Recipe', either," Rambo had warned as he had loomed over me while I had sat in my computer chair. "Call it something else. Something like 'Parking Fine Letter' or 'Mortgage Application'. And don't email it to me as an attachment, either, boy. Email isn't secure. I read it in a newspaper so it must be true. I'll take the recipe home and copy it on to my computer separately. Then I'll destroy it. Then I'll get the same antivirus stuff as you."

"Antivirus first, data entry second. And don't just rip it up and chuck it in your green bin," I had warned. "Destroy it properly."

Rambo had nodded earnestly. "I'll eat it," he had promised. "Chew the fucker up and eat it."

Looking back, I think we were both so cranky about the whole process because of how Pup had acted during the handover of hardware and recipe. I reckon we had been contaminated by his madness; his bizarre behaviour bludgeoning us both into becoming a bit bait barmy.

Firstly, he had been like an old hen, clucking round our heels, while we had moved out his bait-making hardware. He had constantly hectored and badgered us to be careful and not to damage this and not to damage that because he had used it for over twenty years and never put a scratch on it, let alone wrecked it, like it was clear we were bound to do any moment soon. Even more annoyingly, he had also given us a running commentary on the best practice usage of each and every single piece of equipment. These blunt technical directives were punctuated with hyperbolic bait-making anecdotes of the 'I remember the time I had to mix a last minute one-hundred-kilo order' kind, and more generalised 'You never want do so and so like that, you want to do it like this' patronising bait-making tips. If it hadn't been for the fact we were getting our hands on all his equipment plus the recipe for our exclusive, revolutionary, indented, dirty brown bottom bait boilie, I think Rambo would have decked him. If the truth were known, I suspect the passing on of a lifetime's worth of equipment and knowledge was secretly killing Pup, however much, deep down inside, he wanted to be rid of it. Sometimes it's hard to let go of the rope, even when you know it's pulling you to certain death.

Secondly, when we had returned Pup back home and it was time to pass over the recipe details, his behaviour had become even more bizarre. Thanks to some kind of weird internal jurisdiction, Pup had steadfastly refused to write it out himself on the grounds he regarded such an act as sacrilegious.

"I've *never* committed a single recipe to paper! They're all in my head," he had blustered, tapping at his temple when I had asked him to put pen to paper for us. "There's no way they can get lost or stolen from in there."

"Well, they could. Alien mind probe and early onset dementia. That's two ways for a start," I had told him, rather sarcastically.

"Shut up, Matt! Do you want the recipe or not?" Pup had angrily retorted. "You just don't get it, do you? This is like cutting one of my fingers off, giving a recipe, a *whole* recipe, to you two." Despite feeling increasingly niggled by Pup's superior attitude we had both nodded obediently. "Right," the ex-boiliemeister had declared, his condescension clear by the tone in his voice. "I'll *dictate* it then, shall I?" He gestured towards the two non-matching chairs in his kitchen. "Sit down the pair of you. You'll be fucking gobsmacked when I tell you what the revolutionary ingredient is."

For all of Pup's bait diva histrionics, I have to admit he had been *so* right. 'Fucking gobsmacked' had barely covered it, hardly touched the surface of our combined stupefaction. That! *That* was the revolutionary bit! Holy fucking hell! It was as if Che Guevara, Vladimir Lenin, Fidel Castro and Karl Marx had been bundled into a big vat together, minced up and then processed down into a single liquid – or powder (no clues) – ingredient. I would never have thought of *that* to put into a carp bait in a million years. Nobody would. Nobody except Pup, the man who had spent over half his life striving for boilie perfection. Amazing! He might have spent the entire handover of his previous life being a sanctimonious cantankerous arsehole, but there was no denying he was a highly gifted sanctimonious cantankerous arsehole.

As Pup had dictated the recipe, with me constantly telling him to slow down so I could keep up, he had detailed the exact amount of ingredients required by weight and the exact order in which to mix those ingredients; the exact amount of additives, flavours and enhancers by volume, the revolutionary bit by [*undisclosed specification*] and the exact order in which to mix them; the exact amount of eggs, what sort of eggs and the exact way in which to mix the whole lot together; the exact amount of standing time for the mix; the exact rolling and indenting techniques and the exact amount of boiling time for an exact amount of baits; and finally, the exact amount of cooling and drying time before bagging up the finished product. He had even insisted on me writing down 'Freeze as soon as baits reach ambient room temperature' in case we forgot. He had then gone through the same process for the legendary pop-up version of our bait.

Normally, I'm pretty sure Rambo would have gone up like Mount Vesuvius at this demeaning slight, splattering all immediate organic life forms into paste in the process. But he hadn't. The giant bucket of ice cold water that was the revelation of the revolutionary bit had rendered him dormant. Rambo had sat motionless on the chair, lifeless and unblinking, like a powered down automaton, one lost in a world of secret bait additives. It was like his brain had been switched from its default setting – 'violence' – to the one marked – 'ruminate' – and all he could do was focus on the fiendishly fantastic awesome additive.

It wasn't only Rambo who had been blown away. So detailed and precise were Pup's instructions, so steeped in mystic and magic, that as I had written down his words I had felt them take on the form of an incantation. It was as if I was chronicling a forceful spell, one brim-full of the preternatural power to entice carp to pick up a hookbait. Pup's recipe was always a wonder but now, entrusted with the knowledge of its contents, it seemed heightened to an even greater status. Now I knew how the trick worked, now it had been finally disclosed, I felt like an all-powerful sorcerer.

So consuming was the feeling for both of us that we had been given a key to open the box to one of the great secrets of the universe, the day afterwards, when all Pup's equipment was stored and the recipe was on both our computers, Rambo and I had felt much more paranoid over losing control of it than we had previously. And we had been bad enough then! It was a strange phenomenon, all those years of using the exclusive, revolutionary, indented, dirty brown bottom bait boilie with the constant background hum of trepidation – over the loss of exclusivity – and now we knew, really knew, what made it tick, the fear factor felt far more frightening. The only way I can explain it, to myself as much as anybody else, is when Pup had made the bait it seemed a single entity. Now we knew all of its ingredients, there seemed so much more to spin out of control. So many more things to go wrong. So many ingredients to stop being manufactured, to be lost in the post, to be intercepted, to be noted and correlated and pieced together by a shadowy master bait thief.

It did make me wonder if Rambo and I were going through a kind of midlife carp fishing crisis.

On the subject of ingredients, as the consummate professional, Pup had sourced the best outlets for purchasing not only the revolutionary bit but all the other items in the bait. These firms' contact details had also been dictated to me – the phone numbers, website and email addresses and personal contact names. Pup was nothing if not thorough. Once it was done and the whole process was over, Pup had lightened and returned to his more usual self, mirroring how he had reacted when he had initially started to clear out his house.

"That's it then," he had said. "It's over. Time to move on. Once you've got Hobbes, there's nothing left of my old life."

"You've still got those other recipes in there," I had said, feeling sorry for him, pointing to Pup's head and thinking about what Eccentric Ed had told me.

"We've got your bait-making gear, boy," Rambo had added, also with a consolatory air. "But only on loan. If you ever come back or need it again, just say the word and we'll get it to you."

Pup had breathed in deeply and sighed. "Thanks lads. I appreciate the sentiment. I don't think I will be needing it."

When it had come to Pup parting with Hobbes, a different set of his emotions had come into play. Gone was the attitude and strops and in came genuine sadness. Giving me all of his fishing kit, which I had put in my garage, hadn't seemed much of a wrench to him. When he had taken Hobbes and his blanket-lined wicker basket into our house, it had been a different matter. Tears of sorrow had poured down Pup's face.

"Goodbye, Hobby-Bobby. I promise I'll visit," he had snuffled, rubbing the ginger ninja's head. "Check Matt's bait for him. If they're careful, him and Rambo might get it somewhere about right."

"We'll do our best, Hobbes. We'll try not to muck it up and poison you," I had said directly to the cat, easing to one side Pup's continuing low estimation of my and Rambo's bait-making capabilities.

"God, this is awful. Long goodbyes are no good to anybody. I have to go. Goodbye, Hobbes," Pup had said, giving the cat a final tickle under the chin before turning to me. "Goodbye, Matt. Here's all the house stuff. Keys, documentation, paperwork… Oh, and one last thing," Pup had said, wiping away his tears, "I've decided not to sell the house just yet, after all. I *am* going to rent it out for a while. I've decided to take your advice. I've put it with an agency, given them your number and told them to deal directly with you. I haven't signed up for the full package, so you will still have to show people around and sort out any repairs needing to be done once the tenants are in. I've signed a letter to say you can act for me. It's all in there," he had said, nodding towards the large envelope he had just given me. "They know the score and will be in touch if they have a prospective tenant. Don't let them rent it out to a bunch of anarchists or a terrorist cell, will you?"

"Right… Okay. Er, sure. No anarchists or terrorists. All the 'ists' are right out!" I had said brightly, trying to mask my inner conflict concerning this latest major change of direction. I couldn't imagine for one second it was solely because of what I had said. Something else must have happened. "If there's anything I'm not sure of I'll send you an email or a text."

"Thanks, Matt," Pup had said offering his hand and nodding at Hobbes. "Look after him."

"Don't worry, I will," I had said shaking Pup's hand. "You concentrate on looking after yourself, Pu… Pete. Give my love to Daisy."

Pup had smiled. "I'll do my best."

Once he had walked out of the front door and left, I had wondered how long it would be before I saw him again. Three months, I had originally reckoned. It seemed about right.

I heard the screech of furniture being moved over a tiled floor and hurried to the kitchen to see what was happening. Once there, I saw Adam standing on a chair, leaning on the worktop and stretching over to open up the kitchen tap. Hobbes, who was already alongside him, moved on to the sink's draining board and started lapping at the water as soon as it started to run.

Adam squealed his delight. "Drinkies for Hobby!"

"You be careful on that chair, young man," I said, lifting my son down and putting him safely on terra firma. "And don't let Mum see Hobbes up there or she'll go ballistic. She doesn't think it's very hygienic, a cat walking on the worktops. She'll have me cleaning every square inch of them."

Once free from me, Adam squealed with laughter again. "Hobby, come!" he shrieked and ran out of the kitchen.

To my amazement the cat stopped lapping at the water, jumped off the sink and ran after him.

Shaking my head in bewilderment, I turned off the tap, put the chair back under the kitchen table and glanced at my watch. I had a couple of hours to get my arse down to The Pit. It was time specific because I was meeting a prospective new member to show him round and interview him as the replacement for Pup.

The prospective new member had already been vetted by phone. I had spoken to him, and the three others I had regarded as the most suitable candidates on the waiting list, a week ago. All four had been on the list for some years and all had made the effort to flag their continuing interest with brief phone calls at the time of the annual renewal. Nick, the person I was meeting, had simply come across as the most suitable angler. If he turned out to be as genuine as he sounded, once I had met him in the flesh, then I was going to offer him a place on The Pit. These remote, first-stage, non-personal initial screenings were a much cleaner, quicker and easier method of thinning down applicants rather than hauling all four in for a personal interview. Chatting to each of them for a half hour or so gave me a feel for them, a frame of reference where I could happily make a primary judgement before meeting them face to face.

Over the years, I felt I had become quite adept at sorting the wheat from the chaff.

I had managed to perfect what might at first seem to be a trivial, casual line of questioning, which in fact was quite subtly revealing. My line of patter – Easy Going and Slightly Lapse Supreme Fishery Owner – would successfully lull the would-be member into a sense of false security to the point where they would often unintentionally open up. Without realising it, they would end up being a tad more candid than they might ideally have wanted. It was from these tiny unguarded snippets of conversation, the bullshit-free bits, where I had formed my decision on whether they were worth a face-to-face interview.

As an alternative, I suppose I could have insisted on dragging them into my house and wiring them up to a lie detector, or employed a more proactive method, like waterboarding or genital electrification techniques to winkle out the truth, but frankly I couldn't be arsed. At home on the phone, sipping a cup of tea was much easier. Especially when it came to the 'thanks, but no thanks', bit. Some took it on the chin, others got the hump. A tiny few got abusive. It made little difference to me – remote and untouchable, like a super villain safely ensconced in his lair.

During our telephone conversation, Nick had assured me he had the money to hand (no point continuing otherwise) and I could tell by the way he spoke he was a proper carp angler as opposed to an improper one. (One who casts in your swim, seems to be on average at least fifty yards from his rods, gets pissed and falls in, asks to borrow your landing net, baits up at bite-time, only fishes the Chod Rig – there are shades to this – believes fish off the top don't count, previously a member of ECHO… The list is as long as the arguments about what ought to go on it.) He had been more eloquent than the others and more passionate about his love of nature and carp angling. And I had believed him. Today was my chance to get an upfront and personal look at him, and take advantage of getting a second opinion, seeing as Dr Rambo would also be attending the consultation. Dr Rambo's presence was always useful. It wasn't the fact he was a better judge of character than me, it was more a case of any would-be member quickly realising if they played up at all the big motherfucker dressed in camo clothing would snap them in half like a Twiglet.

More importantly, today was also to be my first session of the year on The Pit. And boy was I gagging to get down there and have the chance to reacquaint myself with some seriously big fish. The Lake was great, but The Pit was better.

"'Bye everyone," I shouted. "See you in a couple of days."

I quickly made my way out the back door and made a dash for my van. Sneakily, before Sophie had the chance to ask me to do something else for her, or for one of her friends, like she had the other night. The favour for her friend was always going to be a pain to have to do, but it had become more annoying thanks to its timing. It was why I was only going fishing for two days.

"What do you think, then?" I asked Rambo, after we had finished interviewing Nick and he had left. "He seems sound enough."

Rambo nodded. "Yeah. Decent enough bloke. Are you going to offer him the place?"

"Yeah, I think so. You happy with that?"

Despite being Supreme Fishery Owner of The Pit, I still liked to run things by my trusted lieutenant.

Rambo nodded. "If he fails to make the grade, we'll just fuck him out. Not that I think he will. Everyone on here knows the management reserve the right to refuse admission." Rambo walked to the door of the functional wooden clubhouse and quickly took a peek outside. "I've ordered in all the stuff," he said, once he knew no one else was in earshot. "According to Pup's instructions I've got enough for a hundred kilos. I can't see the point in going to the trouble of making any less. The Eye has said he doesn't need any at the moment so we can share the lot. My freezer can take fifty if I lever it in with a crowbar, what about yours?"

"I'll find a home for it. I might have to throw some food away, but you've got to get your priorities right," I answered, smiling.

"Too right, boy. How soon do you need some more bait?"

"I won't be using much this session. Early season singles, and all that. I reckon I'll start baiting in earnest on the next one."

"Let's pencil in a bait-making session next week, then. I've only got less than ten kilos and Sylvester's keen to go back on The Lake as soon as possible."

"Sounds good. Let me know what I owe you and I'll square you up then, if that's all right?" Rambo indicated it was. "What do you think about me bringing Hobbes along to check the mix?"

Rambo's face hardened like super-quick post mix cement. "Not a lot."

"Not just to…"

"Matt," Rambo interjected, "I don't need a fucking mangy moggy to quality control my bait mixes. We've got all the information we need, all the equipment we need and we will have all the ingredients we need within the next few days."

I held up both hands and surrendered. "No worries. No cat." There was something else I wanted to ask Rambo. "What was the lowdown with Luke? Fishing on a *Sunday*? He was still at it when I left. Worked though, he finally got one."

Rambo scratched the stubble on his chin and a couple of sparks flew off. "Odd. Very odd. After you had gone, when it was Sylvester's turn to hit a take, I had a walk round The Lake. I had a little chat with Eccentric Ed, Ryan, who had turned up by then, and then with Luke. Fuck me, was the boy buzzing. He wouldn't stop. Started rambling on about how he had taken a new path in his life, how he now realised how wrong he'd been and what a waste of time it had all been. It was like he had seen the light, only in reverse. He'd fucking turned it *off*!"

"What his religion?"

"I reckon so, boy. Funny what catching a carp can do to some people. I think he's joined the massed ranks of us unbelievers!" Rambo shook his head with distraction. "You know those stainless hangers of his?"

"The cross ones? The ones where he can add on a crucified Jesus if he needs a bit of extra weight?"

Rambo nodded. "I noticed they were hanging the other way up. They were inverted."

"Maybe he's got into Black Sabbath," I suggested.

"Or become a Satanist."

"Blimey! I guess desperate men *do* do desperate things. Especially when they're desperate to catch a carp. Incidentally, did Sylvester show you the sew-on badge he'd found?" I asked. Rambo nodded. "What did you make of it? He said he found it round by Luke's swim. Unusual font, wasn't it?"

"No idea what it was, boy," Rambo said, dismissively.

"Could be the initials of some group Luke's joined," I postulated. "Badly Misguided Christians. *Bygone* Misguided Christians. No, wait! Bygone *Mistaken* Christians!"

Rambo gave me a cold hard stare. "Enough, boy. What swim are you going to fish?"

"I'm not sure yet."

"Well, my recommendation is you put some mental energy into deciding rather than letting your brain go acronym crazy."

"Fair enough," I agreed. "One last thing. How do you think the weed growth will be this year?"

Rambo's voice took on a formal air. "Oh, I think I can confidently state it will be much like it has been for some time now. Minimal and therefore not obstructive to angling."

"Yes. I think it'll be like that, too."

We knowingly smiled at each other. I didn't exactly tap my nose with my index finger and wink at Rambo, but I might as well have. Weed growth on many waters up and down the country, especially gin clear gravel pits, had been problematical since the EU directive banning aquatic herbicides had been put in place. The Pit had been no different and the combined effects of not using Casoron G annually, plus the prior removal of the ghost's murder weapon from its watery location (my pet theory), had permitted a gradual increase in weed growth. Over the time since treatment had ceased, Canadian Pondweed and other weeds had gradually started to make life increasingly difficult to the point that by the third year of non-treatment, the sheer volume of weed had started to cause frequent lost fish through hookpulls and lines parting due to its abrasive qualities. As the weed had become even more predominant, certain areas had become unfishable and at the height of its growth in summer several swims had been put out of commission.

The situation was far from ideal on many levels and Rambo had told me it was time for us to get our fingers out and take matters into our own hands. Large, priceless fish with tackle left in them, however careful and educated the anglers fishing for them had been with their end tackle set-ups, was not a good situation, Rambo had reiterated. I had agreed and following the dynamic of our entire relationship, I had further agreed we had to act unilaterally. Bolstered and emboldened by Rambo's rhetoric that no faceless foreign bureaucrat should dictate what I should or shouldn't do on a water I owned, we set about a plan of action. One involving breaking the law.

At the back end of the last season where weed had been an issue, we had shut The Pit for three days and brought in an outside contractor to clear it. During that period the weed cutting boat and its crew, along with myself and Rambo as labourers, had cleared the vast majority of the weed. There had been a mind-boggling quantity of it, literally tons and tons of it, and it had been hard graft for all concerned to shift it from boat to bank and then to an area away from the water where it could be left to rot down. However, once this labour intensive task had been achieved and The Pit's waters were virtually clear, we had the first part of our duplicitous plan secured.

The following February had seen Rambo and I out in the boat, our boat, with Rambo rowing it and me putting in Casoron G again. Rambo had managed to source the herbicide in granule format from a company he had found on the internet in sufficient quantities for our needs. Behind closed doors – we had shut The Pit to all members on the grounds of 'swim maintenance' – we had done the dirty illegal deed. That first year, I had felt a bit ill at ease, the second less so. By the third year of our forbidden weed-killing felony I couldn't have cared less. The fishing was back to normal and The Pit was perfection personified – just the way we liked it. The spin we had given to the members was the weed boat had done wonders and uprooted the weed so well it hadn't grown back. Whether they bought it or not didn't matter, we were all as one in not wanting to fish a weed-choked Pit. If any members did house doubts over how three days' work with a weed boat could be so continually effective, then they never voiced them.

This February we had once again maintained our annual illegal water-based herbicidal ritual. Interpol hadn't swooped, the EU thought police hadn't dawn-raided our houses and a reporter from Watchdog hadn't doorstepped myself or Rambo asking awkward questions about gin clear weed-free gravel pits. We had got away with it again. Happy Canadian Pondweed-free days! Long may they continue.

Rambo closed the padlock through the hasp and staple on the functional wooden clubhouse door and we made our separate ways to our respective vehicles. We were going to have a drive round The Pit, stop off at a few swims experience told us were usually productive early spring, and have a look to see what took our fancy.

"Have a good session, mate," I said to Rambo as I climbed into my van. "No going catching anything bigger than I do."

"I'll make sure to ring you if I do, boy. Get you to reel in and come round and photograph it for me."

I laughed, shut the door to my van and started her up. A tingle of anticipation ran through me as I drove off clockwise around The Pit's perimeter grass track. Another new yearly campaign on the water of my choice was about to begin. Like thousands of other carp anglers, my aspirations and desires ran high, lifted by the optimism of the warm weather and lengthening days to come. Visions of the carp I might catch, flicked across my mind's eye and filled me with expectation. Naturally, I was aware for many, me included, the expectation might never materialise into reality, and disappointment might usurp all original hope. If that wasn't the case, if every carp fishing dream did come to fruition, then it wouldn't really be carp fishing at all. It would cease to be the uneven pursuit where so many variables beyond an individual's control could so massively influence the outcome. Perhaps that's what made it so fascinating, so compelling, so able to burrow deep under your skin, the utter unpredictability of it. Sure, you could swing the percentage points in your favour by the things you could control, but ultimately you were dealing with the capture of a creature totally beyond it.

The big hitters on my team, those swinging the percentage points my way, were – in no particular order – my angling knowledge and that of The Pit, gained over many years of fishing, my bait and The Carper's super trick rig. Three of those awesome rigs were ready and in place, tied on my rods, made up last night in preparation. The Pit was the only place where I fished The Rig, the only place secluded enough to make me feel happy I could use it without the fear of its discovery by other anglers. Looking at it again, as I had last night, after not using it all winter, it was evident The Carper had been a fantastic and forward thinking angler – a genius of all things hook and hair. Not such a genius elsewhere, seeing as he couldn't avoid getting sliced in half by machinegun fire and couldn't catch The Seventy from the MoD pit located on the live fire range, but a rig genius nevertheless. Such was the step forward in rig design he had accomplished, I can only relate it in terms to the days of side hooking baits as compared to the latter Middleton/Maddocks hair rig improvement. It wouldn't catch you fish if you were in the wrong place, but it certainly did if you were in the right place with the right bait.

The consequences of having The Rig in our corner, throwing heavyweight knockout uppercuts, meant I was left with only one out of the big three to deal with. The same applied to Rambo. It was why we were the two most successful anglers on The Pit. Our bait was better than everybody else's, our rig was better than everybody else's and we were good enough at the last bit. Good enough at sorting out the right place and the right spots within the right place. The thing was, and I'm not ashamed to admit it, Rambo and I quite liked being the two most successful anglers on The Pit and, I'm double not ashamed to admit it, we rather wanted it to stay that way. We didn't *actually* want to give our edges away to anybody if we could help it. The Eye might have our bait – but he didn't have our rigs.

Sometimes, for around a nanosecond, I had considered whether we were terrible people for hugging our ace cards so close to our chests the print came off on our skins. Oughtn't we to have downed a bottle or two of neat altruism and shared our riches with the rest of the carp fishing fraternity to the benefit of all? Hailed our discoveries (well, Pup's and The Carper's, anyway) via a vividly sensational magazine article or two?

To be honest, I hadn't ever mentioned the possibility to Rambo because the feeling invariably passed the instant I thought about it. I doubt it had ever flitted across Rambo's mind in the first place. So there it was. We still tenaciously hung on to the secret of our bait – the one we had only just had revealed to us, like a butchered body giving up its vital organs – and when fishing The Pit, we furtively concealed our end tackle.

Please don't judge us harshly. I mean, come on, what would you do given the same circumstances? Are *you* thanking Lenny Middleton or donating to his PayPal account every time you catch one? Exactly. No further questions, M'lud. I rest my case.

# Chapter 6

The fish I had seen roll had put me in a dilemma. The swim I had been standing in at the time was not one of my preconceived early season favourites. A 'carp fishing conflict of interests' alert had flagged in my head and I had stood at the water's edge wondering what to do. (Keep taking the money and say nothing to The Standards and Privileges Committee. Sorry, wrong scenario. That's the line for MPs on the take, not wavering carp anglers.) The show had been only seventy or so yards out, had looked a good fish, and was the only carp action I had spotted so far. If it had occurred in a swim I did consider to be a preconceived early season favourite, I would have been unloading the gear from the van right now quicker than a delivery driver on 'job and finish'. Instead, I was still looking, waiting for a second showing or a flash of inspiration prompting me to go somewhere else. Neither had happened.

I stood in the swim procrastinating, gripped by inertia and indecision. I needed to get this right. What I didn't want to do was set up, not see anything over the next twenty-four hours, fish with a diminishing confidence in my location skills and the swim itself, and then have to think about a last night move. A last night move with less options because it was highly likely a few Pit members would be crawling out of the woodwork over the next day or two. Historically, the third and fourth week of April was when the fish came out of their winter torpor and started to feed a little. Results were still patchy, early May was a far better bet for more consistent action, but getting one under your belt early doors, setting you up for the year, was always a fantastic feeling. The pull of being in with a shout of hooking a carp from The Pit was always strong after a winter's abstinence.

The fact I was on an enforced forty-eight hour session, rather than the usual seventy-two, also put me under additional pressure. (I can hear the sarcastic violin and tissue quips from here!) The reason for the twenty-four hour loss was Sophie had promised a friend of hers I would nip round to her new house and move a few power points for her. It was the only day Sonia could be there to show me what needed to be done and, unfortunately, it had clashed with my arrangements to interview Nick and fish on from then. (Remember, I *was* a fully qualified electrician in my past life, a bit like Pup *was* a fully *un*qualified boiliemeister. You show me where you can get hold of a Higher National Certificate in carp bait manufacturing.)

Sonia was in a new residence with, unluckily for me, incorrectly positioned power points, because she had recently divorced from her husband, George. According to Sophie, George had left Sonia, which I had found a bit odd from my simplistic male default viewpoint of thinking how extremely attractive she was. I had wondered how bad it must have got between them for him to want to walk away from such a gorgeous woman. Evidently, bad enough. For all my sexism, ravishing beauty clearly couldn't compensate and George had called time on their relationship. Why remained a mystery, not that I really cared for analysing who had ditched who, or what the reasons were, only in the respect, thanks to the split, Sophie was helping her friend through the difficult process of rebooting her life by offering out *my* electrical services FOC. As if moving a few poxy power points was going to make her feel any better. It certainly wasn't going to make *me* feel any better.

I had always liked Sonia on the few occasions I had met her – *not* in that way, that was the old Matt Williams from a long time ago, in a galaxy far, far away when I had no self-control – but moving her power points, *any* power points, was a chore. And the fact I was having to cut my session short and come home a day early, constituted a double whammy I could well do without. For a start, there was all the palaver of taking my fishing gear out the van, digging out my tools from the garage, getting the right materials, putting them both in the van, going round there, doing the job, tidying up, coming back, taking all the tools and leftover materials out and putting them back in the garage. It was too much like in the past when I had a proper job, before I had rather unexpectedly moved into the carp fishery game. Sure, I might still drive a van – Peugeot Expert Professional, 130bhp, air con, central locking and deadlocks, Bluetooth hands free kit with USB input, electric doors and mirrors, sliding side doors on both sides, steel bulkhead, ply lining kit, two cup holders and a unique internal microhabitat originally populated by a myriad of migrant creepy-crawlies, snails and slugs that had hitched a ride on my rod holdall, bivvy and unhooking mat – and quite liked the 'couldn't give a fuck', fear factor kudos of being a White Van Man. However, it didn't mean I wanted to have to conform with the stereotypical manual worker/delivery driver condition going with it. The van was a dedicated fishing wagon, designed to get me and all my gear to the venue of my choice. Delivering fishing tackle to The Lake or The Pit *didn't* make me a delivery driver.

"Face it, Williams," I mumbled to myself, "you're becoming a right whinging tart in your middle age."

Intently, I scanned the water where the fish had last shown, the sun's reflection off it making me squint into the glare. To ease my eyes for a while, I looked down into the deep margins and spotted a couple of boilies through the clear water a few yards out. That was surprising. As far as I was aware, from what I had been told by other members and by Rambo, nobody had fished this swim this year. Maybe the explanation was someone had come in and done a quick overnighter and hadn't mentioned it, or simply hadn't been seen. After all, The Pit was twenty-nine acres and, exactly as Michael Brown had originally set it up, had only twenty members to fit into twenty extremely well-spaced and secluded swims. In all my time on The Pit, the most anglers I had ever seen fishing it at one time was sixteen, during the 'Pulimov's Prize' madness, but typically numbers would sit at around ten less than that. It wasn't exactly a superstore on Black Friday out there. Members could come and go and not talk to a soul if they didn't want to and could easily avoid being seen by fellow members. Seclusion was part and parcel of the attraction of The Pit, what with so many waters rammed with anglers bivvied up and other anglers bivvied up behind them waiting for the swim to be vacated – the swim eight yards to the left of the one next door and nine to the one to the right. In retrospect, I decided it wasn't so surprising the swim had been fished unnoticed, especially so early in the year when hardly anyone was about.

I looked back up just in time to see a carp top out almost in the exact spot as the first one. I gave a little fist pump, hissed 'Yessss!' under my breath, thanked the Great Carp God for the miracle of sending me a sign, spun on my heel and went back to the van. Time to unload the gear and deliver my carp tackle at 'job and finish' intensity.

In a couple more hours, I was set fair, wind in my sails, three rods out, portable home built and the van back in the car park. Tactics: Two single bottom baits around thirty yards apart in the general area where the two shows had been – both on a nice feathered down 'donk' – and another closer in to my left, at forty yards, with a tight-to-the-deck pop-up plus a small PVA bag of chopped boilies – *not* chopped finger tips.

Perched inside my bivvy, like a vulture waiting for the death cry of a Delkim indicating a run to feast on, I had no idea where Rambo had opted to fish. I decided to give him a call to see which swim he had chosen.

"I'm in Big Island, boy," he said, referring to the swim directly in front of the largest of the two islands closest to the north bank of The Pit. (We're nothing if not logical, prosaic perhaps, when it comes to swim names.) "I haven't seen anything, I just really fancied it for some reason."

"Okay, nice one," I answered.

I told him about the margin baits I had seen in my swim, one called East Ender, thanks to it being at the end of the east bank. (See, I told you.)

"I bet it was Rob. He likes that swim," Rambo answered.

Rob was an original Lake member who had been promoted six years ago. He was an ex-military man who had fought in the first Gulf conflict and now earned a living as a security expert. Rob had been in thrall to Rambo from the moment he had met him and always addressed Rambo as if he was his commanding officer and they were both still in the army. Secretly, I think Rambo was rather charmed by it and I'm sure their shared military background had contributed to making Rob one of his favourite members. 'Blue-eyed Rob', I would call him to his face and he would struggle to hide his delight at being considered one of Rambo's favourites. Sometimes I would stretch to calling him 'Brown nosed Rob', but only when pulling Rambo's leg about his army buddy 'love in' and never to Rob himself. You have to be careful, you never know who's got a Kalashnikov down their trousers and what might prompt them into using it.

"That's fine, I only mentioned it in passing. How many others are on your bank?"

"Just the one. Astrological Jim."

"There's one on mine, too" I responded. "It's odds-on The Bookie's in Old Wood, so that's everyone accounted for."

The Bookie – we're no better with nicknames – to give you even more Pit membership background (there'll be a test at the end), was a betting company manager, not that I could remember which one as there are so many of them. (It had become ridiculous of late. Not seeing a betting company's ad on satellite TV during an evening's viewing was harder than avoiding anything to do with football, and that's saying something. I hadn't put a bet on for years, but it seemed a host of others were more than making up for me and creating an industry growth boom.) Surrounded by odds all day, his working environment seemed to have created an aversion to bucking them in regards to his approach to carp fishing. He was a stickler for playing the percentages and rarely deviated from what had been successful for him in the past. The Bookie was a punter of habit, betting on his own personal favourites with the reactionary zest of a dyed-in-the-wool Conservative pensioner. If the Old Wood swim was free, he would fish it nearly every time.

Astrological Jim was a much older member, predating both Rambo and myself by some years. His passion for amateur astrology had been reflected in his naming of forty-plus fish. (Any member catching a first-caught forty had the right to name it, this being a Pit tradition established in the Michael Brown days. In due course, the successful member would pin a photograph of the fish, with a name tag, on the functional wooden clubhouse's notice board. In times past, Alan, the resident artist, had painted these fish, each one adding to a wonderful pictorial history of The Pit's carp. Sadly, ill health had caught up with Alan and he was no longer well enough to carry on fishing and had left The Pit five years ago. It was an awful shame, his fantastic paintings were far superior to any photograph, and there had always been a buzz of eager anticipation on the day he revealed another of his piscatorial masterpieces.)

Jim had caught and named Orion, Half Moon and Milky Way amongst others, although the latter was coined thanks to the snack Jim had been eating at the time of the take, rather than through any celestial connection. Jim was a decent guy, in his early sixties now, and very supportive of how I had ran The Pit since Michael Brown's zipped-up-in-a-bivvy, death-by-carbon-monoxide-poisoning demise. It was why he still had a ticket.

"You'll never guess what," Rambo told me, chuckling to himself. "Steffi phoned me up a short while ago to tell me Sylvester got in a fight walking home from school today. It involved the big brother of a kid who goes to his school who both live down our road. She said the older lad kept pushing Sylvester and shouting 'sufferin' succotash' at him until he punched him in the face. That shut him up."

"Oh no! That's not nice having an older boy pick on you. Good for him for sticking up for himself… A bit weird, though," I said, thinking as I spoke. "A teenager having that frame of reference for the abuse. Those cartoons were made decades ago."

"Whatever, boy. At least he sorted the kid out. I don't think Sylvester will have to worry he'll be picking on him again."

"No. I guess not. Are you going home to see if Sylvester's all right?"

"Of course I'm not going home to see if he's all right. He's fine. I've spoken to him."

"What did you say?" I enquired, wondering how Rambo had consoled his son and helped him deal with the unsavoury incident.

"I asked him if he put his body weight into the punch and made contact before full arm extension. Like I'd shown him."

"Oh... Right. Had he?"

Rambo gave a loud guffaw down the phone. "I reckon so, boy. He said the other lad went down like a sack of shit! When Sylvester squared up to him the other lad said, acting all tough, 'If you hit me, Puddy Tat, you better make sure I don't get back up!' Well, he *didn't* fucking get back up!"

"What did Steffi say?"

"Oh, she won't ever condone violence. She said he shouldn't have got involved and should have walked away. I quietly told him I'd take him fishing as soon as possible as a reward. I told him not to listen to all his mother's nicey-nicey crap."

"It's a difficult line to tread," I replied cautiously, not wanting to voice an opinion.

"Decommission first, debate after. That's my line of thinking, boy. Always has been, always will be."

"Here, I thought of this earlier. It's a joke. What's the name of Danny Fairbrass's favourite film?" I said, changing the subject.

There was a brief silence. "Come on, then. Let's have it," said a resigned voice.

"The Munga Games."

"How old are you, boy?"

"Not old enough to know any better."

"You're not fucking wrong... Anyway, got to go, I've got a Mars bar needing eating,"

"Sophie won't let me buy Mars bars to take fishing anymore. I've only got low fat Rich Tea biscuits," I moaned. "If I catch a first caught-forty having a snack, it'll be called 'Rich Tea Light'."

"And I bet you know how much fat percentage is in each biscuit as part of your adult reference intake."

"Yeah," I admitted, dolefully.

"You're making a big mistake, boy. Life's too short to worry about making it last a bit longer," Rambo advised. "Remember, *everything* kills you in the end."

Rambo's so wise at times.

I had been fishing for a little over three hours with no action when my mobile rang. I immediately assumed Rambo had caught one and was surprised to see an incoming number my smartphone didn't recognise. Probably another bloody wannabe member trying to get hold of me, I thought, as I answered it.

"Hello. Is that, Matt, the electrician?"

It was a female voice. One seeming vaguely familiar. "Yes, speaking."

"I believe you've got me booked in to do a little job? Some electrical work?"

I knew who it was now. "Yes, that's right, I have."

"I know this seems a little strange me asking, but would it be possible for you to come round and look at it tonight? So I can show what needs... doing," she added in a way seeming to hint at something.

"*Tonight?*" I asked, my previous thought dissolving. Not tonight. I'm on fish tonight.

"I know it's a bit earlier than we both expected... It's just that... You see, I'm all alone tonight."

"*Alone?*" I asked, the earlier intimation back on my mind.

"Yes. All alone. There's nobody else here except me."

"Okaaay," I replied, cagily.

"Do you know what I'm wearing at the moment?" the voice asked, now very alluring.

I felt my mouth instantly dry. "No," I managed to say, desperately trying to keep my tone level now the conversation had veered off into such an unexpected area.

"I'm wearing my new Agent Provocateur lingerie. I only bought it two days ago. No man has ever seen me in it."

"Haven't they?" I managed to ask, a strange feeling of excitement coursing round my body. An excitement I hadn't felt for years.

"Would you like to be the first man to see me wearing it?"

"I think I would," I said, my self-control leaving.

"And be the first man to take me out of it?"

"Yes. I would definitely like to do that," I answered, my self-control by now long gone and  miles away.

"I thought you would. I'd like you to be the first man to do that as well." By now my phone was pressed so hard against my ear, I thought it might shatter into a thousand pieces. "Do you know what else I've also bought?" the female voice continued, teasing.

"No," I admitted because I really didn't have a clue what else she had bought.

"I've bought some silk rope so you can tie me up. When you've tied me up, I won't be able to stop you from doing whatever you want to do to me, will I?"

"No, you won't," I gasped, unable to believe what I was hearing and knowing what she had said was *inescapably* true. I was an angler. I knew knots! I could five turn grinner her to the bed and she would never wriggle out. Not in a month of Sundays. Not even if she was a direct descendant of Harry Houdini. I felt my hands start to shake in raw undiluted sexual anticipation. After all these years, one of my fantasies was going to come true!

"No. I know I won't," she agreed.

"You definitely won't," I reiterated.

"I know I definitely won't," she said.

Having absolutely, comprehensively established, once she was tied up, she wouldn't be able to stop me from doing what I wanted to do to her, there was one last thing I had to ask.

"Just so we're perfectly clear, what is it I'm allowed to do to you that you wouldn't be able to stop me from doing if I wanted to?" I queried, my heart pounding like a jack hammer on amphetamines.

The phone went quiet as if it was making up its mind. "Anything you like," it eventually answered.

"*Anything?*" I responded, staggered. Surely, she didn't mean *anything?*

"I've got something to help," she said in a voice so quiet, despite the phone virtually touching my eardrum, I could barely hear. "It'll be a slippery slope, the one leading into depravity."

I think I sort of grunted, what with my brain being so deprived of blood flow on account of the massive flashing diversion sign directing it all to my groin. Wow! Who would have thought fantasies were like London buses?

"How soon can you get here?" the female voice asked.

"I'll leave now," I said. "I'll be as quick as I can."

"You know where I am, don't you?"

"I know exactly where you are," I confirmed.

"I'll be waiting."

Suddenly, being on fish didn't hold quite the attraction it had a few minutes earlier.

I wound in furiously and stripped the three rigs from my rods one by one, placing them inside my rig box and putting the box inside my rucksack. With the rods back on their rests and everything stashed inside my Fox Euro Classic Easy Dome, I hastily zipped up the mozzie mesh and then the porch door. With my head torch now on in the gathering darkness, I strode off around the Pit's perimeter grass track at a pace somewhere between a walk and a run. Undoubtedly, I looked as stupid as any Olympic 20K walker scurrying back towards my van, but at least I was chasing a bigger carrot than something as unimportant as a gold medal. By the time I reached the Peugeot, I was wet through with sweat and my head was throbbing. My whole body seemed to be generating steam, the roaring fire deep inside me – lit by the telephone call – was boiling water at a rate Robert Stephenson would have approved. Realising there was no way I could turn up on the doorstep and expect intimacy in my current saturated state, I opened the back of the van and grabbed the bag containing my spare set of clothes; the Falling In, Caught in a Thunderstorm, Sudden Onset of Hideous Vomiting/Diarrhoea set. Shutting the van, I hurried to the functional wooden clubhouse, went inside, stripped off, showered and put on the clean clothes.

My new outfit hardly consisted of first choice garments for turning up on a hot date and expecting to proceed, James Bond-like, to fantastic sex. An ensemble comprising an old T-shirt, old sweatshirt and old Adidas tracksuit bottoms could never depict a suave and debonair spy about town, although, crucially, the pants and socks were pretty new. The important factor, though, was they were all clean and fresh, like myself now – provided I didn't boil down into a globule of grease on the journey to her house. I needed to remain calm, I told myself as I pulled off the farm track and on to proper tarmac. That, above all else, was paramount. And not only on the drive, but later when things got even more thrilling. What I had to avoid, at all cost, was the biggest firework in the box going off prematurely before I had the chance to put on a nice display/foreplay with lesser ones.

The Journey to the Centre of my Fantasy seemed to take forever, in spite of my constant speeding and occasional, vitally necessary, manic overtaking manoeuvres – you know the kind, ones shaving whole *seconds* off hour-long trips. Only after what seemed like three days and fifteen hundred miles, did I complete it. As I parked the van, I thought of all my past sexual misdemeanours and wondered how they might stack up against this one. Pretty well, I thought as I rung the bell. This was as electrifying as anything.

She answered the door quickly, easing it open to reveal herself in her new lingerie and 'fuck me' high heels – a superfluous set of shoes in terms of making a statement, if ever there was a pair. She looked so different from how I remembered her, I had to double check to make sure it definitely was her. Her hair and make-up made her look so different. She looked incredible. So different. So sexy. So gorgeous.

"Hello, you," she purred. "There was no need for you to dress up," she added, eyeing me up and down.

"It was all I had with me. The tuxedo was at the dry cleaners," I answered.

"You'd better come in," she said.

No sooner had I stepped over the threshold and shut the door, she flung her arms around my neck and kissed me, grinding her groin into mine.

"This is so exciting," she gasped as she came up for air, unclamping her mouth from mine.

"I know. Why haven't we done this sooner?" I gasped back.

"I had to get rid of that husband of mine," she replied, peeling my sweatshirt over my head. "Now he's not around, this mouse can play." In response, I grabbed hold of her butt and squeezed both cheeks, pulling them apart. "Were do you want me?" she murmured.

"Where's the rope?"

"Waiting on the bed."

"Take me to the bed."

We both moved off and ascended the stairs, her first, me second. I took off my T-shirt during the climb up the first flight of stairs and on the half landing, kicked off my trainers. I clambered free from my tracksuit bottoms as I strode up the last few treads to the first floor hallway. Reaching out to take my hand, she lead the way into the bedroom. On the bed was the rope. Next to the rope was the lubricant.

You know how directors zoom in on a male actor, in a really tense scene from a film, and he swallows so hard you can see his Adam's apple bob up and down? Well, that's what mine did.

She turned to face me. "I don't think I need this on, do you?" she said discarding her bra. "Or these," she smirked, see-sawing the tiny pair of knickers over her hips and down her silky thighs, letting them drop on the floor.

My jaw pretty much went with them. Shaved! She had shaved! What was this woman? Probably only the sexiest woman on this earth.

She kneeled down in front of me and teased off my pants, took hold off my...

There was a sudden almighty smash. The noise of breaking crockery coming from downstairs.

"Jesus Christ! What was that?" I asked in alarm.

"Shit! It's him!" she replied.

"What, your husband?" I blurted, so caught up was I in the performance.

"He's coming up the stairs! I can hear him," she said.

I strained my ears. She was right! I could hear him coming up the stairs. *Bounding* up the stairs. Both of us looked at each other in terror, unable to move, ensnared in the shock of the moment. We were going to get caught with our pants down! Both of us were going to get caught with our pants well and truly down! Our heads turned in synchronisation to look at the closed, yet slightly ajar, door to the bedroom. Gradually, horror film-like, it started to open.

"He's coming in!" she cried in alarm. "He can't see us like this! It's all wrong!"

The door opened a little further, enough for Hobbes to push through the gap and run in to us, purring and nuzzling around our bare legs.

I looked down in dismay at my drooping manhood. "Fuck me, Soph. It's no good. I can't do it with him watching."

"I don't think we *want* to do it with him watching, do you?" Sophie asked, as if it was a no-brainer. "Put him downstairs in the kitchen and give him a bit of food to keep him quiet, then come back up to me. We are *not* going to lose this moment! Do you know how much organisation went into getting Amy out of the house and Adam over to my mum's. That's before buying everything else?"

I kissed her gently on the cheek. "I know. It's fantastic. You're fantastic. You look even fantasticer. And I know it's not a proper word, but it sort of sounds right. I loved the mobile phone number thing, by the way. It made it so realistic. What was it, a cheap Pay as You Go one?"

Sophie nodded. "My sex date mobile!"

I laughed. "Stay there. Don't go away... I'll be back."

"Okay, Arnold," she said, coquettishly and smiling.

I scooped Hobbes up, cuddling his furry body close to my bare chest so he couldn't escape, and took him downstairs to placate him with food. As I shut the kitchen door and turned off the light, I told him not to start caterwauling or there would be big trouble. The broken dish on the tiled floor I could deal with later. "Mind your paws on the sharp bits," I warned.

Cat sorted, and with renewed rising enthusiasm, *I* bounded back upstairs to take my part in Sophie Williams' new initiative: to spice up her and her husband's love life through role-play, a bit of bondage and… I know I don't have to spell it out.

By the time I got back to The Pit and had walked to my swim, it was nearly four in the morning, I was dead on my feet and feeling really hungry. These were only secondary attributes, however, because, above all else, I was elated. What a night! Sophie had really pushed the boat out and it had been brilliant. So exciting, so fresh, so different and so wonderful. Why hadn't I ever thought of having an affair with my wife before? Albeit with the pair of us masquerading as different personas. It would have saved an awful lot of trouble and maybe stopped both of us from doing it for real.

The past can never be undone, of course, but tonight had been a huge underlining of the continuing success of our relationship after all the ups and downs of yesteryear. Sure, we argued and moaned at each other at times over day-to-day matters, what couple doesn't, but tonight had shown what we could recapture when we put our minds to it. When both parties played their part, it seemed we were capable of inventing a Hot Sex Time Machine; one capable of transporting us back to the early days of desire, lust, thumping hearts and shaking hands.

I wasn't so naive to imagine we might ever top tonight, not with its first-time-ever shock value of plunging into previously uncharted sexual waters. The second time would obviously be a variation of 'more of the same', the very problem leading to stagnation in the first place. Yet 'more of the same' of what we had experienced tonight was light years ahead of more of the same from the past. Tonight set a new standard, a new dimension promising sexual longevity with the capability of it becoming an integral part of our lives. There were simply so many endless variables for either party to embrace in order to spice things up. All that was required was the imagination, the time and a willingness to embrace our individual parts. As I walked over to my rods, pleased to see them, the rod pod and my Delkims still present and correct – although I hadn't for a minute expected otherwise – I considered the interruption to my session to have been more than worth it.

"Let's get you boys back out there, have a bite to eat, and then I can get some kip," I said to my rods, as I picked up the left-hand one.

After propping up the left-sided Torrix of my front three forward line on the side of my dome, I unzipped the porch door and rolled it up, securing it with the two elastic loops and toggles to make a Polyester lintel. With access now acquired, I did the same with the mozzie door and knelt down by my bedchair, virtually in the same spot as Sylvester when he had half scared me to death. I shone my head torch around the dome's interior and experienced a strange feeling creep over me. I couldn't put my finger on why I felt like I did, I just did. Everything inside looked exactly as I had left it, as far as I could recall, having left in such a hurry in the dark. I scanned the bivvy more carefully, perusing my rucksack, bedchair and other equipment and tried to convince myself I was imagining it. I told myself to stop being so stupid and look at the evidence presented before my eyes. Regardless, I couldn't stop myself being wholly convinced somebody had been inside my bivvy while I was gone.

# Chapter 7

My Delkim, my blue LED Delkim, or rather the blue channel on my Delkim Rx Pro had turned into an alarm clock. Remarkably, given the volume at which I had set it, one struggling to wake me up. After a disgustingly long response time, so dead was I to the world, the nagging, repetitive tune eventually permeated into my auditory cortex and elicited a response. As disorientated as an attractive fourteen-year-old girl disembarking from a fairground waltzer ride – the waltzer guys always spin the pretty girls the most, it's a fact of life – I escaped my sleeping bag, staggered barefoot over my loosely-laced-trainers-ready-for-a-run-in-the-middle-of-the-night out to my middle rod, tightened the Basia's clutch and hit the take. Eighty odd yards away, a carp pulled against the strange resistance in its mouth.

The bend in my rod felt good. Last night's feeling in my other rod had also felt good. It was true to say each held a special place in my heart. However, now was not the time for my mind to start evaluating differing pleasures. It was not the hour to log on to comparethethrill.com, but was the time to focus solely on the underwater leviathan I had hooked on a clipped-up, cast-in-the-dark, feathered-down-with-a-'donk', single, exclusive, revolutionary, indented, dirty brown bottom bait boilie attached to The Carper's super trick rig.

With full CPU locked on to playing the fish and a cold, wet feeling soaking up my socks, I initiated the first opening gambit in a game of chess. I quickly rescinded the order. Idiot! I didn't know how to play chess! Or what a 'gambit' was. Instead, I played a little straight overhead strain on the fish. There. Much better now I knew what the hell I was doing. On a long line, it's always difficult to ascertain the size of the fish you're fighting and this occasion was no different. My adversary chugged away in The Pit's depths, in a low key kind of manner, and I, trying to keep equally as unflustered, was quite happy to let it do so.

I took in a deep breath. The first take of the season, I thought, savouring the moment before acknowledging my mood would be entirely decimated by not converting the opportunity into a fish on the bank. (Rule of carp fishing: A take is only an elevator ride to heaven; it doesn't give you the key to the lock to open the gates, go inside and start knocking back the free drinks, eat the sandwiches and fraternise with the in-house supermodels.) With this absolutely vital concept uppermost in my mind, I gently eased back, lowered and wound down, each time slowly gaining line over the ensuing minutes; ever mindful each pump of the rod was shortening the time until the battle would kick in for real. When I had successfully eased the fish back to a distance approximately twenty yards from me, as predicted, events took a more lively turn.

Producing its most powerful run to date (think: favourite wide player – Gareth Bale, Cristiano Ronaldo or Sadio Mané getting on his bike and charging down the touchline), the fish surged down to my left, taking line from my clutch as it did so. Impressed by its power, I held on tight because, to chuck an expletive into an old carp fishing cliché , there was 'fuck all I could do about it'. Disconcertingly, during this burst of raw power, the fish had picked up the closer-in line of my left-hand rod and I had to perform the old 'up and over' trick of getting it clear and resetting it on the pod's middle rod position. The 'up and over' – not to be confused with Grandstand relic commentator Eddie Waring's 'Up and Under' – is always a mildly traumatic manoeuvre and I was pleased to complete it without incident. Especially once I definitely knew the carp I had hooked hadn't completed a preposterous logic-defying barrel roll around the other rod's line as carp sometimes, inexplicably, manage to do.

Having shuffled to the extreme left edge of my swim, with only the fish to contend with, I could now apply more hefty side-strain. I was keen (desperate) to avoid letting the fish get too far down to my left, where it might kite into the bank. There were several trees growing near to the water's edge with overhanging branches and I certainly didn't want them entering into the equation. Consequently, as an angler firmly established in the 'Nah, never backwind, mate' camp, I tweaked the clutch a bit tighter as the fish was still resolutely refusing to buckle to my will. Then, with the rod's butt in my left hand and my right hand positioned way past the reel fitting, arms at full reach and body leaning out over the water, I gave it the full monty. The clutch gave way at first, but a couple of seconds later the fish turned and started to swim back towards me. With everything more or less under control, I let the fish move up to bore around directly in front of me, keeping it ideally positioned with the odd application of solid side-strain when required. Now it was closer, I could feel the weight of it and the boils of water, as it resisted the upwards pressure, were testament to the amount of Pit liquid it was displacing. My heart gave a little flutter, the beats spelling out 'big fish' in Morse code.

After some time of carefully nudging the reel handle around, ever decreasing the distance between me and my quarry, the carp was close enough for me to catch my first glimpse of it in the gin clear water. Seeing a big carp in clear water is always a thrill, even more so when it's attached to your line. Watching it dive and roll, twist and turn, powering away only to be subdued by your tackle's resistance is a fascinating experience. To actually see what you often only experience in touch feedback through your rod; to correlate the bend and bumps and sudden brief episodes of slackness with a visual picture of how a carp is creating those moments, is a true privilege. Landing it, it goes without saying, is an even bigger one. Only then will you know if it's as big, or bigger, than your earlier estimation.

It's a fundamental aspect of our pastime when we play a fish – guessing how big it is. Fantasising over whether or not it might be a twenty, a thirty, a forty, or perhaps, jackpot of jackpots, a PB. Of course, if you recognise the fish in the water you will already have a pretty good idea of its size. If it's one of the 'A' list, your adrenaline levels will soar as your mind ponders on how much it may have grown. Will it be at its biggest ever, or will the time of the year, or its condition, conspire to bring it down in weight? This was the position I found myself in as I was pretty sure the fish I had on was The Olympian. Named thanks to the five huge scales on one side, so positioned they mimicked the circles on the Olympic flag, it was an original stock fish and a definite A-lister. The last time it was out, over two years ago now, it had weighed fifty-nine six. I couldn't see it having lost any weight and dared to wonder how big it might have grown in the time since its last capture. Whatever the size, it was a great fish to catch, not only in general terms, but especially for me personally. The Olympian was one of the few originals I had never caught before.

The temporary periscope of the hooked piscine submarine, my anti-tangle tubing, broke the surface of the water while the shimmering bulk of it lay directly underneath. With my heart racing, I kept everything smooth and consistent, applying continuous pressure which eventually caused the fish to come up and take a gulp of air. It rolled over and doggedly went back down again, only for me to carefully force it back up to the surface a short time later. The fish looked spent, it must have been fighting for over twenty minutes, so I readied my net. Now on the surface, its broad flank undistorted by water, it looked enormous. As chance would have it, five huge scales glistened in the morning light and my original notion was confirmed. In the cavernous mouth coming straight towards me, I spotted my boilie deep inside, my hook, by definition, must have been nailed in the bottom lip. This fish wasn't coming off. The Carper's super trick rig had done the business again. With increasing confidence, I leant back and eased The Olympian over my net and lifted. She was safely in. I had now scored twice in the same session!

With mission accomplished, my body relaxed and as my CPU opened up to other inputs I realised my feet felt really cold and wet. It was uncomfortable, so I left the fish safely in the net and dashed back to base to dry my feet and put on my spare socks and boots. Back quickly, I went through the familiar procedure of unhooking the fish and transferring it to somewhere safe in preparation for weighing and photographing. Once she was safely in the staked floating weigh sling I used on The Pit, I phoned Rambo and asked him if he could come round and do the honours with the camera and help me with weighing the beast.

(One of the few additional rules Rambo and I had added since we had taken over The Pit was to do with the photographing of fish. Popular opinion often has it anyone refusing to wind in and photograph a fish for a fellow angler, when asked, is a bit of a carping pariah. A right grumpy arsehole. Rambo and I had always thought otherwise. Fish get caught at bite-time and being asked to wind in during the 'window of opportunity', to accommodate another angler's photographic needs, is tantamount to being asked to write off what could be a whole day's fishing. It's certainly a waste of bite-time and means a three rod recast, with all the associated disturbance, on the camera wielder's return. And for what reason? None other than the lucky angler hasn't the correct equipment to photograph his fish for himself. With modern digital cameras, a cheap tripod and a remote shutter operator it isn't hard to get perfectly adequate photos of any fish. Do it a few of times and it becomes second nature.

The problems when photographing fish solo truly come into their own when the carp get really big. The physical process of handling a very large carp, of getting it out of the water safely, of weighing and photographing it, is much easier when undertaken double handed. Therefore, with fish safety uppermost, Rambo and I decided any fish over fifty pounds should always be weighed and photographed with assistance. Fish under that weight, although obviously still large by anyone's standards, we felt could be safely dealt with by an individual. These weights weren't set in stone, clearly we were banking on the successful angler being able to guestimate his capture reasonably accurately, and were only intended as guidelines. Equally, if an angler felt he needed help with a fish, irrespective of size and in exceptional circumstances – a physical issue, for example – then it was okay to ask. But *never* purely on the grounds of wanting to get better pictures.

For our new rule to be successful, it needed membership responsibility. Fish safety was the priority and with so many fifties, sixties and seventies in The Pit, help was often a necessity. The onus on the membership was simple; to gladly give the help they themselves might one day require and the nous not to take liberties and bother fellow anglers unnecessarily. Everyone knew the score and what was expected of them, whether they were the one who had made the capture or whether they were the one who had asked for help. As it transpired, the rule worked perfectly as most anglers found themselves a 'fish buddy'. An angler who would help them and one who would receive help in return. A reciprocal arrangement between two friends, causing no disturbance to others, the main criteria of which, for a happy and continuous arrangement, being two anglers pairing up who caught roughly the same number of fish per season!)

Rambo was impressed as he held up my scales. "Sixty-four pounds and four ounces. Nice fish, boy. The Olympian has always been a looker."

"Yeah, no doubt. You can't mistake the scale pattern."

"And from the spot where you say you saw fish when you were looking round?" Rambo asked, as he lowered the leviathan on to my unhooking mat.

"That's right. I was well pleased to hit it because I had to cast out in the dark."

"Why?" Rambo asked, sounding confused as he moved the fish back into the water.

"Oh… I had to nip back home early evening. I didn't get back until the following morning," I answered, not wanting to tell Rambo what I had been up to.

"Everything all right?" Rambo enquired, concern in his voice.

"Yeah. Perfectly fine… Just one of those unavoidable things."

Rambo seemed happy with my answer and dismissed it from his head. "Where's your camera?"

"I'll get it."

Once retrieved, I handed Rambo my Eos and the pair of us set about photographing my first capture of The Olympian. Job completed, Rambo helped me get the fish back into the weigh sling and carried it to the water's edge.

"Want to do the honours?"

I nodded and took over from Rambo, gently easing open the floatation weigh sling's zip and clearing it from The Olympian's head. The huge fish slowly snaked its bulky body out of its temporary home and cruised off into the clear water. What a sight it was.

"Fantastic. Thanks for coming round. Much appreciated," I said to Rambo.

"No worries, boy. Nice to see such a great fish on the bank." Rambo wiped his huge hands on his camo trousers. "Rob's fishing now," he informed me. "He came and saw me yesterday before he set up."

"Brought you an apple, did he?" I teased.

"He brought me some *info*, boy," Rambo continued, ignoring my gentle piss-take. "He hasn't fished East Ender this year and as far as he knows, nobody has."

"Really? That's a bit weird. I suppose it could have been someone baiting up. They could have easily gone unnoticed." I weighed up whether to tell Rambo how I had felt on my return back to my bivvy and decided, on balance, I ought to.

"So, no physical reason to make you think someone had been in there? Just a gut feeling?" Rambo asked, once I had told him.

"That's it in a nutshell."

"Were your boilies all still present and correct?"

"Funny enough, I didn't perform an inventory on all my kit before I left. Certainly not down to the level of counting all my baits out and logging them," I answered.

"Maybe you should have done," Rambo replied.

"*If* I was suffering from paranoia or OCD it *might* have been a runner…"

"But you are. *We* are, aren't we?" said Rambo, cutting in. "And now we've got the recipe we're worse than ever! You've only got to take a step back and look at what we've been doing to hang on to all our little edges. To keep them safe and away from prying eyes. I bet you took the rigs off your rods before you left."

"Yeah," I admitted.

"I'm glad you said that, boy, otherwise I'd have been really pissed off with you," Rambo remarked.

"I guess you're right about the paranoia," I conceded. "Trouble is, there's no way of knowing what has happened, or if it has even happened at all. I put my rigs in my rig box and put the rig box in my rucksack, but I suppose someone could have still looked at them."

"I don't like it," Rambo confessed. "You're probably right about someone having a nose in all your gear. You've got a track record for predicting this sort of stuff. A one hundred per cent track record. Let's hope they never had the nerve to start rummaging in your rucksack and found The Carper's rig."

"This was nothing like that," I quickly corrected. "This was no vision. This was just an odd sort of feeling. I was knackered by the time I got back. Perhaps we're both getting a bit carried away."

"Possibly... I wonder if it's some member from The Lake doing a bit of poaching and trying to copy what we're up to," Rambo mused aloud, undeterred by my doubts. "I'll tell you what, boy, they are going to seriously fucking regret it once I find out who it is."

"If it is, who would do it, though? Who would be mad enough to risk chancing their arm?" I asked.

"I don't know. Maybe somebody who's been through a personal upheaval. Some fucker who's just dumped a lifetime ethos and thinks they're a bad boy."

"You mean, Luke?" I spluttered. "No way."

"Got any better suggestions?"

"No, I haven't got anybody any better. How could I?" I answered, slightly exasperated.

"I think I need to have a word," Rambo insisted. "See what's going on in that newly-formed, non-believing head of his. I'm taking Sylvester to The Lake soon, I think I'll coincide our trip with his usual Friday start."

"Okay," I agreed. "But go easy on him. No pulling out his fingernails with your forceps."

"I like it!" Rambo exclaimed. "That's the best idea you've had in weeks, boy."

The trouble with Rambo is, you never know if he's joking or not.

Rambo departed and I fished on in an odd state of mind. On the one hand, I was elated at having got off to such a cracking start with the capture of The Olympian, on the other, I had fleeting feelings of trepidation and insecurity mixed with a sense of incredulity. Was it credible to even think someone had poached The Pit or gained access to my bivvy and the secrets within? My conversation with Rambo had made it seem all the more feasible and yet what real evidence was there? A couple of boilies in a margin and an odd feeling I'd had when utterly exhausted. It would hardly stand up in a court of law. It was more likely we *were* having a midlife carping crisis.

In an attempt to make myself feel better, as if I was 'doing something about it', I spent fifteen minutes mucking around with my landing net fishing out one of the rogue boilies. It was an awkward job as the margin was deep and the only two boilies I could see were lodged in little dips on the bottom. Eventually, after using some highly evocative language of an Anglo-Saxon origin, I succeeded in dredging one up. Plucking it from the corner of my net with the same satisfaction as if I had reclaimed an ancient artefact from the depths of the ocean, I held it between my thumb and index finger and examined it. Then I went and got my reading glasses and examined it again, rolling it between my thumb and finger as if it was a lustrous pearl.

It wasn't ours. That was the first thing I established – although why on earth I had considered it a possibility was beyond me. Paranoia yet again, I guess. Taking on the air of a forensic scientist, I sat in my sitting-outside-the-bivvy-in-the-sun-during-the-day chair and decided to perform an autopsy, making notes as I did. Before putting the boilie under the knife, I regarded its shape. It wasn't as perfectly round as it should have been had it been rolled in a machine and it had a less commercial look to it, if that makes sense. Size-wise it was a good eighteen millimetres, possibly a bit bigger, although it would certainly have swollen up in the water. With these observations in mind I noted down: 'Hand rolled, 18mm?' on a clean page in the wire bound pad I kept with me to log fish captures. Moving to the external colour, I jotted down exactly what my eyes told me: 'Washed out pink.' I squeezed the boilie gently and, although hamstrung by not knowing how hard it had been in the first place, I estimated how long it had been in the water and noted it down: 'Two days in water, tops.' I then photographed the boilie as a whole with my phone.

It was time for the surgery to begin. Cutting the bait carefully in half, I noted down the internal, and thus the original, colour of the bait: 'Dark pink, but *not* a fluoro.' I took another photograph with the two centres facing towards the lens and next observed the mix. The bait seemed to be a very smooth mix, there were no little bits of this and that, only a uniform consistency to what I perceived to have been a very fine series of ingredients. I noted down: 'Fine mix – no additional bits.' Finally, I sniffed it. The flavour was still apparent, supporting my earlier assumption of it not having been in the water too long, only what the hell was it? Smell is a such a bastard to put a tag on. Compared to animals, we truly are the poor relations regards to using this sense. Despite the ability of smell to provoke a huge reaction in us, one where a pungent whiff can transport us back in time to a moment long buried in our memories, we still find it hard to categorise. Something may smell fruity, meaty or fishy, but defining which individual group it belongs is difficult. I lifted up my nose in agitation and shook my head at my non-cognition. Pup might know. He might be able to sniff out the answer, quite literally be able to sniff out the answer. Pity he wasn't around. An idea shimmered into my brain. Yes, I would do it later, once I didn't need it anymore.

In the end, I could only decipher the flavour as fruity, with what I thought might be a subtle undercurrent of something a bit creamy. I noted down: 'Fruity + hint of cream?' Once I was done, I wrapped the boilie in a small piece of silver foil used to keep my sandwiches fresh, carefully putting the two halves back together (I didn't use sutures), and placed it in my cool box for safety and preservation. If there was anything going on, it was our only link to it and Rambo needed to take a look while it was in a good state. God help Luke if Rambo found him fishing with a similar bait, I mused.

At three in the afternoon, I was considerably perked up by a show in the same area from where I had caught my fish. This seemed to augur well for another take, possibly at the same time the following morning. As daylight faded and the weaker evening chance for a bite came and went, it became apparent this was to be my best chance of bagging a brace. Two of my rods had been out since my early morning, completely knackered return to The Pit and I had taken the opportunity to recast them before the evening light had faded. The other rod, the one that had produced the take and been recast straight after, I left alone, confident in its positioning and how it was laying on the bottom. Apart from its great presentation and perfect hook-up ratio, I had never wound in The Carper's super trick rig and found it tangled. Not once in all the years I had used it and Rambo had reported the same infallible success rate. It really was the rig that broke the mould; the best thing since sliced bread; the bee's knees, so much so it had become the apple of my eye because it cut the mustard and could go the distance and the extra mile. It was the rig that never stopped giving… No more. I'm all idiomed out.

I was up at first light the next daybreak, boots on in anticipation for another seven-thirty take. As the clocked ticked past my appointment time and headed on towards eight, I fired up the kettle in a desperate attempt to provoke a take. Ten was my absolute, can't-leave-it-any-longer, got-to-go wind in time. Even then I was cutting it fine to get home, get my tools and trek over to Sonia's as I still had to pop in and see Rambo on a 'long way round' trip back to the functional wooden clubhouse. At nine I started clearing out my bivvy, stacking all my gear under a tree. By half past it was time to go through the process of breaking down the EuroDome – a thirty second job – and shoehorn it into its carrier bag, which was a much longer chore.

With everything ready to go, I stood a yard from the butts of my rods and accepted it was unlikely another chance was going to be coming my way. By five past ten, I told myself, no, really, another chance *wasn't* going to come my way. Fuck Sonia and her power points, I thought, and reluctantly wound in my left-hand rod and stowed it away in my rod bag. The right-hand rod went next and only then did I move on to the Take Giver rod. Doing my customary starting from twenty countdown, I stood with the rod in my hand and on reaching zero wound in like a demented spodder. From hanging it out, I turned about face and went at it full throttle, packing the last rod away and yomping off to retrieve the van in double quick time. Once everything had been bundled into the back, I drove off to Big Island, parked behind it, took the operated upon boilie out of my cool box and went to see Rambo. He was standing outside of his bivvy eating a Mars bar.

"Fuck me! How many of them do you bring with you?" I asked, nodding at the sweet that in days gone by apparently helped you work, rest and play.

"More than what I used to," Rambo answered. "The fucking things are shrinking on a weekly basis."

"Have a look at this," I said, offering Rambo the tiny silver ball.

He took it from me gingerly, pulling a face. "You haven't castrated yourself, have you, boy? I always wondered if you only had one."

"Bloody cheek! No, I haven't. And if I had, it'd be much bigger than that," I insisted.

"Okay," Rambo said smiling. "Think I hit a bit of a nerve there."

"It's one of the baits from the margin. I fished it out. I've taken some photos and made some notes."

Rambo pulled the corners of his mouth down, nodded approvingly, unpeeled the foil from the boilie and inspected it. "At least it's not one of ours," he said.

"Nice one," I said, sarcastically, secretly pleased Rambo's first comment had been much like mine. We were like a pair of paranoid old men. "But what is it? Do you recognise it?"

Rambo shook his head. "I don't think it's a commercially available bait somehow. More a homemade effort, I think, judging by its shape." Rambo held one half of the boilie up to his nose and sniffed it.

"That's the hard part. What flavour do you think it is?" I asked.

"A bit pineappley? There's something else going on as well. Coconut cream, maybe. Whatever it is, I'll be able to recognise it if Luke's using it. Why don't you take a look at the stored baits in the clubhouse freezers and see if anyone on here is using it."

"That's a good idea. I'll keep you posted. Look, I've got to dash, I'm late as it is. Can I have it back?"

Rambo shrugged and handed it back. "You didn't have anything else, then?"

"No. I had another show over my middle rod, but nothing came of it."

"I haven't had that," Rambo admitted. "Not seen a thing. You've done well to wangle one out, boy. Very well."

I nodded. "Yeah, I'm well happy…. Right. Sorry to be rude, but I've got to go. I'll give you a ring. I might come up and spend a bit of time with you and Sylvester at The Lake if I get the chance. If you don't hear from me you'll know I haven't found anything like this in the freezers. See you later!" I said, holding up the washed out pink bait.

"Bye, Matt," Rambo said, lifting up a huge hand.

As I left him, I imagined both of them around Luke's neck.

To my surprise, I hadn't poked my head in them for years, there was a fair bit of bait in the freezers. Clearly, quite a few members weren't fussed about other anglers knowing what bait was going in The Pit. I was pleased to see there were a number of bags of bait from the recognised quality bait manufacturers; Mainline, Nutrabaits, Sticky Baits, to name a few, and there were no shelf-life baits nor any sneakily frozen tiger nuts. The well-known ten-kilo bags, with their contents blatantly marked, I could quickly dismiss as the dark pink bait I was looking to match wasn't a commercial. With rapidly cooling fingers, I humped those frozen monsters to one side to see what else was in amongst the frost. The 'what else' consisted of a roughly equal number of various sized plain bags of boilies. There were some ten-kilo bags, but predominantly the sizes were smaller, usually five kilos, with the odd single-kilo bags. Some were bags from firms who offered rolling services and others were probably homemade mixes rolled by members, although none of the bags had names on them. These were the baits slaved over and created in a kitchen at home, with a nagging partner never too far away. Pushing to the back of my mind the notion Rambo and I would be doing something very similar very soon, I carried on hunting. By the time I had gone through all the chest freezers my fingers were numb from the cold and none of the baits I had looked at were dark pink in colour. Blowing air into my cupped hands in an attempt to get some feeling back, I knew there was nothing left for me to do but shut the lids and leave the boilies in peace in their pitch black freezing environment.

Driving home, I considered the search for the dark pink bait had been a bit of a pointless task to some extent, but nevertheless one that had to be undertaken. It was all to do with the process of elimination. If it had turned up, then it would have been game over and case closed with everything returning to normal. It hadn't and it meant the situation remained unresolved.

Essentially, there were still a lot of Pit members who didn't want to keep their baits in the clubhouse freezers. I had reckoned on there being at most only five or six anglers' worth of bait in the freezers. As such, eliminating them didn't equate to the dark pink bait definitely belonging to a poacher, only in the fact it shifted the odds towards that possibility. Even so, it was hardly conclusive. What I didn't want to do was start phoning up all the members – there was no way of knowing who was keeping baits in the freezers and who wasn't – and asking them if they were using a dark pink bait. That seemed far too premature at the moment. Best to see what Rambo turned up with Luke.

Once I was home, there was one thing I was keen to do before I rushed off to Sonia's. I went indoors via the back door and found Sophie in the kitchen putting on some washing. For a split second it was hard to adjust to seeing her in jogging bottoms and an old top loading the washing machine with how she had looked and what we had done yesterday.

I kissed her on the cheek. "Hi, darling. Good to see you again. I hope you've been behaving yourself while I've been gone?" I asked, keeping up our little pretence.

"Oh, yes. The same old routine. Cooking, washing and hanging around the house looking dowdy," she said, returning my peck on the cheek, a knowing smile on her face.

"I'm just off to Sonia's in a minute," I said, getting it in before she could ask. "Only I wanted to do something before I go. Where's Hobbes? Is he with Adam?"

"Isn't he always? They're in the living room. He's playing cars with him."

In the living room, I found Adam pushing his toy cars around on the floor while Hobbes watched intently from the top of the settee.

"Hi, Buddy Boy," I said, bending down and scooping my son up in the air. "Are you playing with Hobbes?" Adam giggled with delight as I swung him around. "Here, look. I've got a sweet for Hobbes. Shall we see if he likes it?"

Adam nodded vigorously. I put him down on his feet and took the boilie from my pocket, still rewrapped in foil from earlier.

"Hobbie got sweetie," Adam said, pointing to the shiny orb between my fingers. Nodding and grinning at my son, I removed the foil and placed the two halves of the pink bait on a cupped right hand and offered it to the Sphinx-like mass of ginger fur on my settee. Hobbes' nose slowly inched out and sniffed it. The effect was immediate. His eyes dilated instantaneously and the cat got to his feet in a flash, his whole body bristling, tail thrashing with anger. An almighty hiss came from his mouth, his ears flattened and then a low warning wail emanated from a tooth-bound mouth. With the speed of a striking cobra, Hobbes grabbed the two halves of the boilie off my hand and jumped down to the floor in one continuous movement. Once there, he scuttled under the coffee table and devoured the bait as if it was his first meal in weeks.

Fucking hell, I thought. Whoever's bait it was, they were good. Damn good.

# Chapter 8

Pup had prospective tenants. The company who were dealing with the letting of his house had phoned to arrange for me to meet and show them around. Jotting down the time and date we had agreed on, I cursed the inconvenience. Why Pup hadn't gone for the full package, one where the letting firm could deal with everything, I had no idea. Part of me suspected the motivation lay in him getting his money's worth in return for his bait-making gear and continued access to our exclusive, revolutionary, indented, dirty brown bottom bait boilie. The other theory, when being more kindly disposed towards the ex-boiliemeister, was his need to have a more personalised contact with his old life. With me directly involved I could tell him what his tenants were *really* like and, thinking ahead, what they were getting up to in his house on a regular basis. For example, I could pop by to see if they were growing marijuana in every room after bypassing the electricity meter, if they had turned the place into a crack den or were using it as a sex house hosting orgies for transgender ethnic minorities. Whatever the true reason, I was only guessing at it. The truth was in Pup's brain, or at least the illogically linked nest of writhing worms passing for his brain.

The prospective tenants turned out to be a couple in their late twenties and didn't look the type to get involved in skunk, cocaine or aggravated pimping. I could also confirm, after careful visual inspection, both were traditional gender White British – although, thanks to an ever-changing society, there was no telling how soon that description might put you on the outer edges of sexuality and ethnicity. She was a legal secretary, very nice and chatty, and he was a store manager for a large high street retail chain.

Showing them around Pup's past shrine to all things round, smelly and edible for carp, I was struck by the plight of their generation. With an air of resignation, she told me wherever they decided to rent would be their first home. They were still living with his parents at the moment, as it had been impossible to raise the deposit to go the mortgage and buy route. Despite both having reasonable jobs, buying a house was beyond them and only now, thanks to his recent promotion, could they consider renting. In East Sussex. Not London. East Sussex.

Virtually having to force myself to remember to say phrases like, 'living room' and 'dining room' instead of '18-22mm drying room' and '25mm plus room', as I walked into each miserable magnolia-smeared monstrosity, all still with the hint of peculiar olfactory affront, I found myself empathising with them and their contemporaries. What chance did these kids have? Too many people and not enough houses, poor interest rates making money pour into buy-to-let schemes and the super rich gobbling up London – pushing exorbitant prices outwards like a lobbed stone's ripple on a pond – were creating the perfect shit storm.

"How much have they said the rent will be?" I asked.

She told me. Fucking hell. All that for an ex-boilie factory.

They seemed excited enough, though. Maybe I was so out of touch with rental rates Pup's pad was a bargain. To be honest, I thought it needed to be, looking at the state of it through fresh eyes. That was my take on it, but maybe their youth and enthusiasm could ignore the house's current grimness. Maybe they imagined breezing in, redecorating it, furnishing it, decking it out with personal knick-knacks and making it into a proper home. A cosy little nest affording them true independence; one where they could have sex on the stairs and watch whatever they wanted on the TV without forever being judged by his parents. Rather strangely, I wondered if I would want to be in my twenties today and decided, on the whole, I was more than happy with my lot despite being well into my forties.

Once they had seen all they needed to see, I locked up and phoned Rambo. "Are you there, yet?" I asked the undoubtedly camo-clad Terminator with Tackle.

"Yeah, all set up, boy. The Lake's looking good."

"What swim?"

"I'm in Silver Birch, where you fished on your last trip. I saw lots of bubbling on my walk round and thought, that's good enough for me."

"Is you-know-who there, yet?"

"Just turned up. Looks like he's fishing right down the other end."

"Okay. What time does Sylvester have lunch?"

"One o'clock. I've told him a strange man in a white van will be waiting for him outside the school gates. I told him when the driver waves a packet of sweets at him, he's got to get in!"

"Steady!" I exclaimed, unhappy with the picture Rambo was painting. "Is it all right him bunking off for the afternoon?"

"Sure is, boy. He's got an appointment."

"Yeah, with some fishing tackle and hopefully a few carp."

"Exactly. His Mum doesn't know, so keep it under your hat. Don't go blurting it out when we're bait-making at mine," Rambo warned.

"Will do... Look, I'm just going to leave Pup's now, so I should be bang on time to meet Sylvester. I'll see you later."

"Okay, boy. I reckon I'll have had one by then."

"Don't doubt it, mate! Bye!"

I was doing Rambo a favour by picking up Sylvester from school. He had promised the lad a two-nighter on The Lake, but had wanted to get there in the morning rather than after school to beat the Friday just-finished-work rush. For my part, I wanted to be present when Rambo interrogated Luke. Partly as a stabilising device to stop Rambo from tearing him apart if he had been poaching The Pit – something I still couldn't get my head around – and partly because I was chomping at the bit to find out the truth. Rambo had suggested letting Sylvester leave school early to give all concerned a bit more breathing space. Naturally, Sylvester was more than up for it and I didn't mind if his father didn't – the scam was only depriving him of a few hours of his education, it wasn't as if Rambo was taking him on a three-year world fishing tour.

On the journey to the primary school, I had an incoming call. On the van's display the name 'Pup' appeared.

"Pu... Peter! How's it going?" I answered, enthusiastically.

"Great! Really great! How's Hobbes?"

"Yeah, he's fine. Him and my Adam have really struck up a bond. They're always together. Adam loves him. He carries him around and everything. He couldn't have settled in any better."

"Brilliant! Lovely to hear. He's eating okay, then?"

"Tucking it away. No problems there at all."

"Excellent... Don't overfeed him," Pup said sternly. "I don't want him getting fat."

"I won't overfeed him. I promise."

"Good. How did the viewing go. The letting firm sent me an email to say they'd got someone who wanted to have a look."

"It went well. I've literally just left your place after showing them around. I think they liked it. Nice couple, both got good jobs. They'd be ideal. I can't see them trashing the place," I added, thinking in its present state it would be pretty hard to tell if they did.

"Good. Good. Let's hope it all goes through. I could do with the extra money. Daisy's come up with a fantastic idea. She wants the pair of us to start up a business on the back of it. All it needs is a cash injection and I've said I can supply the syringe and the liquid loot to go in it... There's something else as well," Pup tacked on the end.

"Right," I said, dourly.

I had tried to keep the negativity out of my voice, but the alarm bells were ringing so vividly in my head I had almost slowed down and pulled the van over to let them pass. She was setting him up for the sting! Getting her claws into him already! What was it I had said? That he would arrive back home a single, broken, penniless ex-boiliemeister within three months.

"Daisy's wonderful, Matt. I think I'm in love with her and want to marry her," Pup eulogised, not noticing, or perhaps not caring, about the tone of my answer. "I said to her Daisy, Daisy please answer me; I'm going half crazy being in love with you. I said to her, it won't be a stylish marriage; I can't afford to hire the boat equivalent of a Rolls Royce *and* put money into your business, but you'll look sweet, upon the seat, of any mode of transport whatsoever."

I suddenly felt a bit delirious and the road swam in front of my eyes. "What did she say in response?" I managed to ask.

"She said, Peter, Peter, I'll level with you; I'm not as fast a mover as you in this type of matter. There won't be a marriage unless we can do it properly. I'm not having my special day ruined by going to church in any old boat. Promise me the equivalent to a Roller and I'll think about it."

I was so mentally disrupted I said the first thing popping into my head. "Sounds reasonable. I can't imagine any woman wanting to go to church on a tandem," I gabbled, my mind whirling like a gyroscope.

"A tandem! What the fuck are you on about? A tandem?" Pup shrieked.

"A Trabant. I meant a Trabant. Those shit old East German cars. A boat equivalent to a shit old East German car. I was only making a point," I said, finally getting a grip and mentally high-fiving myself for the good save.

"Oh, right. Yeah, I see what you mean... Sorry. Okay, love! Just coming... I've got to go, Matt, Daisy's calling. We're going out for our weekly Cornetto and Gondola trip."

What the fuck was Pup on about *now*? "You can buy Walls Cornettos in Venice?" I asked, flummoxed.

"We buy *any* local generic ice cream, Matt, and *pretend* it's a Cornetto," Pup answered as if I was a moron. "Like in that old ad. *So* romantic."

Then he hung up, leaving me feeling dazed and bemused. All my recent interactions with Pup were getting so increasingly surreal it was like tripping on LSD. And I *have* tripped on LSD (Lac Fumant, the mind-meld mirror), so I do know what I'm talking about. I wondered if he was cracking up and having some kind of psychotic breakdown. He was certainly sounding unhinged – a bit like a barn door hit by a fucking great tank – and, the most worrying bit, he seemed totally unaware of what was happening to him. This Daisy seemed like a right piece of work – a real manipulative, gold-digging bitch. Good job he hadn't sold the house, then he really would be kissing goodbye to everything. Maybe it was why he hadn't. Maybe a tiny part of his head had managed to put a veto on it – despite his heart holding the whip hand in all other matters.

I made it to the school ten minutes early. I think my conversation with Pup had tipped me into a state of hypertensive fervour and thanks to it, my right foot had become more twitchy than normal. I parked the van twenty or so yards down from the school's gates, on double yellows, and waited for Sylvester. As the stress of Pup's conversation gradually faded I began to feel somewhat uncomfortable. Rambo's little joke was playing on my mind a little too much and unfortunately I had forgotten my 'Hey, I'm a parent, too!' badge and my old official NICEIC 'Electrician on emergency call' laminated card to take the curse off it. Ridiculously, I felt a bit like the Child Catcher in Chitty Chitty Bang Bang, only with a white van instead of a horse drawn cage to store the fruits of my evil deeds. Feeling clammy, I tried to cleanse my soul by blaming the Catholic church, the child care industry, nineteen seventies TV presenters and an overzealous police force for the absurdity of my situation.

As a handful of kids started to emerge from the school gates, I tried to look out for Sylvester without directly eyeballing any of the other children. It wasn't easy, but thankfully Sylvester's keenness to go fishing and his shock of spiky blond hair helped tremendously. Amongst one of the first children out, Rambo's son came bolting through the school gates, spotted me instantaneously and sprinted towards the van. I pressed the unlocking button on the dashboard and let Sylvester in.

"Hi, Uncle Matt," he said, his face beaming with delight. "Thanks for picking me up."

"No worries. Dad's got all your clothes and food with him so we can go straight to The Lake. He's fishing already."

"Cool!"

I pressed the button to relock the doors – a force of habit from taking both Amy, when she was younger, and Adam in the van – and started it up. Before I had chance to pull off a heavily tattooed man in his thirties, dressed in a scruffy T-shirt and jeans, thumped his fist aggressively on my driver's side window. I pulled a face at him as he gestured for me to put the window down.

"That's the dad of the boy I punched," Sylvester whispered.

Deciding the guy didn't want a friendly chat, I cracked the electric window down a couple of grudging inches.

"Out the fucking van, pal. I want a word," he threatened, working the door handle up and down to no avail.

"I'm not getting out. What do you want?" I answered as strongly as my wavering voice allowed.

"Your son punched my lad in the face."

"Your son was provoking him," I protested, ignoring his mistake. "He was pushing him around and verbally abusing him."

"I don't think so. Get out the fucking van. We need to sort this out now!"

"I've told you I'm not getting out the van," I said once again, quite truthfully, as it was the *last* thing I intended doing. "Why don't you go away and teach your son to respect other people and treat them decently. Then they won't lash out at him."

Not surprisingly, my advice wasn't well received and his attempts to open the van's door became more ferocious.

"Don't fucking lecture me, you piece of shit!" he shouted. "Get out the fucking van and we can do this now!"

"Piss off, loser!" I said, easing the van away.

"I know where you live!" he said, jabbing a finger at me as he ran alongside the van. "I'll be round to see you. You won't be able to drive away next time!"

"Twat!" I told him as he disappeared backwards. Once we were out in traffic, I turned to Sylvester. "I can see where his son gets it from. What a dick." Sylvester nodded. "Luckily, I can leave it to your dad to field any further developments. That's his particular sphere of expertise, not mine I'm afraid. I can't see it being a problem for him, can you?"

Sylvester laughed. "No way! Dad'll kill him!"

I laughed, too. Not for the first time in my life, I wished I could be a bit more 'Rambo'. What a great thing to have in your locker – the absolute undeniable confidence of knowing, if needs be, you could batter the living daylights out of any stupid prick you wanted to.

The trip to The Lake seemed to fly by and took no time at all. It was rather enjoyable having Sylvester for company and I found myself relaying, at his request, numerous fishing anecdotes about situations his dad and I had been embroiled in. Many of the stories cracked him up and he laughed loudly at them, his enthusiasm egging me on to further recollections. The only areas where I had to rein myself in, and be much more circumspect, were with tales involving his mum. I had no idea whether he knew how she had met his dad, or if he knew how she had previously made a living. I had certainly never asked Rambo for clarification. Whatever the case, it didn't matter, omitting the carp fishing adventures including Steffi hardly ate into my repertoire. If we had been travelling to John O'Groats there would still have been more than enough material to last the entire journey.

As we started our walk up the path to The Lake, Sylvester insisted on one last story. I decided to finish on a good one and told him about the time The Eye had predicted a take while we had all stood around watching and waiting for the decreed moment to arrive, chanting his name like he was a famous footballer.

"And it came on time?" Sylvester asked, incredulously.

"More or less to the second," I confirmed. "He was, still is, one crazy guy, The Eye. Me and him got drunk on absinthe during that session," I said, chuckling at the memory.

"What's absinthe?"

"The most disgusting drink you can imagine," I replied with utter candour. "It's bright green in colour, but if you drink enough of it everything goes black! The Eye used to use it to help him predict when he was going to get a take. Mental."

Sylvester nodded. "Dad has mentioned his name before. He still uses your bait doesn't he?"

"The only other person... Apart from you," I said, smiling at Sylvester.

Sylvester's face beamed. "Dad said you saved The Eye's life. Is that right?" he asked, more seriously.

"Sort of. With the help of a Dutch neurosurgeon. He had a malignant tumour in his brain, I spotted it and told him to get it checked out. Because it was caught early enough it was still operable and he made a full recovery, pretty much. He can't predict takes anymore, but our bait has helped him get over the loss. He's catching more fish now, he just doesn't know when the bites are coming," I said, grinning. "Like the rest of us."

"How did you look into his brain?" Sylvester asked, mystified.

"That, as they say, Sylvester, is another story."

"Dad told me how you saved *his* life once," Sylvester said, unexpectedly.

"Really," I answered, taken aback. "When was that?"

"Only the other day. When he told me off for taking his real Glock... The night I put it against your head," Sylvester said sheepishly. "Dad said if it wasn't for you, I wouldn't have been born. He said you were a special friend and I should never take liberties with you."

My cheeks flushed red, I could feel them glowing, and not from the exertion of the walk. Rambo had fobbed off the incident when I had told him and yet here was proof he hadn't taken it in such a blasé manner. He had clearly decided to tell Sylvester of my intervention much earlier than anticipated to underline a very serious point.

"That and a whole lot of other things wouldn't have happened," I replied, not knowing what to say. "The Lake wouldn't..."

"What did it feel like?" Sylvester interrupted. "Killing that man?"

I stopped walking and turned to face Sylvester, whose eyes were burning with intrigue. "Awful afterwards," I admitted. "I threw up. Not because I regretted killing him, I was glad I had, purely from the shock of seeing what I had done to him. At the time, when I saw him right on the verge of shooting your dad, I was so angry, I never even thought about it. I just took aim and kept pulling the trigger until all the bullets were gone."

"All seventeen?"

"All seventeen."

"I love my dad. I'm glad you did it," Sylvester stated with childlike simplicity and conviction.

I ruffled Sylvester's spiky hair and smiled at him. "I'm glad I did it, too. I wouldn't have my best friend or my favourite nephew to go fishing with otherwise."

To my surprise, Sylvester moved forward – my testicles did flinch at first, they couldn't help it – grabbed hold of me around my chest and gave me a hug. Despite him not yet being ten years old, I could feel the power in his arms.

"Danke vielmals, Oncle Matt."

"Sorry?"

"Thanks very much."

"No problem. Come on, let's go and see if your dad's had one."

As predicted by his good self, Rambo had had one. A nice upper thirty common from the spot where he had spotted the fizzing on his earlier Lake reconnaissance mission.

"It fought well," Rambo commented. "Went berserk in the margins."

"Good angling," I said. "You did everything 'they' tell you to do. You didn't fish a preconceived swim, especially not the closest one to the car park, you had a walk around, you spotted fish and fished for them. You'll make a proper carp angler yet!"

"There's a chance," Rambo agreed. "With another ten years of experience." Rambo turned to his son. "Go and get changed, Sylvester. You know what you're mother's like if she sees anything unexpected on your school uniform. Like too much mud."

Sylvester nodded and went into their two-man bivvy to do as he was told.

"Won't the school text her to say he's absent?" I asked.

"They'll text *me*, boy," Rambo answered, smiling and lifting his eyebrows. "I made sure I'm the parental contact point."

"Well, I can see you've got it all under control, so how about I give you another little problem to deal with?"

Rambo scowled. "What's that?"

I told Rambo about the altercation at the school gates and the ensuing threat that had come my way but was, in fact, intended for him.

"Huh! Should be a laugh," Rambo commented. "I'll look forward to hearing what he intends to do about it when he knocks on my front door."

"I don't think it'll involve much respectful considered adult conversation," I observed.

"Thank fuck for that," said Rambo, sounding genuinely relieved. "That means I can just punch *him* in the face and that'll be the end of it. The last thing I want to have to do is invite him indoors and *talk* about it."

"That'd tie things up neatly. You hitting him. Like fathers like sons, so to speak."

"Exactly, boy."

"When do you want to go and grill Luke?"

"As soon as Sylvester's changed we can leave him in charge of the rods and go and see what he has to say… Oh, and once I've got my fishing stroke torture kit out of my rucksack."

"I was joking about the forceps."

"I know *you* were."

"All done, Dad," said Private Sylvester, reporting for his watch, dressed in British Army camo from top to bottom.

"Good. Now, quickly remind me again *exactly* where you found the sew-on badge. Have you brought it with you like I told you?"

Sylvester put his hand in his pocket, pulled the item out and gave it to his dad. "It was inside his bivvy, on the floor, right next to the leg of his bedchair."

I snorted at Sylvester's impudence. "You told me you found it *outside* his bivvy!"

"That's what he told me to begin with. He thought he was in enough trouble as it was, what with going inside your bivvy," Rambo said with austerity.

"Not a problem," I said, waving a dismissive hand. "The gun thing did put the wind up me, though," I admitted. "More so when I found out which gun it was!"

"I've had a word," Rambo said, giving Sylvester an evil eye. "Anyway. Obviously Luke's," Rambo stated, waving the sew-on badge. "Whether it has any significance, what it means, we have no idea. Let's go and find out. Come on, boy."

Dutifully, I followed Rambo's lead. "Don't catch too many while we're gone," I said, winking at Sylvester.

Retracing my steps from twenty minutes earlier, we made our way anti-clockwise around The Lake, past the point where the path from the car park emerged and around to the bottom bay. There were two other anglers on apart from Rambo and Luke. Eccentric Ed was round further than Luke in a swim called The Wide and Marcus, a retro angler, was right at the opposite end to the bottom bay in a swim called, View, as it afforded a clear line of sight right the way down the centre of The Lake on its longest dimension. Marcus had been a member for five years and fished exclusively with late seventies and early eighties tackle regards to rods, reels and buzzers. All the rest of his tackle was modern, but his eleven foot 1¾lb test curve Jack Hiltons, ABU Cardinal 55s and Delkim Optonic Conversions still floated his boat. That and his flared waterproofs and butterfly collared rain jacket. Just kidding. Marcus was a top angler – the antithesis of 'all the gear and no idea' and more 'tackle mart' than 'tackle tart' – and an all round good guy. 'Why change if you love it?', was his viewpoint and apart from having his rods rewhipped and revarnished, all his tackle was 'as good as the day it was made' according to him, although he had admitted to putting new batteries in his alarms every season or two.

"I'll let you off on that one. I don't think new batteries counts as the abandonment of a principle," I had once told him.

As we approached Luke's bivvy, Rambo turned his head around and spoke. "Leave the talking to me, boy," he insisted. "I'll only call on you if I need you to hold him down while I pull something out."

"Sure thing. Did you bring earplugs? I can't stand the sound of screaming. Puts my teeth on edge," I said with a false world-weary air.

"Teeth! *Another* good idea, boy. You're on a roll."

Rambo poked his head into Luke's bivvy. "All right, Luke? How's it going?"

Luke swung his legs off his bedchair and got up out of his bivvy. "Hello, Rambo. Hi, Matt. Fine thanks."

"We'd like to have a little word, if it's okay?" Rambo started.

It was an innocuous enough start, yet somehow it still exuded menace – a point not lost on Luke.

"Yeah, sure. Of course. I haven't done anything wrong, have I?" Luke asked, worriedly.

"That's what we're here to find out." Rambo replied. "First things first. I need you to show us your bait."

Now, asking a carp angler, right out of the blue, to show you their bait is tantamount to walking up to a stranger and asking them to show you their genitals, right there and then, in the public domain. However you dress it up and for whatever reason, it's just not protocol. It's not the 'done thing' by any set of standards. You would probably offend a carp angler less by asking him to reveal his deepest sexual perversion rather than ask to look at his bait. It crosses a line. It's taboo. It steps over a mark. It breaks an unwritten rule. It quashes the right of entitlement of every carp angler to keep his bait secret should he want to. A right that is sacrosanct. Inviolable and hallowed.

"Okay. No problem," Luke answered. He went back into his bivvy and returned with a five-kilo boilie pouch. "There you go."

He's bluffing, I thought, as Luke handed the bag to Rambo. He's given in too easily and must be pulling a fast one. He must keep a handy rogue bag of diversionary bait in his bivvy for this very circumstance. Then I took a rain check, looked at Luke's drained face, and realised he was too shit scared of Rambo to try and pull the wool over his eyes.

Once he had looked at it himself, Rambo showed me the opened pouch. A cursory look from myself proved there to be no dark pink baits only dark brown ones, transpiring, after an equally cursory sniff, to be a fishmeal of some description.

"Thanks," said Rambo, handing the pouch back. "I know it's a bit rude me asking," Rambo admitted, his tone softer, "but the reason I did is we think someone might be poaching The Pit. We found some boilies in the margins of a swim. A swim we're pretty sure no one has fished this year. Plus no member, as far as we're aware, uses the bait we found."

"But why me? Why did you think it might be me?" Luke asked, confused.

"That's only my personal theory," Rambo owned up. "You've had a bit of a life upheaval of late, boy. Started fishing on a Sunday. Discarded a lifetime's belief just to catch a carp. I thought you might have turned into a bad boy... And, we found this." Rambo showed Luke the sew-on badge. "Is it yours?"

If Luke had looked sickly before, he was positively bilious now. "Yes. It's mine. I wondered where it had gone. How did you get it?"

"That's not important. What's important, is, 'What's it all about, Lukie?'" I said, singing the last bit of my question and simultaneously disobeying Rambo's orders.

"I got it when I joined," Luke blurted, frightened. "They sent it to me. It was my free joining gift. I was really struggling, you see. That's why I joined. I hadn't had a take in over a year. I know it sounds ridiculous, but I was getting so desperate and *He* wouldn't help. Not that I think He exists anymore." Luke wiped his mouth self-consciously with the back of a hand. "Matt tried to help as well, but when I lost one, I knew I had to stick with what they'd suggested. If I'd landed the first fish who knows what I might have done. Possibly gone home Saturday night and carried on as normal? I don't really know. Instead, I cocked it right up. You saw me cock it up, didn't you?" Luke asked me directly and I indicated with my head he had indeed cocked it right up. "Then I *knew* I had to do what they said I should. Once I had, once I had fished on and caught on the Sunday, I realised they were right. *So* right. It's their creed you see. It's one of their fundamental teachings. You have to push yourself if you want to catch. You have to put in the hard yards."

"Whose creed? Who are they? *What* are they?" Rambo asked.

"They're very underground. I only got to meet one of them and then only purely by chance. I told him how I was struggling and he said he might be able to help. He told me it was lucky we had met because he was a member of this new radical carp fishing movement that was going to change everything. He said all the retail bullshit was dead in the water because the BMC were going to cleanse carp fishing of commercialism and give it back to the real anglers. He said it was an underground movement devoted to spreading the vision of the BMC. A vision taking carp fishing out of the hands of the corporate, handing it back to the individual and helping every angler who joined the movement to catch more carp in the process. He said the BMC would also introduce a new carp fishing etiquette, one detailing the direction carp fishing must head if it wanted to provide a better fishing experience for all anglers. He then gave me the address of a PO Box where I could pay my membership fee, in cash, and said once I had been ratified I'd receive personal guidance. After I'd coughed up, one of the Higher Associates contacted me within a couple of days and asked me to relay my problem to him. 'Go the extra mile, Luke', was the message I got back. 'Luke, you must do whatever is necessary' I was told."

I glanced over at Rambo at this point and hitched up my eyebrows. All the ex-Christian carper needed to say now was the BMC had told him 'to use The Force, Luke' and we could all fall about pissing ourselves with laughter.

But Luke didn't. He was deadly serious and neither myself nor Rambo were cracking a smile, let alone convulsing in mirth.

"So I did," Luke continued. "I gave up God, fished on a Sunday and I caught. That was my personal challenge, to believe in their guidance and really go for it. It's what they're all about on a personal angling level. Getting you to push your boundaries and work hard. To take the necessary steps in order to achieve what you want. One of their Daily Directives, I get one every few days is, 'Who dares catches – BMC'. Another was, 'Don't believe what you read – believe in the BMC'."

"But what is the BMC?" I asked.

"The Black Mirror Cult," Luke replied.

"And did you tell them where you were fishing?" Rambo asked, his voice angry again. "And mention The Pit."

Luke nodded once again. "I told my Higher Associate I was a member of The Lake when I was explaining my problem. He said he'd already heard of The Pit. Once I mentioned The Lake he mentioned The Pit straightaway. 'It hasn't escaped the Black Mirror Cult's attention' was how he worded it. But then anyone in the know has heard of The Pit. It's the best water in the UK."

"'Worded it?'" Rambo asked.

"A WhatsApp message. I've only ever been contacted by my Higher Associate on WhatsApp."

"Okay, Luke," Rambo said, imposing his giant frame over the ex-Christian carper and laying a huge bear-like hand on his shoulder. "Let's hear it from the top. Don't miss out a single thing and you might get to hang on to your ticket."

# Chapter 9

I sat with Rambo and Sylvester, a mug of tea in my hand, and contemplated everything Luke had told us. The first thing that sprung to mind was the realisation Luke had almost certainly been telling the truth. The second was not getting a take for over a year may have nudged him into the arms of a very strange carp fishing cult, one we little understood, but it hadn't made him a monster. Not from our standpoint, anyway – to religious parents or a partner, maybe. The biggest effect caused by Luke's desertion of his religion and signing up to the Black Mirror Cult, regards The Lake membership, was the likelihood of future Sundays being a bit busier.

Luke hadn't exactly been brainwashed into embracing a world of carping terrorism, but had been coerced into taking a momentous personal decision. His shift away from religion and into a world permitting Sunday fishing might seem laughable to the vast majority of a secular carping community, but to Luke himself it was a massive shift in direction and a colossal lifestyle change. If a WhatsApp message from a Black Mirror Cult 'Higher Associate', whoever the fuck he was when he was at home, could motivate him enough to make such a radical move, what might the BMC convince some of the more – how shall I put it? – 'colourful' anglers within the carping fraternity to get up to? Carp fishing already had a history of anglers going about their fishing on the edge of what might be termed 'respectability' and the Black Mirror Cult seemed to be an organisation that could encourage the fringe minority to participate in unsavoury actions.

The counter argument to that line of thinking, one Luke had strongly argued for, was the BMC's carp fishing etiquette agenda, which if it was to be accepted at face value, appeared to promote a sensible, respectful and wholly appropriate way for carp anglers to conduct themselves when on the bank. What the BMC appeared to have done, rather cleverly, was to have aligned itself with the vast majority of history's cult/sect/terrorist organisations in that it was founded on offering hope and a counter culture to the struggling, the disaffected, the disenfranchised and those simply bored with the status quo – the Latin phrase, that is, not the aging boogie-rockers.

If the BMC could continue to trade on a combination of shadowy mystic and the undeniable street kudos of an 'out with the old and in with the new' mentality, I could see them gathering quite a following. And to be fair, the BMC had flagged up the demise of one of carp fishing's most contentious issues as a primary mission objective: Commercialism – carp fishing's 'C' word. You only had to go on any carp fishing forum to read anglers constantly bitching about how bad they thought things had become. Sponsored anglers writing magazine advertorials full of blatant product placement and plugging; company videos showing overcomplicated rigs, spod mixes with ten ingredients, gear you must have for this and gear you must have for that, all designed to make you buy more of their wares, and greedy fishery owners sticking massive fish in small, overcrowded lakes with too many swims were a few examples. Never mind carp fishing only mirrored how every other business in the capitalist First World operated, carp anglers still moaned about it!

Of course, a lot of the time the biggest gripe of all, the one surpassing commercialism, was other carp anglers. What haters we all are! Not that I could see how the BMC could address that particular problem, short of organising the genocide of all those deemed to be chav anglers or Noddies, or anyone brave enough, or stupid enough, to pop their head above the parapet and voice an opinion on any aspect of the finer points of carp fishing – from the thorny issue of ranking carp captures to the merits of the barbless hook rule. Sure, there was an element of a 'keyboard warriors' vibe surrounding the whole forum scene, but no one could deny many underlying sentiments were often genuinely and widely supported. If the BMC's carping etiquette agenda could change chav anglers into upright pillars of the carping community, then fair play to them for getting blood out of a stone.

My take on it, as I sat on Rambo's stalking chair, was the Black Mirror Cult, for all its rhetoric, was nothing more than a modern, tech-savvy, fully-paid membership required stroke-pulling club. I mean, fifteen fucking quid for a sew-on badge and one WhatsApp contact? Come on! There was the stroke being pulled right there. I bet those Higher Associates were raking it in.

Or were they at fifteen quid a pop? One of the questions Luke couldn't answer was how long the BMC had been in existence and how many members it had. There were no clues as all his WhatsApp messages had come from the one single point of contact, his Higher Associate. Being a shadowy underground movement hardly anyone knew about didn't seem conducive to becoming a carp fishing institution with clout, so that led me to speculate on what its true primary motives were and I decided to plump for 'milking sucker anglers'. It did make me wonder where the money went, although, admittedly, fifteen quid was hardly a fortune –and Luke had insisted it was a one-off payment, which I couldn't believe, solely on the grounds of the old adage of it 'sounding too good to be true'.

Whatever the truth, there was money sloshing around somewhere and it was only human nature to speculate on how it was used. Were all the fees spent on tackle and bait, or on booze, cigarettes and porn site subscriptions? Most likely there wasn't a great deal of cash and it all got frittered away on chocolate bars and scratch cards depending on how many Higher Associates there were to divvy up the money. Moving on to other matters, how did anyone even become a Higher Associate? Were there BMC meetings in pubs with an accompanying slide show? Did the BMC have their own poorly produced magazine – hard copy or online – littered with typos, low resolution pictures, but, crucially, without a single advert? Was social media too social for them? Were they on the Dark Web, instead? Did members have a special clandestine handshake for when two of them met on the bank, or was the way they set their rods up the giveaway clue – splayed rods, for example, rather than parallel rods? I suppose a member could simply sew their free-on-joining BMC badge on to a beanie hat, jacket or rucksack. That would do it. That would give a heads up you were one of the tribe.

I sipped my tea. 'You know nothing, Matt Williams' I said in my head – with the hint of a female northern accent.

Of course, all these generalised enigmas wrapped up in a page ripped from a Bumper Puzzle Book and sealed with Sudoku Sellotape and Riddle Ribbon were of little consequence when offered alongside the big personal ones. Had it been a Black Mirror Cult member who had poached The Pit and been inside my bivvy on the night I'd had a secret affair with my own wife? If the dark pink bait was a BMC member's bait, considering Hobbes' reaction to it, then there was little doubt the angler was a good one and knew his baits. Then again, it could be a coincidence and nothing to do with the BMC and our possible mystery poacher might be a 'name' looking to drum up inspiration regards writing material. There had been articles/chapters in books over the years, some anonymously written, some not, concerning the subject of 'guesting' waters.

I had a sudden thought. What if, taking it one logical step further, the BMC was a vehicle for a single bloated carp fishing ego? A device purely set up as a self-promotion exercise? The Pit was the best carp water in the UK, so undoubtedly would be a target if that were true. Nicking a big one out of The Pit would make a great story. And how could a water containing so many big carp not have escaped this individual's attention? *Finally*! A question I did know the answer to: It hadn't escaped the BMC's attention.

"I've got too much going on in here," I said, tapping my temple with an index finger.

"No change there, then, boy," Rambo answered, deadpan.

"I can't get a handle on it," I confessed. "It's all a bit bizarre. Nothing seems to add up or make much sense."

"Yeah, it is a bit of a fucking teaser," said Rambo. "An underground carp fishing cult distributing sew-on badges with its initials plastered across them, once you've sent fifteen quid in cash to a PO Box, issues individual carp fishing advice on WhatsApp, proclaims to have the ultimate carp fishing etiquette agenda and is on a mission to cleanse commercialism from carp angling and hand it back to 'real' anglers. Whoever the fuck they are."

"I've Googled them on my phone, Dad, and there's nothing online," Sylvester chipped in. "They could be on Facebook, but if I'm not a friend I might not be able to see them."

Rambo pulled a face to signify he had little idea what Sylvester was talking about. "Have you put what I need on my phone, yet?" Rambo asked his son.

"Nearly. It's still downloading. It's well slow."

"The thing is, do we need to care about the Black Mirror Cult?" I proffered, as much in hope as anything, glancing at the plain green icon on my phone. No messages forwarded on by Luke so far. "We've been in our own little carping bubble for years now, so much so I'd probably go into anaphylactic shock if I had to fish a single session on a day ticket water. We've been in the eye of the storm for so long we've probably lost track of the mayhem going on outside it."

"That's a fair point, boy, but what if our bubble's been popped and the mayhem's already upon us?" Rambo asked.

"But how can we be sure our bubble *has* been popped?" I replied. "The shit's hardly hit the fan. Two boilies in a margin and my gut feeling someone had been inside my bivvy, when I was knackered, despite nothing being touched to the best of my recollection. And we still can't say one hundred per cent the dark pink bait isn't a genuine member's."

"Again I take your point, boy, but I still don't fucking like it," Rambo countered with agitation. "Flip your argument on its head to a worst case scenario and someone could have poached The Pit a day or two ago, stolen some of our bait for analysis and taken a photo of The Carper's super trick rig. Bang! All our edges gone in one foul swoop. For over a decade we've had them to ourselves and now some slimy bastard might have waltzed in and taken them from right under our fucking noses. There's an outside chance they might even have caught a Pit carp! What a fucking liberty! How can that have happened on my watch?"

Rambo's words permeated into my head like an SDS masonry bit attached to a rotary drill. He was right. It could actually have happened how Rambo had described it. I just hoped and prayed it wasn't possible to deconstruct a boilie and work out, back to front as it were, what was in it. Rambo and I couldn't even put a definite flavour to the dark pink bait, but maybe someone else could, given the right equipment and the right knowledge. I would have to ask Pup if it was possible when I next spoke to him.

"What can we do, then?" I asked.

"Not much at the present," Rambo admitted. "Everything revolves around Luke passing on his messages." Rambo turned towards his son. "What is it I've got to do to get them, Sylvester?"

"It's installed now. Your phone's got WhatsApp on it now like Uncle Matt's," Sylvester answered, holding up Rambo's smartphone. "That means Luke can share any messages, pictures, videos and stuff he gets from the Black Mirror Cult."

"Have you used it much?" Rambo asked me.

I puffed out my cheeks and nodded. "Quite a bit. Amy put it on my phone for me and Sophie a year ago before the pair of them went to Portugal with some of Sophie's friends for a girls' holiday." I said. "Once it's installed, it automatically updates the contacts list on your phone and shows who's already got it. It's easy to use and you can WhatsApp those people straightaway. It works like a text message, but you can do more. You can send a text message with a picture you've taken, send a video, record and send a voice message. You can even make phone calls with it. In 'Group Chat', once a 'Group Administer' sets it up, whatever any participant of the group sends goes to everyone in that group. Only the Group Administer can add participants, though. I think I remember Amy saying you can have up to a hundred people in a group chat and you can have as many groups as you want. If the BMC ever wants to scattergun a message out to lots of members and let them interact within their own group, then it's the ideal tool. And it's got end-to-end encryption, so it's very safe," I added.

Rambo waved a dismissive hand. "Sylvester can show me what to do later, I'll soon pick it up. As for Luke, he had better stick to his promise," Rambo rumbled. "If he doesn't pass on the BMC's messages he's in big trouble."

"It was good idea of yours to tell Luke he could only hang on to his ticket by passing on all his BMC correspondence to us," I conceded.

"I have my moments of genius," Rambo confirmed. "And your insistence of making him forward *his* to you, means you'll get all the messages he sends to them. As long as he plays the game we'll be up to speed on everything. He knows what'll happen if he tries to pull a fast one."

"Yeah, it was probably the bit you added about the hanging on to his ticket also applying to his front teeth that sealed the deal."

"I think you subliminally planted the idea of teeth," Rambo replied.

I laughed. "I'm going to make a move now. I promised I'd look after Adam tonight so Sophie can have a night out with some girlfriends. What evening do you want to make the bait?"

"How about Wednesday? Around half five?" Rambo answered.

"It's a date. I'll see you guys later. Bye, Sylvester. Don't go outfishing your dad and make him all grumpy!"

"I'll try my best! See ya!" Sylvester answered.

I flicked the dregs of tea from my mug and handed it to Rambo. "Thanks for the drink. I wonder if they'll eventually do Black Mirror Cult mugs?" I asked.

"Why wouldn't they? Every other fucker does their own mug," he answered.

"My grandad used to have a ceramic tankard and on the side it said, 'Lord grant that I may catch a fish so big that even I, When speaking of it afterwards may have no need to lie'. The Angler's Pray it was called. I wonder if Luke's got one?"

"Not now, I wouldn't have thought. It's in pieces in his dustbin if he did have one!"

I laughed."Yeah, you're right. I'll see you two Wednesday."

The weekend Rambo and Sylvester spent on The Lake, I spent with Sophie, Amy and Adam very much in family mode. Late on the Sunday, I got a WhatsApp message from Luke telling his Higher Associate he'd had two more fish, both caught that morning. Good for him, I thought. He was flying now. How strange. All that time spent struggling and then he turns the corner and now he appeared to be on a roll. How very carp fishing! An hour later, Luke forwarded on his Higher Associate's reply. It was a single word 'Congratulations'. Sparse and to the point, I thought, but probably all that was needed. Luke's BMC-inspired change was paying dividends. For the record, Rambo and Sylvester had three between them. Sylvester outfishing his dad by virtue of him once again shotgunning the first take.

On the following Monday, Sophie and I went on our own for a day's shopping at Bluewater. It was when I was listlessly hanging around outside the female fitting rooms in Dorothy Perkins, waiting to give my verdict – always a dangerous procedure – on an outfit Sophie was trying on, when the first non-Luke specific BMC message came through on my phone. It was one of the Daily Directives he had mentioned and it said, 'Don't be a c**t – follow the Black Mirror C**t'.

"What do you think? Do you like it? The vertical pattern doesn't make me look too thin, does it?"

I jolted my head up from my phone and eyed Sophie up and down. "Too thin? I definitely don't think it makes you look too thin," I responded.

"What do you mean?"

"That it doesn't make you look too thin," I replied, slowly.

"So not fat?"

"No. Of course not fat."

"It's quite nice, but I'm not sure about the length. I should have brought my heels to try it with," Sophie said, standing on tiptoe and looking at herself sideways on in a mirror.

"It looks nice to me," I said, earnestly. "It fits you really well."

"You think so?"

"Yeah."

"Flattering?"

"Very flattering."

"Hmm… You know, I think I'll try the red one I saw in Apricot. Maybe the one in Hobbs as well, even though it was a quite a bit more expensive. We can always come back to this one if I don't like them as much. Okay?"

"Sure. Whatever you want," I answered, my spirits flagging at the thought of more dresses and more shops.

As Sophie disappeared back into the changing room, I looked over to another guy, standing a few yards from me, who was also waiting for his partner to come out and show off her new ensemble. I shot him a weak grin and he gave me one back – kindred souls hanging on to the lifeboat, cast adrift on the high fashion seas.

Head down and back on my phone, I mentally counted off the shops we had visited so far; Dorothy Perkins, Apricot, Hobbs... Ha! Hobbes. Rolling bait was going to be a breeze compared to this.

Bait-making day, I arrived at Rambo's a bit before five, parked my van on his drive, got out and went and knocked on the front door. Steffi answered dressed in leggings and a slimfit jumper. The past allure and slight scariness of seeing her had long faded. I actually felt comfortable in her company now – admittedly an event not occurring often – and could relax enough to be myself. She was aging elegantly and had gradually morphed from 'sex bomb' to 'classical beauty' as she had entered her fifth decade. I could easily imagine all the younger mums at Sylvester's school admiring her and the younger dads fantasising about sleeping with her. If they knew her as well as I did, they would fantasise even more!

"Hello, Matthew," she said, smiling. "Rambo von't be long, he has just gone down to ser corner shop because ve haff run out of milk. I know how you men must haff your tea ven you are togezzer." She turned her head and shouted back into the house. "Sylvester! Kommen Sie hier, bitte! Oncle Matt ist hier!"

"How's everything?" I asked, as she turned back to face me.

"Pretty gudt. My beautiful boy is growing bigger and stronger vitt every day. I am getting *older* vitt every day," she added, ruefully.

"You still look great," I told her, truthfully.

"Sank you," she replied, lowering her head graciously. "And your family are all okay?"

"Fine. Amy will be off to university after the summer. It'll seem strange not having her around and Adam will be starting full-time primary school just before she leaves…"

"Hi, Uncle Matt," said a slightly breathless Sylvester, making two shocks of spiky, blond hair within the confines of doorway. "I've got the garage keys. Shall I open up? Dad'll only be a couple of minutes."

"Sure," I answered. "Go for it."

Sylvester ran off to the adjoining garage where all of Pup's bait-making gear was stored, Steffi's adoring eyes following him all the way.

"Vell, I'll let you get started," Steffi said. "Sylvester is very pleased to help, I know. Gudtbye, Matthew. Say 'hi' to Sophie for me."

"Will do," I acknowledged.

As Steffi shut the door and Sylvester came back out of the opened garage, I heard a squeal of brakes followed by the unmistakable sound of a car reversing quickly. The car in question stopped right across Rambo's drive, blocking my van in as it did. Before the driver had a chance to get out, I knew who it was.

"I said you wouldn't be able to drive away next time, didn't I, pal?" the cretin from the school gate altercation gleefully shouted as he walked down Rambo's driveway towards me. "Now what was it you called me when you ran away last time?"

"Look," I said to the fast approaching threat. "There's been a mistake. You're making a big mistake."

"Oh, I don't think so," said the father of the son who Sylvester had smacked in the chops. "*You've* made the fucking mistake, pal," he corrected, now right on top of me and jabbing a finger hard into my chest just below my collar bone. "One I'm going to put you straight on right now."

"Don't you threaten my uncle!" Sylvester warned, bravely pushing himself between myself and Punched-son.

Punched-son's face clouded. "What?" he demanded looking down at Sylvester and then up at me.

"He's not my dad. He's my uncle!" Sylvester shouted.

"Oh, I get it," Punched-son sneered, his face now clear and full of intent. "You really are a pathetic prick, aren't you? Trying to hide behind this little charade."

Over the top of Punched-son's shoulder I saw Rambo returning with two litres of semi-skimmed milk – on a white horse, in shining armour, hoisting aloft a banner with the words 'The Cavalry' written on it.

"Not really, mate," I said, relaxing and nodding my head in Rambo's general direction. "Here's Daddy now."

Punched-son spun round to see Rambo stride down his driveway and come to a halt inches from his nose.

"You wanted to see me?" Rambo asked, looming over his adversary like the dark shadow of death. "Hold this, son," he said, passing the milk to Sylvester. "Not that I think I'm really going to need *two* arms here."

Now as a mere extra, one happy to be spectacularly demoted from leading man by Rambo's return from the milk run, it was interesting to note Punched-son's body language deflate from a strutting, thinks-he's-the-bomb, cocksure cage fighter to a crushed, out-of-his-league, hesitant, asthmatic librarian.

"Er, your, s-son, um, punched my son in the face after s-school the other day," he stammered.

"I know. He asked for it by mouthing him off. What's the problem?" Rambo countered.

"Well…"

"Listen," Rambo interjected, laying his hand on Punched-son's shoulder, much as he had Luke's. "Is that your car blocking my drive?"

Punched-son looked up at his car – either to remind himself because he had forgotten where he had left it, or to make absolutely sure it was his car he had arrived in, I couldn't be sure which – and nodded.

"Good. Get it, and yourself, out of my sight, right now. If I *ever* see you round my house again, or if either of your two boys give my son any more grief, I'll be round to see *you*. And it *won't* make for pretty viewing, I can tell you that for nothing. Now, fucking jog on, boy," Rambo said flicking a thumb up the drive.

Without another word, Punched-son ascended the driveway quicker than he had come down it, got in his car and jogged on.

"Incredible," I said with admiration. "You scared the bejesus out of him without having to lift a finger. Why can't I do that?"

Rambo rolled his eyes. "The next time the pair of us are standing in front of a full length mirror, I'll explain it to you."

I laughed at Sylvester. "Your dad's a lad, isn't he? Do you want to hear the story about the very first time we made bait together?"

Sylvester nodded eagerly. He liked my stories. To him, being so young, they were probably like hearing medieval history.

"How long ago was that?" he asked.

I cast my mind back to the night of the old SS Syndicate meeting in the Black Horse pub. The night when Rambo had asked me to come in on bait with him and the ensuing mixathon in his flat at Plenham Place.

"A lifetime ago," I answered. "A different lifetime ago."

"And thank Christ it is," said Rambo. "I wouldn't want to mix up a hundred kilos like we did in those days. We never had electricity, gas or running water back then," he said, with false seriousness to Sylvester who immediately got the joke. "You two elves," he said, flicking a finger at me and his son in turn. "Come on into my bait grotto," he urged. "You can tell Sylvester the story while we crack on."

Once I was inside the garage, I could see Rambo had been busy over the last few days. When we had originally shifted Pup's bait-making gear we had put all the equipment up the far end, standing it in as tight an area as possible against the garage's rear wall. Rambo had since moved it and now it was much more spaced out, connected electrically where required and with ample space to work with each bit of kit. There was the large propane bottle and burner with the stainless pan for boiling baits, an industrial food mixer, the compressor, plus the air-powered sausage guns, and the electrically powered rolling machine capable of puking out a dozen or more boilies in one go once a suitably-sized sausage of mix had been inserted within it. The rolling machine, fitted with Pup's special indenting 18mm roller set on this occasion, was on a large sturdy bench and therefore at an easy working height. Underneath, in various bags, boxes and bottles, were the ingredients for our exclusive, revolutionary, indented, dirty brown bottom bait boilie Rambo had previously ordered.

Pup had upgraded his kit over the years, but had shied away from ever investing in an all-in-one type machine which mixed, sausaged and rolled bait within the one unit. It had never crossed my mind to ask why, but standing there in front of all of his kit, I had the feeling such a machine might have been too 'impersonal' for a mentalist baithead like Pup was at the time. I imagined what we had here was equipment as far down the automated road as Pup could allow himself to go. It still maintained enough hands-on human intervention to satisfy Pup's love of his boilie-making craft, without going back to the ridiculously tiresome and inefficient long winded ways of converted mastic guns and hand rolling tables.

I told Sylvester how much easier Pup's gear was going to make the process of creating a hundred kilos of our bait compared to when his dad and I had made fifty kilos all those years ago. A process that had physically exhausted me, if memory served correct.

"It was brutal," I told Sylvester. "Your dad knocked up the mix in his kitchen sink and I used converted mastic guns and an old type of boilie roller called a Sidewinder to make up the baits. And we were making two sizes! Sixteen millers and tens! *Tens*! What a killer they were! We boiled them in an old tin bath straddled across the four burners of the cooker and your dad had to regularly top it up with hot water from the tap to stop it boiling dry." I shook my head in disbelief at the vivid recollection. "The mess we made! The bloody mix got flung all over the place, from the powder in the bags when we opened them up to the finished mix getting flicked up the walls and on the floor. It was a red bait and there were footprints all over the flat from where we'd walked it everywhere. Like footprints on a Martian desert, I remember thinking! We both stunk of it by the time we'd eventually made it all. We didn't get to finish until *three* in the morning. When I got home and had a shower it took me ages to get clean and get rid of the smell. I even pulled out a mini boilie's worth from my left ear that had been making me deaf! That night, after I'd gone to sleep, I must have been so consumed by the effort of making them, I had a dream all the boilies were attacking me. I was trying to swat them off with cricket bats, baseball bats, tennis rackets and fence posts," I explained, vigorously swinging an imaginary lightsabre through the air, "but they kept splitting up and I kept swinging and missing right through the middle of them. They parted like the Red Sea did for Moses! I couldn't hit a single one! At the end of the fight, they formed a giant grotesque fist on the end of an all-powerful invisible arm and they swept down in a full-blooded swing with the intention of decapitating me... and then I woke up."

Sylvester, who had been laughing all the way through my little story, had suddenly stopped. "Who's Moses?" he asked.

"Time to get started, you two," Rambo suggested, a half smile on his face.

"Sorry," I apologised. "Getting carried away. What do you want me to do?"

"This is it," said Rambo, ignoring my question and holding a large plastic container up to my face, one he had just taken out from underneath the work bench.

I took it from him as if I was handling a priceless and extremely fragile antique. "Is this the revolutionary bit?" Rambo nodded. I unscrewed the top and sniffed the contents. "Wow! Who'd have thought?" I stated, reverentially.

"Who indeed, boy? Who indeed."

"Have you got Pup's instructions with you?" I asked.

"Printed off in my pocket," Rambo replied. "I'll destroy them after."

"I guess we better get started then."

"It's why we're all here," Rambo agreed. "You get the hose pipe from round the back, run it through the rear door of the garage and fill up the boiling pan," Rambo advised. "Then we can get the burner on the go. I'll start weighing and measuring out the ingredients into the mixer. Sylvester, you're on egg-breaking duty. They're indoors in the fridge. Go and get four dozen. That should do for a start."

Duly instructed, we set about our individual tasks and began the ritual of the making of our bait. Surprisingly, seeing as we had never worked as a bait team before, we soon got into a rhythm. One where we wove our way around each other without colliding in a syncopated session of swing; an elaborate series of dances –

the Boilie Hop, the Boilie-Woogie, the Boiliero, the Mixarena plus a soupçon of Michael Jackson Mixwalk – with Rumba Rambo as the choreographer. Within an hour and a half, the first batch of baits were cooling on an old king-sized duvet cover Sylvester had laid out on the garage floor.

As the initial batch had dried, I had gradually experienced a huge wave of relief, one overcoming an initial nagging doubt. At first, much like an amateur decorator emulsioning his lounge wall, the colour of the baits didn't look like it should compared to on the tin. It looked too light. That eventually changed as the moisture came out of the baits and the colour of each one began to look right. Splitting one open and smelling it happily confirmed what I was now thinking – this *was* our bait. The acid test, when Rambo retrieved one from his old stock, a Pup original, proved what my memory suggested and there was no questioning it whatsoever. We had done it. We were still in the game despite losing our boiliemeister. Pup had given us the right ingredients, brilliant instructions and we had successfully followed them to the letter. Job done and pats on the back all round.

"Shall we have a cuppa before we make up some pop-ups?" Rambo asked. "It'll give the last batch a chance to dry and cool before we bag them up and make some more."

I glanced down at the impressive spread of baits on the duvet and nodded. "Sure, I could murder a tea. Here, Sylvester!" I called to the young lad. "How would you like to be able to bait up like that at a hundred yards in a cross wind," I asked, pointing to the duvet.

"Be cool," the young carper admitted.

"Go and ask Mum to make us three teas, Sylvester. A few chocolate digestives wouldn't go amiss," Rambo added, catching my eye.

"I shouldn't really…" I started.

"Treat yourself, boy. I won't tell if you don't," Rambo said, dismissing my negativity.

"Just a couple, then," I insisted. "But no more."

Five minutes later, Sylvester returned with a plate piled high with chocolate digestives and three mugs of steaming tea on a tray. Concentrating heavily, the young lad placed the tray on the floor without spilling a drop and the three of us sat down on the concrete floor, our backs resting against the dividing wall of the house and garage.

By the time I had eaten my fifth digestive – I admit it; not a fucking shred of will power – I had finished telling Rambo and son about Hobbes' reaction to the dark pink bait.

"A good bait, then?" Rambo enquired.

"No question. Obviously, I haven't been around to see the ginger ninja grade other baits, but it was a pretty emphatic reaction. You couldn't have taken it any other way. I might try him on one of ours, to get a bit of a better picture," I reasoned.

At that moment my phone, a Samsung, gave its default 'whistle' to signify an incoming message. A split second later, Rambo's smartphone went off as well.

"Luke!" we both declared in unison.

"You read it out, boy," Rambo instructed.

I swiped my phone and then pressed the green WhatsApp icon, taking me to the chat screen within the app. I pressed the chat at the top of the list.

"It's a message forwarded on by Luke from the Black Mirror Cult," I said. "It says: 'The next step in your BMC membership can now be taken. You will shortly be added to a new group chat. This will be your BMC cell. With this new facility you will be able to connect with like-minded anglers and help push forward the BMC's agenda. The BMC: Working for you to cleanse carp fishing of commercialism and give it back to real anglers. Your Higher Associate'. Well," I said, looking up at Rambo and Sylvester. "What do you make of it? They're using it as I said they might."

"Interesting," Rambo answered, picking up the plate from the tray and offering it over to me. "Another biscuit, boy?"

# Chapter 10

Pup was now a landlord. The couple I had shown around his poorly appointed pad had decided it could be their des res and had signed on the dotted line. Pup was very happy with this state of affairs and once all the necessary legalities were over and it was a done deal, he had phoned me up to express this sentiment.

"How's Hobbes?" he had begun. I had assured him the ginger ninja was fine and dandy. "Great news on the house, Matt," he had continued, excitedly. "Well done! It's a massive relief to know I'll be getting some money coming in from it, what with Daisy's business idea needing more funding."

"No problem," I had answered, thinking, actually, there was a problem – the one of our ex-boiliemeister being manipulated out of his hard earned mullah by a hard-faced, conniving bitch. "Can I ask why you decided not to sell the house in the end and went for renting it out?"

"It was Daisy's idea," Pup had answered. "She thought I shouldn't commit myself so completely at this early stage of our relationship and business venture."

"I see," I had said, seeing straight through Daisy's duplicitous deed. She was smooth all right, pulling the old double bluff manoeuvre – reassuring hand on the shoulder while the other knifed you between the shoulder blades. "So, what's this great business plan Daisy's come up with that needs your money? Can you reveal it yet?" I had asked, keen to know what spin she was putting on the process of scamming Pup out of every penny.

"Oh, no. Sorry. I can't, Matt. I promised I wouldn't tell anyone else. Not at this delicate early stage when we're trying to get everything up and running."

"Are you allowed to tell me how much you've put in?"

"Twenty grand," Pup had said. "For starters."

"Quite a serious amount, then?" I had said as lightly as possible.

"It's a serious plan," Pup had replied. "Daisy reckons, according to her business plan, we could double our money in the first year."

"Brilliant," I had remarked with as much enthusiasm as I could muster. "How are you getting on with her on a personal level?"

"We had full penetrative sex for the first time last night," Pup had admitted with great candour. "Before that she had only sucked me off."

"Okaaay," I had said, reeling somewhat from Pup's graphic honesty.

"She's a swallower," Pup had fired straight back. "So, pretty amazing, but when we did it last night she got in this position, her arse…"

"I wanted to ask you something about Hobbes," I had said, cutting across a mental image I was keen to crowbar out of my brain, while simultaneously appreciating what a fully committed con artist Daisy was turning out to be.

"Oh… okay," Pup had said, his sexual sails suddenly devoid of wind thanks to my Doldrums-inflicting intervention. "You did say he's all right. He *is* all right, isn't he?"

"He's fine. In fact, I fed him a couple of our baits the other night. The ones me, Rambo and Sylvester made from your recipe with your gear. It was an interesting response from him, to say the least. I've still got the deep scratch marks on my arm! The thing is, Hobbes' reaction wasn't totally dissimilar to an earlier one when I'd given him a boilie I'd found in The Pit's margins," I had explained, before going on to relate, in some detail, Hobbes' response to both baits. "If you don't mind, I'd like to send you a photo of the bait I found so you can have a look at it. It's a dark pink one. That okay?"

"Sure. Send it to me if you want," Pup had replied. "But going back to Hobbes' reaction, it's exactly as I would have predicted for your revolutionary bait," Pup had continued. "You obviously did a good job rolling it, even if you were spoon-fed everything by yours truly. It's his response to the other bait that's more interesting. Without being big-headed, I'm surprised Hobbes reacted as he did to the one you found. By what you've told me, I'd say the dark pink boilie is within spitting distance of being in the same league as some of my top baits. Believe me, it's some product to get anywhere near them."

Taking Pup's words in and sifting through them, I had then asked him to grade, marks out of ten, our exclusive, revolutionary, indented, dirty brown bottom bait boilie against the dark pink bait, his other baits and a top commercially-available bait.

"Yours is a nine and a half. It's the best bait I ever made," he had stated categorically. "The dark pink bait I'd hazard a guess at being an eight. It could sit on the next level down from my other top baits like PhD, WTF, Inducer and Pro, which I all consider to be eight and a halves. Now that's what's surprising. Whoever dreamt it up knows his stuff. All the commercial baits you can disregard. The best ones are okay, but in all the tests I did over the years with Wilton, and then with Hobbes, no bait company ever scored more than a seven and a half. It's why you, Rambo and The Eye catch more fish than anyone else."

I had been about to defend our carp fishing skills, but had thought better of it. I had to ask my last question while I still had Pup in this genial mood, one where he was happy to talk about the trade he had left behind. It was probably a combination of renting out his house and the full penetrative sex that had swung it for me so far.

"I know you haven't seen it yet, but if you had the dark pink bait, in a boilie format, could you ever deconstruct it and work out exactly what was in it. You know, with no clues, nothing else to go on other than just the bait itself?"

"You're not really talking about the dark pink bait, are you?" Pup had said, perceptively.

"Okay. *Our* bait. I don't give a shit about someone unpicking the dark pink bait."

"It'd be very difficult even with access to a lot of very expensive laboratory equipment and a high degree of scientific knowledge," Pup had answered. "A top boiliemeister *could* take a punt on guessing some of the likely ingredients, by what he could see and taste in the mix and by what he could smell. In terms of the flavour, he'd have to base it on taste and smell as well, but he'd struggle to get anywhere near the whole picture. You don't have to worry, no one could fathom out your revolutionary bait, not with it containing the revolutionary ingredient. Not unless they steal it from Rambo's house... Hold on. All right, darling. Just coming! It's Daisy, Matt. I've got to go."

"Gondola ride with ice creams?"

"That's Mondays. Doge's Palace tour today and then coffee in St Mark's Square with more loving for Peter tonight."

"Enjoy them all," I had said. But don't expect it to last, I had thought. "I'll email some pictures of the pink bait. Have a look at it when you get the chance."

Pup had never answered back. He had already gone.

Mentally buoyed by Pup's assertion of how hard it would be to get to grips with our exclusive, revolutionary, indented, dirty brown bottom bait boilie, if by any chance it had been nicked from my bivvy, I made arrangements to have a three-day trip to coincide with Rambo on The Pit to start the following day. While I was sorting out my gear in preparation for the session, Luke forwarded me a Black Mirror Cult Daily Directive, 'To Cult or not to Cult – It's not even a question', which, despite myself, I kind of liked on a couple of levels. In the evening, I received an ordinary text message from Luke saying the BMC cell group chat had started a few hours earlier. He was in a group with nine other members plus his Higher Associate as the 'Group Admin'. The messages had been flying backwards and forwards thick and fast. He told me it was impossible for him to pass on all these messages, saying it was difficult enough to keep up with the volume of notifications he was receiving in the first place. He indicated his concern Rambo might look unfavourably on this situation and, as a consequence, might want to take his Lake ticket away as punishment along with the violent removal of his two front teeth. He finished by saying he desperately needed me to get in touch and tell him what he should do.

I decided to phone him. There was too much to say to do it by text.

"How's it going, Luke? The BMC cell chat getting a bit hectic, is it?" I enquired, after he answered his phone.

"You could say that," he replied. "I'm getting snowed under with messages from the others in my cell. It's like being put in a room where the lights are out, it's pitch black and then someone turns them on and says, 'Hi! It's time to meet the others. You're all in the same club. Get to know each other!' It's crazy!"

"Anyone on there you know?" I asked.

"Hard to say, to be honest. We've all played it a bit careful, I guess, and haven't used our real names. A lot of the others did what I did and gave a genuine address, a mobile number and a made-up user name when we sent off our cash."

"No Lake members, then?"

"No. Not that I can say at the moment. No one's mentioned The Lake so far amongst the venues that have cropped up in the chat messages. Most waters mentioned aren't from around here. My cell group seems to be made up of anglers from all over the place."

"What's your general take on them?"

"Most of them seem all right, to be fair. They all have their individual reasons for joining. Most thought it would be a bit of a crack and worth taking the chance for a one-off fifteen quid payment, a couple were like me, going through a bad time and thought some personal advice might help and the rest were the more motivated type."

"In what way," I asked.

"They're really into the anti-corporate, anti-commercial crusade thing. They seem passionate about the idea of giving carp fishing back to real anglers even if they're a bit unsure how it could happen. Plus they like the 'do what must be done', 'got to push yourself' side of it. It appeals to them. I think it helps give their fishing added motivation and encouragement. I know it did for me."

"Okay," I said with non-commitment. "Out of interest, how did they all get to hear about the BMC?"

"I don't know for sure. A few of them have said they heard by word of mouth, but most were directly approached by someone they didn't recognise."

"And you?" I asked, realising it was a question Rambo and I had forgotten to ask.

"The same really. I got talking to this bloke in a tackle shop. He was a customer looking through all the masses of bait stuff, like I was, and he commented on there being too much choice. It sort of went on from there, we got into a conversation, like you do, and in passing he mentioned the Black Mirror Cult and told me a bit about it. He told me how I could join when I said I might be interested and gave me the PO Box address."

"That's a bit weird, isn't it? It's hardly an effective recruiting method, hanging around a tackle shop waiting to get into a conversation with someone," I said, laughing.

"I don't think he was there just to do that," Luke remarked. "It genuinely seemed to be an off the cuff thing."

"How long have the others been members?"

"Not long. A couple of months at most."

A new broom, then, I thought. "Incidentally, have you ever tried actually speaking to this Higher Associate of yours," I asked.

"When I broke my blank I did. I was so excited and grateful I wanted to speak to him personally. He didn't pick up, but did message me saying he couldn't ever talk to me and would only ever respond through the 'proper channels' as he put it. You can phone fellow cell members if you want, but to be honest all of us are sticking to messaging."

"Right. Have any of your BMC cell told their carping mates about joining the Black Mirror Cult?"

"Most have. I think quite a few of their mates have joined up since."

"Have you told anyone?"

"No. No way. I don't want to upset Rambo."

"Very wise. You're doing the right thing," I said, thinking it was time to wrap this up. "Anyway, nice chatting, Luke, and I'll leave you in peace. I think it's best if we carry on like this. You can either update me or Rambo on the BMC cell banter front by giving either of us a call every week, not unless something really interesting crops up, and in the meantime keep forwarding on your and the your Higher Associate's messages. One thing I will stress is don't let these others know where you're fishing. No mentioning The Lake or The Pit. We're still not any further on with establishing whether someone has poached The Pit or not and certainly don't need the potential problem of 'highly motivated' BMC members hearing about it. You know where your bread is buttered, so don't go putting the BMC above me and Rambo and your Lake membership. The big guy won't like it, you know."

"I haven't. I won't. Not a single word about what water I'm on."

"Good. I'd keep it that way if I was you. Bye for now."

"Bye," Luke responded and hung up.

I went back to preparing my gear, idly wondering how much momentum the Black Mirror Cult might be able to gain through its underground style of modus operandi. There was no doubting its unusual methodology might appeal to some and I could see the potential for rapid expansion if enough initial members could rope in their mates and convince them to part with fifteen quid. The big question, undoubtedly, was would enough carp anglers pay to be part of an ideological think-tank with few tangible benefits? An idealistic notion of ridding carp angling of commercialism and supposedly giving the sport back to 'real anglers', a carp fishing etiquette and the active encouragement of a 'do what must be done' mentality when it came to members' individual carp-catching were all well and good, but what else did BMC members get? A bit of carp fishing advice, oh, and a free sew-on badge. It was evidently all bollocks, but somehow, even to a cynic like myself, it was entertaining bollocks. On a French restaurant menu it would be 'Bollocks Élan' served with a side dish of brio and a glass of red pizzazz. Ultimately worthless and unworkable, yet somehow tantalisingly cool and trendy. The big proviso being, from our viewpoint, the BMC wasn't a front for a bloated carp fishing ego who had poached The Pit, stole our bait and nicked our rigs!

When I checked my rigs – The Carper's super trick rigs – I hoped the nonsense of someone poaching The Pit, taking our bait and seeing the secrets in my rig box would turn out to be nothing more substantial than phantoms founded in my palpable paranoia. Rambo and I had baulked at asking all members to notify us about their bait choices and as such the two dark pink baits I had spotted in the margins of East Ender had to remain, for the moment, an unsolved mystery. Luke was our only pathway to discovering if there was a link between the BMC and any possible Pit poaching and it seemed we had that base covered. As long as Luke co-operated – his fear of Rambo and losing his ticket was our insurance – we were as informed as we could ever hope to be.

The following morning, I was up early, breakfasted and off to The Pit by seven. Hobbes had been curled up in his blanket-lined wicker basket as I had eaten my cereal at the kitchen table, all snug and toasty, a basketball-sized mass of fur determined to get in a straight sixteen hours of sleep. The most animated he had got was to gingerly (get it?) lift his head to watch me with apparent disinterest when I had first walked in and turned on the light. How different from when I had offered him a couple of MRS (Matt, Rambo and Sylvester) produced exclusive, revolutionary, indented, dirty brown bottom bait boilies. On that occasion he had sprung into life, as if jolted by a cattle prod, physically assaulted my arm in a flurry of hissing and mewing malevolence and devoured the two baits I had offered up in sacrifice with manic gusto. With hindsight, it was a probably a good job Pup had never produced a 'ten'. The chances are he would have lost an arm as a consequence.

By mid-morning, I was all set up and back in East Ender. I had experienced a really strong pull to fish it again after my previous success, one purely based on that most odd fishing instinct, the 'gut feeling'. There were no carp shows to make me want to occupy the swim again, no climatic diktat forcing my hand and no fellow angler 'carp in the vicinity' tip offs of the 'I've seen fish jump/roll/show/crash/ bosh/top/head'n'shoulder/lump out/bubble/fizz/muddy/colour/stir (we're like fucking Eskimos and the word 'snow' with this sort of stuff) in such and such a swim' kind. All I knew was I had caught from there last session and a repeat performance meant I could do so again. I had still engaged in the professional-carp-angler-approved activity of walking round and looking, but only in the confines of my swim and for rogue pink baits, rather than carp activity. Thankfully, there were no dark pink baits to be found anywhere.

At two in the afternoon I was striding my way out of East Ender; rods wound in with baits removed and then placed back in the margins to hide my rigs. I pulled my phone from my trouser pocket as I walked anti-clockwise around The Pit's grass perimeter track, exactly as I had when answering the call from Rambo ten minutes earlier. A notification alert had sounded and I worked my way through a few screens to get to the new WhatsApp message. It was a BMC Daily Directive forwarded on by Luke. It read, '(Don't Fear) The Cleanser – Black Mirror Cult', which, although equally as derivative as the last one, seemed a lot less accessible. One likely to be met with a blank expression by someone not that into music; specifically, mid-nineteen seventies American rock music. Possibly someone like Rambo, for instance.

"Did you get the reference in that last BMC Daily Directive?" I asked, as I arrived in his swim, pointing a finger at my phone."

Rambo shook his head. "No. I have to say it went over my head, boy."

"*Blue Öyster* Cult had a pretty big hit with a track called '(Don't Fear) The Reaper' way back in the seventies," I explained.

"Oh, yeah," Rambo said, unsurely. "That sort of rings a bell now you've mentioned it. I think I've heard the song before. Years ago, though." Rambo clapped his hands together with an air of finality. The noise of it echoed across The Pit. "Still, it's a relief to be set right and finally know. Now I'll be able to sleep tonight. You're officially the fount of all useless knowledge, boy," my camo-clad mucker stated. "Can't remember if anything's been moved in his bivvy or not, but can remember pop trivia from forty years ago."

"Long term memory's always the last to go," I pointed out. "Anyway. Enough of all this nonsense," I said, dismissively. "What've you had that's meant you've had to ask for my photographic assistance? I know you didn't want to tell me over the phone, you tease."

"It's a good one, boy," Rambo beamed. "A true gnarly original monster. Have a guess."

"Pugwash?" I ventured.

"Nope."

"The Black Pig?"

"Nope."

"The Paddle?"

"Wrong again."

"Not *Orion*?" [The biggest fish in The Pit.]

Rambo gave me the smile I imagined he normally reserved for those pitiful souls influenced by The Ladbroke's Life ads and Jehovah's Witnesses, shortly before slamming the door in their face. "You didn't listen to what I said, boy. A true gnarly original *monster*. I've caught, Frankenstein. And before we go any further, don't give me your usual lecture about how it was the *doctor* whose name was Frankenstein."

I held my two arms up to indicate I wouldn't. "Nice fish," I cooed. "How big?"

"Clickety click on the nose, boy," Rambo answered.

For a second I was confused and then realisation dawned. "Sixty-six pounds dead! What a fish! It's well up in weight from the last time it came out," I enthused. My effervescence faded and I scratched the back of my head self-consciously. "How come you're fully conversant with bingo nicknames, but know fuck all about American rock bands?" I asked.

Rambo scrunched his nose and hunched his massive shoulders. "Guess I'm just one of the cool dads."

"Yeah, you're a pretty cool dad. I'll give you that," I admitted, grinning. "Shall we do the honours?"

Rambo nodded and moved down to the water's edge to lift Frankenstein from the margins of his swim. The leviathan had been resting up in a flotation weigh sling since losing a 'two falls, one submission' bout to the Terminator with Tackle. The victor effortlessly extracted the fish, placed it deftly on his unhooking mat and eased the giant carp out into daylight and clear of the sling. With its full bulk now apparent, I gorged on the scaly creature's size and glory. It was a remarkable beast, not a pretty fish by any means, more an ugly one if anything, which impressed by virtue of its very dark colouring – almost jet black along the upper sections of its flanks – and its squat, deep, muscular shape. And its size. Black, and with a physical appearance suggesting battle-scarred, Frankenstein was a true old warrior; a fish reeking of history, hardship and brutality. A monster indeed.

The fish had been originally named by ex-Pit member, Rocky – a fish-stealing bell end who Rambo had crushed in a fist fight – yet as much as I had disliked him, I had to admit he had captured something of the fish's essential essence.

As Rambo held Frankenstein in a traditional pose, I wielded his digital SLR, snapping at will. Once I had confirmed the suitability of the images on the camera's rear screen, Rambo re-wrapped the fish in the sling, move it back to the margins and from there released Frankenstein into The Pit's clear waters. Should he have written one, I imagined Frankenstein's diary entry for the day reading; 'Bad day at the office. Hunger got the better of me and I slipped up. Don't know why, but I couldn't stop myself; sort of got pre-occupied with eating the round things and must have picked up a wrong'un. It's still as weird as ever on the other side. Hard to breathe. Impossible to move, too. Thank Mother Nature the creatures always put us back. Still can't quite put a pelvic fin radial on how it is they do it.'

"How do you fancy a day's shopping with me, Matt?" Rambo enquired as he rinsed off his hands in The Pit's waters.

"If it's going to be anything like when I went to Bluewater with Sophie, then no," I replied. "I spent so much time hanging around outside fitting rooms, some of the customers started handing *me* back the clothes they'd just tried on saying, 'Sorry, no good.'"

"I'm talking about shopping for something a little more interesting than *clothes*," Rambo explained.

"Guns?" I asked.

"I've got enough guns."

"But can a man like you *really* have enough guns?"

"I've got enough guns," Rambo confirmed. "I'm talking about rods."

"Ooh, rods!" I said, childishly. "Now you're piquing my interest."

"It's Sylvester's birthday soon and I want to get him a set of rods as a present. He's been using mine up till now, but it's not the same."

"Good idea. He'd love that."

"That's what I thought. He's old enough now to warrant having his own set. In a few years I'd like him to be a member of The Lake in his own right and be able to go on his own. A set of rods can be the start of him having all his own gear for when the time comes."

"Where are you thinking of looking?" I asked.

"I haven't bought a set of rods for a fair number of years now, so I really need to see what's out there in the flesh. Viewing them on a computer screen's no good. I want to have a close look, touch them and see how the rod feels in my hands." I nodded my agreement. "I don't know whether you've seen it advertised anywhere, or if any of the members have mentioned it to you, but there's a big tackle show this weekend down in Hampshire, near Eastleigh, just off the motorway. There are quite a few rod manufacturers and rod builders going to have stalls there and the choice should be good so I thought about going there. I'm expecting there'll be loads of blank options worth considering and if I find one I like I can specify the rings, reel fitting and finish I want and get them made up. There's nothing like having a bespoke set of rods with your name on them."

"You *have* to have your name on them! It's obligatory and the absolute First Law of Tackle Tartery," I chimed, thinking, even if your name is as unfortunate as Sylvester Ramsbottom.

"You're not wrong," Rambo concurred. "If you're up for it, boy, I could pick you up on the way through and we could go together. It'd be a day out and a good chance to have a nose at some of the other gear there."

"Yeah, why not," I answered. "Might be interesting to get out of our bubble and mix with the masses. See what's occurring on the dark side of the moon."

"Pink Floyd!" Rambo said, proudly.

"Very good," I acknowledged. "We'll get you on Ken Bruce's Popmaster, yet. Does Sylvester know what he's getting for his birthday?" Rambo shook his head. "Maybe I can get something for him at the show as well. From me and Sophie. Make it an all-fishing job lot of presents to set him on his way to having his own independent kit."

"Good idea. He'd be very happy with that, Matt," Rambo enthused. "His mother's got other ideas about what to buy him for his birthday and I can guarantee it won't be fishing tackle!"

"A musical instrument?" I guessed. "A grand piano, perhaps? Steffi might shoehorn one into your living room when you're not looking and get him to practise Chopin until four in the morning. Or more books, maybe? Catch-22…" I stumbled, unable to think of any more famous books off the top of my head.

"Christ knows," Rambo said, saving my silence of ignorance. "I let her do her own thing when it comes to that sort of thing. Then it gives me the right to do mine. Just have to warn the boy to make sure he smiles equally as much at both sets of presents."

I chuckled at Rambo's declaration and went off on a tangent. "It's good we've got a fish under our belts on one of the baits we made," I stated. "Not that there was any doubt after Hobbes' reaction."

"Have you spoken to Pup recently?" Rambo asked, his mind jogged to the ex-boiliemeister by the cat's name.

I nodded and informed Rambo about my most recent conversation with our Venetian-based friend. I then moved on to the one I'd had with Luke. Rambo seemed happy enough with how Luke was playing the game, but much like myself, was a bit perturbed at how Pup was being systematically relieved of his money.

"She's a cunning bitch," Rambo stated. "Underhand, too. Fancy a woman using sex as a weapon."

"Pat Benatar," I said, proudly.

Rambo's brow furrowed and he held up a giant paw. "First... Don't bother explaining. Second... Haven't you got a swim to go to?"

As requested, I didn't. In answer, I did. Bidding my buddy goodbye, I left for it. On arriving in East Ender, I recast all three rods and settled into the waiting game. My traps were set, all I needed was a carp to fall for one.

Early the following morning, my prior gut feeling mutated from a promising chrysalis into the fully realised butterfly of inspired choice. My left-hand rod had a slow take, one turning out to have been the work of an immaculate mid-thirty common. It had fallen to one of the MRS made pop-ups made after I had pigged out on Rambo's chocolate digestives. Although I had five kilos of MRS made exclusive, revolutionary, indented, dirty brown bottom bait boilie ready and raring to go in the bivvy, I hadn't put any out and had instead relied on the same tactics I had used on my last session. This time, it had been the tight-to-the-deck pop-up with a small PVA bag of chopped boilies, cast forty yards down to my left, which had produced the take. After dealing with the common, I recast with heightened optimism, convinced more action was coming my way.

Almost a day later, still in darkness, the sun having not yet risen, one of my single bottom baits fished at seventy odd yards ripped off. Extracting myself from my sleeping bag, I put on my head torch, frantically donned my loosely-laced-trainers-ready-for-a-run-in-the-middle-of-the-night and blundered to my middle rod with all the grace and co-ordination of a tap dancing bison who had never made it to stage school. Grabbing the rod, my heart hammering from the sudden exertion, I stood in the cold darkness and eased into the fish. Fifteen minutes later, my third Pit fish of the season was safely on the mat. The fish was a mirror, a bit bigger than the previous one, weighing thirty-eight pounds ten, and almost certainly another second generation fish; one created by the successful spawning of the original stock. Placing my conventional black weigh sling down on the mat, I debated whether to photograph the fish myself or to put it back straightaway.

To most anglers, the notion of not bothering to photograph an upper thirty might seem ridiculous. An act bordering on being so absurd it led to question whether the angler involved was on a massive ego trip of the 'I only bother to photograph *big* fish', kind. Unfortunately, or rather, fortunately, The Pit did have the effect of 'normalising' generally regarded big fish into making them seem comparatively unremarkable. An upper thirty wasn't exceptional – although no one in their right mind could argue it wasn't a wonderful fish – and given the circumstances, it being dark, I questioned the worth of making the effort to get a flash-lit photo. I had umpteen photos of upper thirty Pit fish and I certainly didn't consider sacking it for a few hours, or asking Rambo to reel in and come round in order to get a better picture, a viable option. It was a simple choice; photograph it or return it immediately.

If the fish had been a bit heavier, a forty pound fish and possibly a new-caught forty I could name, then the question wouldn't have arisen and the camera would have come out. As much for the progression of The Pit's history as a trophy shot. As it was, I was still unsure what to do and I moved the weigh sling clear of the fish to have another close look at it – as if looking at it once more might push me into making a decision. To my stupefaction, the inside of the weigh sling was now smeared with excreted bait. I set my head torch to its brightest setting and looked closer. Pink! The excreted bait was pink! I gathered the fish back into the sling, a sound in my head like distant thunder.

# Chapter 11

My accompanying Rambo on the journey to the tackle show gave the pair of us plenty of time to chew the cud. I had previously done my homework – thanks, Mr Google – on digestion times for carp and had passed on my newfound knowledge to Rambo. The general consensus, according to the articles I had read, was carp could eat and then pass out food within a twelve to seventy-two hour window. This considerable variation was caused by two principal factors; water temperature – the colder the slower, the warmer the quicker – and the digestibility of the food in question.

Rambo glanced over to me, momentarily taking his eyes off the road. "Then one of two things must have happened, boy. Either the dark pink bait sat at the bottom of The Pit for the best part of two weeks without being eaten, or someone has put some more in. Probably in East Ender again, and you, being the jammy bastard you are, caught a couple of fish over the top of it."

"It seems that way," I agreed.

"You say you've already sent out a text to all The Pit membership?"

I nodded. "Sixteen have replied back already. No one's using a dark pink bait and no one's seen anything unusual."

Rambo slammed both hands on to the steering wheel. "Fuck! Who hasn't replied yet?"

"The Bookie and Astrological Jim."

"Text them again. Say it's urgent. Say *I* said it's urgent!"

"I'm on it."

I had sent the original text message last night. There had been no point in holding back any longer and baulking at the idea of having to get everyone involved. I had asked the eighteen other members, including new boy, Nick, if any of them were using a dark pink bait and if anyone had seen any unusual activity on The Pit. I had explained some baits of this colour had been spotted in the margins and to date both Rambo and I had been unable to substantiate who had put them there. As a precaution, we had decided to clarify the situation by asking the membership to co-operate with our unusual request. Unsurprisingly, the members had been most helpful and most had got back to me quickly. They all understood the subtext and saw no pleasure in the possibility of someone poaching The Pit for nothing, seeing as they themselves were paying big bucks for the privilege.

I still couldn't see how it could happen myself, not when I thought about it calmly and logically. How would anyone get in and out through combination padlocked gates without being seen, for a start? How could anyone *fish* without being seen?

Especially now The Pit was busier and both the carp and the membership had fully awoken from their winter hibernation.

My phone sounded a notification arriving. Rambo stared across for a good couple of seconds – a bit unnerving seeing as we were doing nearly eighty – and barked out a question asking the news.

I heaved a heavy sigh. "Thank fuck for that!" I told him, "It's The Bookie. He's using a dark pink bait! He's been working a late shift in his betting shop and couldn't answer his phone."

Rambo puffed out his cheeks in relief and the pressure in the van dropped by a momentous amount of millibars.

"Ask him if he's put any bait out early season in East Ender. Let's nail this here and now," Rambo suggested.

I sent off the text. Almost immediately one came back.

"He said he's done a bit of baiting up and down the east bank and not just in Old Wood. That explains it! No one's been poaching The Pit after all! We've been a couple of paranoid old women reading the runes all wrong! We've been seeing things that weren't ever there!" I said. "No offence to old women," I added, doffing my cap to political correctness now I was in a more genial mood.

Rambo shook his head with exasperation. "Thank fuck! That's good news, Matt. Looks like we certainly got ourselves into a hell of a state over it, doesn't it?" he said with embarrassment.

"Never mind," I replied. "No damage done. One day we'll look back on this and laugh."

"Yeah. The day we went to the Eastleigh tackle show," Rambo answered, grinning.

Over the remainder of the journey, Rambo and I discussed the BMC. Now we could discount the idea they might have had something to do with poaching The Pit – because there had been no poaching of The Pit – we both felt a bit more affable and generous towards them. Funny that. The last few Daily Directives, 'BMC – Keeping it non-commercial', 'In order to succeed, we must first believe we can catch – BMC' and 'BMC = GR8 IMHO' seemed a real hotchpotch of ideas, as much to entertain as inform. Interestingly, Sylvester had reported the odd Black Mirror Cult namecheck on a couple of carp forums, Twitter and other social media platforms and I had followed up this lead.

I hadn't found anything directly attributable from the BMC itself, only a low background hum of 'Has anyone heard of this new carp fishing movement called the Black Mirror Cult?' type of questions and a few BMC members spreading the 'anti-commercial, give carp angling back to the real anglers' and 'effort equals reward' themes. A couple of high profile 'name' anglers had also got wind of the BMC as well, and they had mentioned the 'new underground movement' to their followers. Some scepticism had been noted, 'That's all we need, another version of the Carp Society' was one comment I had found along with several, 'What difference can they hope to make?' opinions. On the whole, though, the BMC seemed to have been well received. Dissenting comments had been rare and quickly rebuffed. 'How can anyone argue with an anti-commercial standpoint and a personal motivation viewpoint along the lines of 'putting the hard yards in?' one Tweet had asked. It seemed of those who had voiced an opinion, if not great in numbers, this was the general stance.

The overall impression I now held was one of the BMC appearing to quietly grow and receive more support. Even so, it was impossible to quantify whether this support would manifest itself in actual membership numbers. Membership was only a one-off fifteen quid payment. And you got a free sew-on badge. And it was anti-commercial. And it appealed to those who considered themselves 'real' carp anglers. And it was possible it might appear cool to be associated with them – whatever it might have meant in the minds of those inclined to sign up.

I told Rambo my original thoughts on the BMC might well have been wide of the mark. "Being a shadowy underground movement hardly anyone knows doesn't seem conducive to becoming a carp fishing institution with clout, *to begin with*," I emphasised as we took our exit off the motorway. "But possibly I missed the point. Maybe they're cleverer than I first thought. Maybe they'll take off *because* they're an underground movement. How many underground movements have there been that have grown and eventually become part of the establishment? Loads!" I exclaimed, answering my own question. "Especially in the arts and music. That's the BMC's USP. Nothing is secret and underground in carp fishing today, not like it used to be, not when everything was secret squirrel. Not like when anglers used to hide their rigs and their bait. I can remember one bloke refusing to unhook a fish while I was watching…" I petered out. Rambo was giving me a withering look out the corner of his eye. "Okay. Okay. I know *we* still do that, but what I mean is, in general, if someone finds a new edge nowadays, most can't wait to tell everyone about it. To get it, and themselves, in the magazines, get a consultancy or develop it commercially and make money from it. And whatever you say, there has been a backlash against it and the perceived commercialisation of carp fishing. A commercial side detracting and taking away from the essence of the solitary, at-peace-with-nature challenge of man against fish." I paused to let Rambo shoot me down in flames. He didn't, so I pressed on. "I think that's the BMC's appeal. Younger anglers won't have ever seen anything like it and the old-skoolers will be on a dewy-eyed nostalgia trip! It's like they're re-inventing the wheel. Out with commercialism and give carp fishing back to the real anglers! What does that even mean? Who will even care? It sounds good!"

Rambo seemed less convinced. "It's early days yet. Give it another month or two and we'll see," he argued. "The gullible and deluded are always the easiest ones to convince. Let's see if the BMC can successfully persuade real numbers to part with their cash. Let's see if they can move on to the next stage and come up with some real policies. There hasn't been any sight of this carp fishing etiquette thing of theirs showing up anywhere, has there?"

"No," I admitted. "Are we there, yet?" I asked, diffusing our differences.

"Nearly. Not far now. The sat-nav says ten more minutes."

The large car park for the exhibition hall hosting the tackle show was already busy by the time we arrived. Parking up twenty minutes before opening time, I could see a mass of anglers already waiting by the entrance doors, ready to stampede through and rush to the exhibitors of their choice. The majority of this mass were dressed in green or camo and could just as easily have been waiting at the gates of a day ticket venue for a day's fishing – although the chances of getting a swim didn't look too clever considering how many of them there were. Clearly, the de rigueur attire choice for going to a fishing tackle show was to wear exactly the same as what you might wear on the bank. Rambo was in his British Army camo gear and boots – more by force of habit and lifestyle choice, than anything – but I had opted out, wearing grey cargo trousers, a T-shirt and a Superdry sweatshirt. Being in my forties, I was the ideal age to wear Superdry clothing – much to the great dismay, I suspected, of their design team. Not that a young person's designer brand getting hijacked by the middle-aged was especially high on my lists of concerns. Nor was it on Rambo's.

"I'm going to make a beeline for all the rod manufacturers and try and find what I want as quickly as possible," he told me as we joined the back of the queue.

"I'll tag along," I replied. "I can look for something for Sylvester afterwards. I was thinking of buying him a rod rest system. That'd make up a good starting package, custom built rods and something to put them on. How many are you planning on buying him? Three?"

Rambo nodded. "I know The Lake is a two-rod venue, but hopefully one day he'll move on to The Pit. There's no point in buying a pair." My fishing and business partner had a sudden thought and a mischievous look appeared on his stubbly countenance. "Hey, boy. Do you think someone in there will be selling any of those Syndicate books?"

I curled a top lip and furrowed my brow in a diversionary tactic to indicate I was considering this for the first time, which was an outright falsehood because I had contemplated it the moment I had known we were going.

"Possibly. A few of the magazines sell them, so if they have stands…"

"Are you going to announce yourself as the author and offer to sign a few for the excited punters?" Rambo whispered in my ear, stopping me in my tracks.

"Fuck me, no! Of course not!" I answered, as if Rambo had suggested I run bollock-naked around the car park with a bait rocket jammed up my arse. "That's hardly the game plan for writing under a pseudonym," I bleated. "Besides, no fucker would ever believe me if I did try to tell them it was me. Grant has dealt with all of the correspondence and admin work. They've obviously never seen, met or spoken to me."

"So you won't bother to look to see if your books are selling better than any of the other carp books here?" Rambo asked, taunting me.

"Why would I do that?" I asked, uncomfortably – knowing I was being mercilessly teased, like a hungry dog offered a bowl of food from the other side of a chicken mesh fence.

"Come on!" Rambo scoffed. "Because! That's *why*! I bet you check your fucking Kindle sales every day."

"Not every day, I don't," I said, indignantly.

"Liar!"

"I don't check it *every* day, for your information, Mr Ramsbottom," I said very properly. "I actually check it about six or seven times *a* day."

Rambo let out a hearty guffaw. One loud enough for a few people in the queue to look up at him to see what was so funny.

"Ha! I fucking knew it!" he hissed triumphantly in my ear. "Don't let the Black Mirror Cult know who you are. They're out to gun you down, boy. What with your commercial exploitation of our honourable pastime," Rambo goaded.

"Oi! Easy," I said, feigning deep upset. "I'd like to think The Syndicate books are the acceptable face of the publishing opportunities afforded by the popularity of carp fishing. Independent, original…"

"One adult and one *child*, please… Hold on. Sorry. My mistake. Two adults, please," Rambo said to the man in the ticket booth, eyeing me with a twisted smile on his face.

"You're mean," I said as we entered the exhibition hall.

"Mean? I've just paid for you to get in, boy," Rambo retorted.

"That's true," I said. "In that case, I'll let you off. Just this once, though. Which way to the rod exhibitors?"

"This way," Rambo replied, pointing a finger to the right of the hall. "Follow me and don't go talking to any strange men."

"We've all put months and months of our time, possibly years, plus an incredible amount of our money into trying to catch carp, and once we've succeeded, we promptly put them back. *Everybody* here's strange," I pointed out.

"I meant relatively," Rambo clarified, yomping off with purpose.

Shutting my mouth, I quickly dived into Rambo's wake, making sure I remained close enough to him so the parted throng washed either side of me as well. It was like trailing behind an ice breaker.

Rambo was nothing if not thorough in his rod blank assessment. Over the next couple of hours he visited all the main manufacturers present, asked a myriad of questions and handled many finished rods before making his preferred option. Once he had decided on the blank and its test curve, it was on to the rod builders, to see what niceties they could offer. During this procedure, I, being much less focussed, had a more generalised experience, taking in the other non-rod related exhibitors and indulging myself in a bit of people watching. Well, carp angler watching – although I do believe it is possible to be a real person and a carp angler at the same time. Just.

Viewing the hordes of carpers milling around the large hall, I speculated on what carp fishing meant to them as individuals, what sort of venues they fished and the general levels of competence existing amongst them. How many of them could feather down to a tiny rock hard gravel patch at one twenty in a cross wind? Or stick out ten kilos of bait on to an area equal to that of a king-sized duvet cover, as I had once asked Sylvester? How many could tie their own rigs up? How many thought bait boats were cheating? How many could stand fishing day ticket venues on Bank Holiday weekends? How many could thrash in a bivvy peg with a mallet and not hit their fingers? How many thought fishing a venue like Rainbow to be the ultimate thrill, or alternatively, something beyond the pale? How many had experienced other types of fishing before starting to carp fish? How many could shot a waggler? How many had caught a forty? How many had fished abroad? How many *only* fished abroad? How many had had to go to hospital to have a hook removed from their finger? How many had died in a zipped up bivvy from carbon monoxide poisoning? Well, none, obviously, not unless some of his mates were pushing him around the hall, bungee strapped to a Carp Porter barrow.

The questions remaining to be asked seemed limitless. In the end, I supposed the question of chief importance hanging in the air was one unconcerned with carp angler profiling and more to do with commerce – that word again, or a variation of it – and boiled down to a simple, 'How much will each individual spend?' And for each individual exhibitor, 'How much of it will they spend with us?'

I concluded, although I had no idea whether I was correct or not, the hall most probably held a pretty good representation of carp anglers from right across the board; from the inexperienced and casual to the experienced and motivated. Some coming just to look and pick up a few bits and bobs, others more set on making a big ticket purchase – one hopefully under the internet price.

Looking at the stalls we had passed so far, it was evident the big brand names certainly attracted more of a crowd, especially those who had a 'famous carp angler' – something I had always considered an oxymoron – fronting for them. Perhaps it was time to admit I was wrong. Any sport/pastime/pursuit had its 'stars' and, on the whole, the masses did seem to take to them. Was trying to get a professional footballer's autograph any different than getting a signed copy of a carp book? To the wider public, maybe. To a keen carp angler, probably not. A company's advertising, and their association with 'consultants', played out on a host of differing media platforms, helped create vital brand awareness – itself the very life force of sales – whether displayed in the brand of Lionel Messi's boots, Roger Federer's racket or the items in an angler's kit. And I could more fully appreciate that now, despite my prior cynicism, because I could see it being played out before my own eyes. For a giddy second, I wondered if was missing out by not having bought a camouflaged bait bucket, twenty ready-tied chod rigs and a weekend carp fishing tutorial.

Feeling queasy, I eased myself back from the brink.

"I need to get a drink," I told Rambo, wiping the cold beads of sweat from my forehead. "Do you want a tea?"

"I'm good, thanks," he answered with distraction, being deep in conversation over the apparent virtues of a matt finish varnish over gloss.

"Okay. I'll be back in a bit," I said, pushing my way out into a busy aisle and heading for the refreshment area.

The queue time for my tea was fifteen minutes and not having had the option of paying for a Disney-like FastPass, I had no alternative other than to wait it out. Having finally made my way to the counter, I purchased my drink and gladly plonked my bum down on one of the many plastic chairs placed alongside the thirty or so small tables constituting the eating area within the hall. The area was almost full – apparently a carp angler sits around on his stomach, as opposed to marching on it – but I managed to find a table to myself right on the outer edges, one furthest away from the counter. After taking a solitary sip of my tea, I started the go-to activity for my generation, and every other younger one when having a few seconds of spare time, and took out my phone. Astrological Jim had texted back, I hadn't heard the notification, saying he had been fishing and his phone had died, hence the late reply. He wasn't using a pink bait.

"All right, fella? Mind if I join yer?"

I glanced up at a man in his twenties, wearing a faded green hoodie – with the hood up – and made an immediate character judgement based on this single fact. Let's just say it wasn't a positive one.

This may have said more about me than it did him.

"No, sure. Help yourself," I said, going back to the safety of my phone's screen.

"Mental, innit?" Hoodie proclaimed, as he slumped into the chair opposite.

Bollocks, I thought. He wants to talk to me. "Yeah. Busy," I said nodding, hoping my monosyllabic answers might deter him from further engagement.

I returned my attention back to my phone to avoid eye contact.

"It's all shit, though, innit? All this lot. Yer don't need all this lot to catch a carp, d'yer? I fink yer could say we're at peak tackle!"

I looked up, a bit surprised at his last piece of terminology. 'Peak stuff' was a broadsheet term I had only recently read about.

"No. I guess not," I answered, not wanting to get drawn in.

"Yer from dahn 'ere?" he asked.

"No. Not really. A couple of hours away."

"Me neivver. I come dahn from Lahndon... Whot sort of places yer fish?" Hoodie asked, opening up a new line of conversation.

"Club waters and day tickets, mainly," I lied. "The odd trip to France."

He nodded, slowly. "Yer bought anyfink so far?"

"Not yet. My mate's looking to buy a set of rods for his son."

"I ain't bought nuffin', neivver," Hoodie stated. "Don't intend to." I couldn't help myself and I looked up into Hoodie's eyes. They were gleaming. Little dark glinting chips. "I'm *sellin'*, not buyin'," he said, enigmatically.

Here we go, I thought, expelling a mental sigh. There's no way out of this now. "Okay. I'll bite. What are you selling?" I asked.

"A dream," Hoodie replied. "A dream that does away wiv all this shit. All this commercial, corporate bullshit we're wading thru."

"How's that work?" I asked, interested now.

Hoodie leaned in to me and inched his head to the left and then to the right, looking furtively in both directions. It wasn't an especially helpful manoeuvre because although his head moved, his hood stayed stock-still and blocked his vision. "I'm in a new movement, devoted to the cause of anti-commercialism within carp fishin' and of givin' it back to the real anglers."

I half expected to see Hoodie drop his cue card, but he'd memorised the pitch well. "I'm interested," I said. "Tell me more."

"We're a cult movement. Underground, see? We're gonna change everyfink. It's gonna take time, but we'll do it. We'll tell it as it is. Tell people yer don't need all this shit to catch carp. Bullshit rigs, bullshit tackle, bullshit bait, bullshit puddles wiv overstuffed pigs swimmin' in 'em. Bullshit anglers pluggin' this and tryin' to sell yer that. They'll all be on their bikes, fella, when the Black Mirror Cult takes over."

"The Black Mirror Cult?" I said. "Never heard of them."

"Yer will do soon," Hoodie insisted. "We're growing. Membership is up. People are joinin' and comin' to support the cause."

"How do you join?"

"If yer interested, I'll give yer the address. Yer pay a one-off fifteen quid lifetime joining-on fee and once it's gone through yer'll be contacted on WhatsApp by one of our top guys." Hoodie looked me up and down gravely. "Y'know what WhatsApp is, don't yer?"

"I know what WhatsApp is," I said, slightly annoyed. "I'm not *that* old."

Hoodie hesitated, as if he couldn't decide whether or not I was or wasn't *that* old.

"Right," he continued. "So yer've joined and after yer'll get yer messages from a Higher Associate, that's what our top guys are called, advising yer on yer carpin' and answerin' any of yer questions. Then, if they fink yer sound, yer'll get put in a cell," Hoodie frowned and opted for further clarification. "Not a prison cell, that'd be mad... not unless yer break some serious rules and get inna trouble wiv the law. No. See, a cell is a group chat wiv ovver members so yer can discuss BMC matters and ovver carping stuff." Hoodie looked over his left shoulder this time, his head swivelling into his hood so only his right eye remained visible. He swivelled it back, de-cyclopsing himself in the process. "Do it nah and yer'll be in on the ground floor, fella. In at the start. Yer'll be able to say yer was there at the beginin', if yer sign up now."

"Hold on a minute," I said. "How's a few WhatsApp messages going to do away with commercialism?" I asked. "What difference is it going to make?"

"The BMC's gonna educate. Gonna help. Tell yer what ain't worth buyin'. The

BMC will give yer *honest* reviews by *real* anglers. Anglers like *you*, fella. Tell yer the truth. No one in the BMC has an *angle*, know whatta I mean?" Hoodie argued passionately. "It'll be honest and say it as it is. And when there are enough of us, the bullshit won't survive. Can't survive, 'cos it'll be gone 'cos no one's buyin' it. Only the decent stuff'll be left. The bullshit puddles will be gone, too, 'cos no one's fishing 'em."

"That's some agenda," I said, sceptically. "And you reckon you'll be able to convince enough anglers to rigidly stick to your viewpoint that it'll actually put firms out of business?"

"Only the bad ones," Hoodie stated. "'Course, we're not only abaht that. Like I said, the top guys advise yer on yer carpin', proper advice, like, not yer 'yer need to buy this' bullshit advice. They'll always be guidin' yer and answering yer questions, all for nuffink once yer a member. Yer know, pushin' yer to put the extra effort in, consider yer tactics, givin' yer little tricks of the trade. The Higher Associates know their stuff, yer won't get better advice, personal advice, anywhere. They're the best anglers in the country, amazin' catches, but... All. Done. Under. The. Radar," Hoodie said slowly. "Not splashed in a comic, not plastered all over the internet, but all low key and subtle, like."

"So who are they, then?" I asked.

Hoodie forcefully wiped his nose upwards with the back of his right hand. "I dunno much about 'em, personally, but a mate of a mate of a mate of a brother's uncle of mine does the window cleaning at one their gaffs. He said they're part of the legendary Cambridge Mafia. Y'heard of the Cambridge Mafia?" I shook my head. "No. Me neivver. But apparently, they're fucking awesome anglers. One's called Mick the Bait and there's four ovvers. Dunno no names, or nuffin' apart from they all grew up fishin' togevver." Hoodie leaned into me, both elbows planted on the table. "I 'eard on the grapevine one of 'em had a massive fish out of a suvvern pit a few weeks back."

My mind lurched at this and I prayed my face hadn't betrayed me. "Do you know which water it was?" I asked as calmly as possible.

"Dunno much, ovver than it's a secret pit in the sarf. When the BMC really gets up and runnin' there's rumours the Higher Associates and the Cambridge Mafia boys'll start showing BMC members what secret fish they've 'ad."

Using the acting skills I had carefully honed over four decades earlier in my primary school nativity play – third wise man, tea towel wrapped around head, converted blanket as an undergown – I too leant forward, puffing out my cheeks.

"How did you say I can join?" I asked, my mind racing at the new information Hoodie had given me.

"'ere's the address," he answered, giving me a card he'd taken from his pocket. "Send fifteen quid, cash only, to the address with yer address, mobile number and yer name. Don't 'ave to be yer proper name if yer don't want. Real name, made up, don't matter."

"What about my mate?"

"It's open to everyone, fella. We don't judge. We help. If yer like the sound of the cause, yer can join the cause. We ain't elitist like some of 'em in the past. Just say in yer letter Wayne sent yer," Hoodie said, tapping the card.

"Why's that?"

"For every twenty newbies I get, I get a twenty."

Still rattled by the thought someone had poached The Pit and caught from it, I automatically associated 'a twenty' with a carp.

"What a fish?" I asked, dimwittedly.

"Nah. A *twenty*!"

"Oh, pounds! As in cash?" I asked, my mind eventually clearing.

"Yeah. A *score*," Hoodie snapped, getting up from his chair. "Look, I gotta go. Be lucky, fella. Remember, Wayne. Say Wayne put yer on to it. Don't let me dahn, bruv," he added as he walked off.

I was left with the distinct impression he hadn't been impressed by me. That's the trouble with an open membership, you get all sorts wanting to join. All sorts like me.

I drained what was left of my tea, which was virtually cold, and quickly headed back to find Rambo. I found him waiting at the same stand I had left him, his arms folded and leaning against a stand banner strut.

"All done?" I enquired.

"Yep. Really pleased, boy. Got the blanks being delivered to Tom who's going to make them up to the spec we decided on. He works with Harrison's really closely and they send him blanks all the time, so turn around should be quick. Builds a fine rod does that boy, and in plenty of time for Sylvester's birthday."

"Good stuff," I acknowledged. "Now, you're never going to guess what's just fucking happened. It's a fucking disaster!" I moaned.

My manner must have come across as genuine because Rambo's nose wrinkled like a bad smell had gone up it.

"What?" he asked, alarm in his voice.

As I told him and got to the big reveal – The Pit *had* possibly been poached – Rambo bristled with barely contained anger; his whole body taking on the air of a doomsday device about to go off, one capable of wiping out all sentient life.

"This can't have happened," Rambo stated, taking a small stride one way and then another, his whole body alive and animated with the energy of barely suppressed violence. "Not on my watch. Not on my, our, *your* water," he rumbled, on the point of losing control. "This is what I *do*! This is what I *stop*! This sort of thing *doesn't* happen when Timothy Eugene Ramsbottom is in charge of security," he stressed. Rambo spun on a heel to face me. "We, no, *I've* become too complacent," he said, jabbing a pork sausage finger several times into his chest. "I've had it too easy for too long. I've gone soft. I've let you down, Matt. *You* can't be expected to deal with this sort of thing. You're fucking *useless* at dealing with this sort of thing! It's why we're a good team. You're good at your bit, you know, thinking about stuff and predicting the future… Although, you haven't done much of it lately," Rambo tacked on, sounding confused. "And I'm good at mine. *Was* good at mine. I've been slacking. I've taken my eye off the ball. And we all know what happened the last time I did that! *You* had to fucking save me! *You*! This is terrible. This has got to be dealt with. Nobody, I mean fucking *nobody*, does this and gets away with it."

"Look, it's not your fault. You don't have to go beating yourself up about it," I countered, feeling uncomfortable with Rambo's deep self-reproach. "We don't know for absolute sure…"

"Then we find out," Rambo butted in.

"How?"

"We go straight from here to The Bookie's house, check out his bait and see if it was one of his boilies you found. If it wasn't, then we join the Black Mirror Cult, infiltrate it, and find out which *cunt* did poach The Pit. Then I'll deal with him,"

I could see there was no point in trying to persuade Rambo to let it go, to forget about it and take it on the chin. It was already way past that point.

"Fair enough," I said. "But first of all let me get Sylvester's rod pod."

Driving to The Bookie's we sat in silence. Rambo appeared to be in turmoil and it was easy for me to see why. I knew my camo-clad mucker better than anyone else on the planet and I knew, beyond a shred of doubt, the possible violation of The Pit lay deeply entangled in Rambo's self-worth. Someone, maybe, had pulled a fast one in his own backyard and it had hurt him. Deeply. He was now as close as I could ever imagine to experiencing a fully-certified mental meltdown. Rambo prided himself on never being bested and the one time he had, when he had openly admitted to taking his eye off the ball, I had saved him. And now he thought it had happened again.

No one could fairly lay the blame at the door of Hamworthy Fisheries' lieutenant – but he could lay it unfairly on himself. If Rambo was a hard taskmaster regards Sylvester, then I knew he judged himself far more harshly. Sitting next to him, I realised we were in it for the long haul now. Rambo wouldn't rest until he had set the record straight and erased the blot from his copybook. Whatever the carnage or the cost.

"We tell him it's his bait," Rambo suddenly declared.

"Sorry?" I asked.

"Whether it is or not, we tell The Bookie it's his bait. And we tell the membership the matter's resolved."

"Fine by me," I responded, not wanting to argue.

"This *isn't* about my ego, Matt," Rambo declared. "If somebody has poached The Pit they might have got inside help. Let them think they've got away with it."

"Right. Good idea," I answered, wondering if Rambo was only trying to save face. Why on earth would any of our members help someone poach The Pit?

The Bookie was waiting for us in his garage. I had texted him five minutes before our arrival and had asked if he wouldn't mind showing us a handful of his boilies, so I could check they were the ones I had seen in the margins.

"Bit of a funny old situation," he commented, handing me a small sandwich bag containing half a dozen baits.

"I know," I said, looking at the dark pink baits in the bag. "I mean, what are the chances of someone poaching The Pit?"

"If you came into my shop," The Bookie answered. "I'd lay you odds of ten to one for someone poaching it and twenty to one to catch."

"That all?" I asked, disbelievingly.

"We're not in the game to *give* money away," The Bookie reminded me. "Only as a free first bet when you set up an account," he said, smiling. "The Pit *is* the best carp venue in the UK, it's pretty remote and not busy for five months of the year. It's a combination guaranteed to lower anybody's odds on someone doing a bit of guesting. Of course, if one of our competitors did genuinely offer you better prices, we'd match them. Company policy."

I sniffed the bag of baits. "Yeah. These are the same as the ones I found in the margin," I confirmed handing them to Rambo.

"You think those odds are poor," The Bookie stated, continuing to talk about a subject that really engaged him. "Single bets only, settled by the sitting President of the USA making a statement confirming without doubt the existence of alternative, intelligent life beings from another planet, is going to get you what? Have a guess at the odds."

"Five thousand to one?" I guessed.

The Bookie laughed. "No! Way off! You'd need to be betting on Lord Lucan to be found at Clacket Lane services within the next five years to pull those sort of odds. It's twenty-five to one for it happening this year. One hundred to one for next year. It's on our website if you don't believe me."

Rambo had the plastic bag halfway up towards his nose. "How the fuck can the confirmation of the existence of an alien life form be only twenty-five to one?" Rambo asked, grumpily.

"It's a numbers game. The more punters bet, the lower the odds are. Betting on the discovery of intelligent alien life's a popular bet, so the odds go down. It's why England are always well fancied at World Cups. It's not based on how good they are, but by how much money goes on them."

Rambo plunged his nose into the bag. "You're right, Matt. This is definitely the bait you found."

"Sorted!" I exclaimed. "All a bit of a mix-up, really! We only wanted to make sure to be on the safe side."

"That's a good life policy, playing safe," The Bookie agreed.

"Do you mind if I hang on to those?" I said motioning my head towards the bag of baits Rambo held.

The Bookie shrugged. "No problem. It's a new bait my mate's experimenting with. I said I'd try them out for him. You know, do a bit of field testing for him."

If The Bookie's mate had had access to a cat like Hobbes, it would have saved the pair of them an awful lot of wasted time and bother. Some two hours after leaving The Bookie's house, I offered one of his dark pink baits to the ginger ninja ex-bait tester who was now my pet. The cat's nose flared at the pink ball resting in his bowl and he gave it an uninspired lick, then a brief nibble before turning away from it, leaving the rest uneaten.

"I think The Bookie's going to struggle this season, don't you?" I commented.

Rambo never answered, but the vein down the side of his temple pulsed with malevolence.

# Chapter 12

Sitting side saddle on my bedchair, the evening light beginning to go, I wondered if my first session on The Pit as a Black Mirror Cult member would be a successful one. Nothing had happened so far, action-wise, in the first eight hours of my trip, but confidence remained high for a morning bite-time take. Still, I thought, if push came to shove and a run never materialised, I could always fire off a question to my Higher Associate and see what he had to say on the matter. Looking across the water, the sun no longer visible having sunk beneath the gnarled branches of the old wood's trees, I could be certain of only one other BMC member being present on The Pit. As for the possibility of there being any others, it was hard to say. I hadn't seen any BMC badges adorning the two members I had bumped into, not that I was flashing mine and Rambo would never deface his beloved British army camo outfit, so perhaps other potential BMC members were being equally as coy about letting the world in on their secret. As it stood, disregarding Luke and Rambo, the only other BMC member I knew personally was Sylvester. The rest were just meaningless user names on a phone.

I had sent off the required forty-five pounds to enrol all three of us in the BMC to the address Wayne had given me, but hadn't mentioned his name, thus depriving him of three quid in commission. I hadn't done this out of a sense of petty vindictiveness as I had only been following the orders Rambo had given me. He had thought it sensible to avoid anything, however small, that might provoke a flash of recognition as our sole intention was to use the BMC as a means to an end. The end in question being to find our poacher and let Rambo 'deal' with him – a euphemism for an as yet unspecific form of brutal violence. It had seemed an irrelevance to me, whether I had mentioned the behooded BMC chugger or not, but in such operational matters, Rambo always has, and has always had, the final word.

Less than a week after I had sent off the money, I had received a letter in the post containing three sew-on Black Mirror Cult badges and three A4 introduction sheets. The printed pieces of paper detailed the requirements for our membership to become fully operational and the conditions appertaining to it. Firstly, it stated we were members for life and no further payments would be required to maintain our BMC membership. Secondly, we were instructed to download WhatsApp on to our smartphones, if we hadn't already got it, and to contact the Higher Associate assigned to us, via the app, with a brief line using our respective user names. (Interestingly, the Higher Associate contact numbers for all three of us were different, and these three contact numbers were different again from the one Luke had been given. Diligently swapping to the calculator app on my phone, I reckoned this meant there were at least four of them.) Once this had been done and our initial WhatsApp messages had been acknowledged, the introduction paper explained, we were at liberty to contact our Higher Associate with any questions regards our personal carp fishing, although these were strictly limited to four questions a month. The paper went to some lengths to expound that although a Higher Associate could help in many ways, drawing on his experience and long years of carping, the member himself must always remember carp fishing wasn't an exact science. It had a high list of variables, many beyond the manipulation of mankind, and a Higher Associate couldn't always promise to solve these variables and create instant carp catching solutions. However, what the BMC *did* promise was all the advice its Higher Associates dispensed was guaranteed to be genuine, honest, well-intended and *without* a single shred of commercial bias.

I had raised my eyebrows at this and thought it good copy.

The paper also went on to say after a brief period of probation, provided there was no abuse of privileges, each member would be allotted a cell of BMC members with whom they could engage within the WhatsApp Group Chat format. It said it hoped knowledge accessed from Higher Associates, or personally gained in the field, would be freely passed around. Useful carp fishing products could be mentioned by members, but, crucially, anyone found to be commercially associated with any recommended products within the Group Chat format would be named and shamed and banned for life. Equally, the BMC actively encouraged the 'outing' of poor products not fit for purpose.

Taking the rating of current carp fishing products one step further, the BMC said it hoped to produce data for members on all carp fishing products in the near future. 'We hope to set the benchmark regards reviews of all aspects of our sport; whether tackle, bait, fisheries or carp fishing holidays and to become universally recognised as the 'Which' magazine for carping. Our reviews will be based on the independent testing of products and will be completely free from any commercial bias' it had boldly stated.

I had raised my eyebrows even higher at this point and had thought the BMC were even slicker than my recently upgraded opinion.

The final paragraphs of the paper set out the BMC's core directives. It stated: 'The Black Mirror Cult is a non-elitist carp fishing organisation dedicated to the cleansing of over-commercialisation from our sport. The Black Mirror Cult is determined to give carp angling back to real carp anglers by giving them a voice and the power to wrest it from its current enslavement to business and profiteering. As the Black Mirror Cult grows in size and in power, it intends to advise its membership,  not only in the personal pursuit of catching carp, but also in other aspects of carp fishing. The Black Mirror Cult's long-term goal is to become the largest membership-based carp fishing organisation ever seen and to use its influence to strip away the non-essential commercial paraphernalia that pervades in the current climate.

The Black Mirror Cult also intends to introduce a carping etiquette for its members to follow. This document will set out the standards of behaviour expected of its members so that all anglers can enjoy their fishing without the distractions of bankside altercations caused by inconsiderate and anti-social behaviour. The Black Mirror Cult is of the opinion many of the issues associated with modern carp angling are caused by the inherent commercialisation within the sport, which in turn has deeply affected attitudes amongst both 'professional' and ordinary anglers alike. The Black Mirror Cult will seek to discourage the practice of promoting catches for commercial gain as it feels the pressures created by this scenario, whether on consultants or ordinary anglers, has helped contribute towards an undesirable 'catch at all cost' mentality. These commercially-driven goals, however, are not to be confused with aspirational angling. Self-motivational angling, where individuals put in the 'hard yards' to become successful, purely for their own satisfaction and self-worth, is another matter completely. The Black Mirror Cult actively encourages its members to pursue a carp angling agenda where individual success, through dedication, self-improvement and the strict employment of the Black Mirror Cult's carping etiquette, are seen as ample reward in its own right.

You, as a discerning Black Mirror Cult member, hold the power to see these long-term goals materialise. As someone dedicated to the cause of giving carp angling back to real anglers, by virtue of your commitment and enthusiasm in joining the Black Mirror Cult, we ask for your continued support in our quest. Please spread the word and help make the Black Mirror Cult grow. Remember; effort equals reward!'

The Black Mirror Cult was incontrovertibly on the march.

Our first Daily Directive as members had been, 'Ask not what the BMC can do for you, ask what you can do for the BMC', which seemed to me a slight change in pitch compared to some of the earlier ones. The second, 'The BMC – probably the finest carp angling organisation in the world' had me wondering whether to believe them. The fact I didn't immediately laugh at the pontifical portentous pretentiousness of it must have meant something.

Only a week after our induction into a BMC cell came the first trophy shot photos in Carp-Talk with an angler wearing a beanie hat complete with a BMC badge. A shit storm kicked off in all three of our BMC cells, and all the others elsewhere I suspect, when several members questioned whether this was appropriate or not. Like myself, these members had been pitched the notion by their 'first contact' that the Higher Associates didn't 'splash their mugs in the comics' and instead were doing everything 'under the radar'. Equally, for some, the photo didn't sit kindly with the Black Mirror Cult's stance on exploiting carp captures and they subsequently thought the photo a bit hypocritical. The argument had raged on, getting bogged down in the minutiae of what was or wasn't a comic, or whether submitting a catch report with hardly any detail was, by anyone's reckoning, 'a splash' or not. Within the hour, all four Higher Associates we knew of had put out the BMC's line on the matter. 'The angler involved in this week's Carp-Talk is not a Higher Associate. He is an ordinary member using the media to spread the word of the BMC. The BMC does not have an issue with this. As a point of note to its membership, the BMC does not have an issue with any angler sending in trophy shots when not used for commercial gain, as was the case in this instance. The BMC does not have an issue with any of the current carp angling magazines, only with some of their content. Specifically, the articles intended to promote commercial wares by authors receiving remuneration from the aforementioned commercial institution. Many of the other articles in carp magazines are informative, unbiased and useful for BMC members, especially those with fewer years on the bank. It is these types of factual and anecdotal articles, ones free from product placement, particularly when aimed across a wide range of venues, with differing levels of reader-experience expectation, the BMC whole-heartedly endorses.'

I had thought it had been eloquently put and the BMC clearly had no desire to alienate themselves from the angling press. One day it would need them, of that there could be little doubt. Aside from that, and very much in the ethos of the BMC, the angler who had appeared in Carp-Talk had played a nice straight bat. In the catch report it only mentioned the carp's weight. There had been no 'caught at this fishery, caught on this bait, with this hook, attached to this hooklength, by this swivel, inside this lead clip, with this tubing' etc etc ad infinitum.

"You think Daisy's smooth wringing Pup's cash out of him, but this lot make her look like she's riding a fucking skateboard on cobblestones!" I had said to Rambo on the phone. "They're pitching everything pretty much spot on. You've got to admit they haven't put a foot wrong yet. I might have joined up even if we hadn't got a poacher to trace!"

"You're not wrong, boy," Rambo had admitted. "They're making a lot of good calls and who wouldn't support what they've said so far?"

"The whole of the carp fishing trade?" I had answered. "The BMC must be putting their noses out of joint by criticising the whole product placement and commercially motivated carp capture thing. I was thinking about it when we went to the tackle show. How can you draw attention to the stuff your company makes without resorting to advertorials, consultants and marketing? It's how *every* company advertises its products. It doesn't only happen in carp fishing. And as for 'profiteering', the whole world pays top dollar for brand chic. Designer bullshit costs a fortune!"

"There's no denying it, boy, but maybe there's a general consensus carp fishing *has* reached a tipping point. Maybe modern carp fishing has gone too far and needs a sense of rebalancing, a resetting of the scales to take us back to something closer to the ideals of our sport. Perhaps the new way for any carp tackle company to be successful will have to rest on getting the unbiased approval of an all-powerful Black Mirror Cult. If there's a massive BMC-driven groundswell against the status quo, and anglers *have* been whining about it for years, then it really could be a game changer."

"Do you *really* think the Black Mirror Cult can change it all?" I had asked.

"It looks like it might have a chance, boy. If they can get a large enough membership and wield some serious clout it might allow them to rein things in. You imagine if they had, say, ten thousand members and started their review programme off and really went after one big tackle company and slagged off their products. *And* the members backed it. They *could* boycott them out of business!"

"Yeah. I guess it's feasible. It just depends on how much the average angler will buy into the BMC. And how many."

"There's never been anything like this before. All these moralistic ideals that are hard to argue against might appeal to a good percentage of carp anglers, something that's unheard of if the truth be known. Most previous carp fishing organisations ended up being a force for division rather than unity..." Rambo had stopped talking as if he had been thinking. "And nobody knows who or what's behind it. It's very strange, boy, very strange." The big man had paused again. "On to other matters, are you and your clan still on for tonight?"

"Wouldn't miss it for the world."

Sylvester's tenth birthday party guest list had comprised of his mum and dad – obviously – all my family, except Hobbes, despite Adam begging me to let him come, and a group of kids from Sylvester's school. The party had been at Rambo's house and family Williams had turned up to a house full of children, all boys, tearing energetically around the garden and letting off more steam than a cracked Lancashire Boiler. After an hour or two of bedlam, as all boys do, they had got hungry and had descended on the mass of food Steffi had laid out on the large dining room table like the proverbial flock of seagulls/plague of locusts/herd of wildebeest – you choose.

It had been during this fuel top-up when I had got talking to one young lad named James. As I had picked at peanuts and crisps he had forced sandwiches down his neck at a disarming rate.

"Are you frightened someone's going to take them away?" I had joshed.

"No!" he had refuted, eating even quicker as if my suggestion had flagged up a warning.

"Where's, Sylvester? Isn't he hungry?"

"Outside still. Sylvester's well cool," he had said, cheeks bulging with food and some of it escaping as he had spoken his words. "He's my best friend and he's the strongest boy in our year," he had said proudly. "He sorts out the older boys if they ever pick on us."

"Does Sylvester ever pick on anyone?" I had asked, a little intrigued.

James had answered vehemently. "Nah. And we know all about his dad," James had added.

I had pulled down the corners of my mouth as I had nodded my head. "Okay. What do you know?"

"His dad was a soldier. A well good one, who went all over the world on secret missions. Like Tom Cruise in Mission Impossible."

"That's what I heard too," I had agreed. "Except his dad's a bit taller than Tom Cruise and has never had his teeth done. And don't get me started on the Scientology stuff!" I had said, laughing.

James hadn't talked to me anymore after that. None of them had. They had probably thought I was 'weird'.

Despite my inability to interact with Sylvester's mates, the evening had gone well and the birthday boy had been ecstatic when he had received his presents. The rods and rod pod were greeted with fist pumps and squeals of enthusiasm and Steffi's present, perhaps sensing Rambo had pushed the boat out, of a GoPro Hero4 Black with Outdoor Bundle Kit, had provoked a similar reaction. Sylvester hadn't needed to worry about faking his smile at a crap present.

"You can record ser fishing trips and maybe do ozzer sings more artistic," his mother had suggested.

By nine – school the following day – all the youngsters had been picked up and only our two families had remained. It wasn't often we all met up, sometimes it equated to less than once a year, despite Rambo and I being so close and virtually living in each others' pockets. Sophie and I very rarely socialised with Steffi and Rambo as a foursome and it had been nice to see Amy and Sophie slip so easily into casual conversation with Steffi. Towards the very end of the evening, I had gone into the kitchen to make a coffee and Steffi had come with me to help.

"Has somesing bad happened?" she had asked me, right out of the blue like a run on a frosty February night. When you're fishing a swimming pool. That's been drained. And backfilled with concrete.

"Bad? What do you mean?"

"It's Rambo. I sink somesing is playing vitt his mind. He seems distracted somehow."

"We've had a bit of aggro on one of our waters. It's an ongoing thing. Rambo, *wrongly*," I had quickly pointed out, "blames himself for it."

A knowing look had spread across Steffi's elegant face. "Vill you be able to resolve it?"

"I hope so," I had said with little inner optimism. "I won't lie. I don't think it's going to be easy."

Steffi's look had changed to one of mild confusion. "You don't seem sure. Haff you not had vun of your looks into ser future?" she had asked, her blue eyes twinkling up at mine.

I had indicated I hadn't. "No. No help there, I'm afraid. It seems like I've grown out of them. I haven't had one for over ten years."

"Haven't had what for over ten years, Dad?" Amy had asked, walking into the kitchen at that moment. "Or do I not want to hear it?" she had asked with a picture of disgust painted on her face.

I had looked over at my soon-to-fly-the-nest daughter and explained. "One of my foresight vision things," I had answered, a little awkwardly.

"Oh, those," Amy had said dismissively, like I had been talking about a pimple on my chin.

"You don't sink sis is a remarkable sing?" Steffi had questioned her with incredulity.

Amy had stood staring at me with both hands on her hips and had said, "If he could tell me *now* if I'm going to get the grades I need for uni, *that* would be remarkable."

I had put a thumb and forefinger from one hand on each of my temples and shut my eyes as if in deep concentration.

"The future is unlit! Darkness pervades! I can see nothing!" I had said, melodramatically. "Only the bright beam of relentless revision can show the way!"

"Don't ever do anything to make Mum divorce you, Dad, or you'll end up leading a very lonely life," my daughter had sneered. "Believe me, no one else will want you."

I hadn't been overly hurt because I was continuing to have the last laugh. Over the years, I had done just about everything possible to deserve Sophie wanting to divorce me and she still hadn't done it. I was golden!

I clambered inside my sleeping bag and checked my phone. Twenty-two BMC WhatsApp messages! No wonder no one got anything done any more, everyone was too busy fucking around on their phones answering them. I had thought it was bad enough dealing with Pit and Lake members and wannabe members, but being involved in one – *one* – social media group was draining. How did kids cope with being in two or three and following their email, Twitter, Snapchat and Instagram accounts? It was mental. No wonder the real world became wallpaper.

I skimmed the messages. Bollocks. Nothing of any use.

Rambo and I had opted for a 'little and not very often' approach when it came to posting in our BMC cells and neither of us had yet bothered to post a question to our Higher Associate. Sending one out saying, 'Are you the bastard who poached our fishery?' seemed a bit of a giveaway, so we had judiciously held on to our four questions and, for some reason, I had wondered if you could roll them over into the next month. Apparently, you couldn't. Someone had asked the very question in Sylvester's Group Chat. Of the messages we had posted in our respective cells, all had been short positive pieces designed to make us come across as active, if not overly active, and enthusiastic members. We chipped in now and then, when we thought it prudent, but mostly we were watching and waiting, scanning the messages for any hint of something useful.

On a more general level, it was now evident despite Rambo and I being members of the BMC for reasons very much of our own, everyone else was in it for real. While we had barely risen above lukewarm in terms of contributions to the cause, other BMC members fairly boiled with prolificacy and enthusiasm. Many of them proclaimed the BMC was heralding a new golden age of carp fishing, one where all the mistakes of yesteryear would be righted. Others felt a powerful groundswell of like-minded carp anglers, one organised into a coherent, non-divisive force could sweep all before it, changing things for the better.

Perhaps the most amazing thing of all was the complete lack of sneering from within the BMC. Not one member had tried to pick holes in their mission statement, although to be fair, it was hard to see how anyone could. What I had expected, though, was a succession of sniping posts aimed at the Higher Associates, where our anonymous distributors of carping expertise were lambasted with cat calls asking them to 'show us your medals' and severely criticised for their 'puerile' offerings. Normally, nothing rankles an online carp angler more than another carp angler setting themselves up as an oracle and expert. Yet the Higher Associates remained untainted and everyone who commented on the advice they had received had been complimentary about it.

Sitting in my bivvy, as a BMC member for all of two weeks, it was clear the underground group was going from strength to strength. Remarkably, it was recruiting in rising numbers without any advertising in the mainstream and was pulling in members purely by word of mouth and the efforts of 'first contactors' like Wayne. By creating an aura of mystic, of being this cool underground group, it had successfully appealed to carp anglers across the board. By offering them the chance to rewrite modern carp angling, it had somehow managed to avoid the pitfalls suffered by other carp organisations long ago disbanded and dead . Sure it was early days yet, but the whole thing had a feeling of gathering momentum behind it, one where you could sense the positivity and hope of the membership.

Cheap, at a one-off payment of fifteen pounds, it promised the collective power to stick the boot into any commercial company not perceived to be playing the game. Maybe this was the BMC's cleverest trick – to marshal discord and unrest and focus it elsewhere and aim it at the easy-to-locate-in-the-crosshairs commercial targets. As I felt myself start to tire after my early morning start, I wondered what any carp tackle company might have to do, what it might have to stoop to if it felt it might get gunned down by the BMC. The only answer I could come up with was it might have to get into bed with it.

The following day, Rambo came round to see me after the morning bite-time had been and gone. He was still fishless like me.

"Higher Associate time?" I mocked, airing my thought of the previous evening.

Rambo laughed ruefully. "Someone made a fair point in my cell last night. He said most experienced anglers know there are no easy answers to success, but as long as it's honest and got no axe to grind, it's hard to get the hump with someone who's genuinely trying to help you out."

"Whoever's behind the BMC has thought it through carefully," I said with admiration.

"*Whoever* they are."

I sensed the frustration in Rambo's voice. "We're not really any closer to finding out, are we? Members of the BMC or not."

"Not really, Matt."

"All we can do is wait and hope something develops. I'm not too sure I buy into this 'Cambridge Mafia' thing Wayne was rambling on about. He did seem pretty vague. What's less vague is the secret southern pit he mentioned. What with the dark pink bait episode it has to be The Pit. Accept that and then someone *has* fished here behind our backs. Are you still convinced they got inside help?"

"Only because I can't see how you could get on here without it," Rambo answered.

"But why? Nothing ties in. The BMC doesn't advocate poaching, quite the opposite with their carping etiquette agenda, and even if they did, why would one of our members help?"

"Not unless we're the bad guys. I was joking about your books, boy, but what if the BMC views Hamworthy Fisheries with the same disdain as other overly commercial entities. The Pit must be one of the most expensive waters in the country to fish, so perhaps we're tarred with the same brush."

"That's not fair!" I blustered. "We're not milking it or taking the piss. We run the place properly, we've only got twenty members for fuck's sake…"

"Calm down, boy," Rambo encouraged. "I'm only saying it's a possibility. Once I get my hands around the neck of whoever's responsible, I can wring out the answer."

Pup hasn't heard of a Mick the Bait," I told Rambo, miserably. "And he said he couldn't fathom much out from the picture I took of the dark pink bait other than he suspected it was a milk protein base." I looked up at my fishing buddy towering a good five inches above me. "Are you sure you want to pursue this any further?" I asked, forlornly.

"What do you think?"

"I know you don't want to let it go…"

"Well, there's your answer."

"But we're at a dead end. We'll…"

"Something has to change," Rambo insisted. "For the BMC to push on, they'll have to become more open. You don't go to all that trouble of poaching a fish from a place like this and then not tell anyone. Something will come out and when it does, we'll be waiting to act on it."

"Fair enough," I said with resignation.

"I've been coming down here at night, even when I'm not fishing," Rambo suddenly admitted.

"What?"

"I've been keeping an eye out for anything unusual. No one else knows. I was very discreet."

"This is majorly bugging you, isn't it?" Rambo visually agreed it was. "Nothing?" I queried.

135

"Not a thing. Everyone's been behaving themselves."

"That's good."

"Or bad. Depending on how you look at it."

I looked at my watch. "I need to wind in now and go and use the loo and grab another bottle of gas from my van. I can't take a day without tea!"

Rambo nodded and I set to the task of winding in all three rods. As I did them one at a time, I took off my baits and placed the unbaited rigs into the deep margin.

"I wonder if the BMC knows about them?" Rambo asked.

"I bloody hope not," I replied with feeling, grabbing my van keys from within my EuroDome. "Right. I'm good to go," I said once out of my bivvy. "Keep me posted on anything interesting cropping up in your Group Chat."

"Likewise."

"See you later, Rambo." I went up to my fishing buddy and slapped him on the upper arm. "Don't go beating yourself up over this, eh? No one can police a place this size all year round."

Rambo nodded. I knew he thought I was chatting shit.

When I arrived at the functional wooden clubhouse its door was open. Inside were Eccentric Ed and Rob, the pair of them having just turned up for a session. Neither were sporting a BMC badge.

"Hi, Matt, how you doing? Any luck?" Rob asked.

"Fine thanks. No, nothing so far. Not been much movement. I've only seen a couple of fish bosh out at extreme range right out in the middle."

"What about my commanding officer?" Rob enquired, pulling his own leg.

"Rambo's blanking as well."

"Sir Rambo blanking!" Eccentric Ed boomed, coming back out from one of the two toilets. "Whatever next?"

"It does happen from time to time," I said, laughing.

"Not often, mind. He's a good angler is Rambo," Rob stated.

"Easy, Rob," I said, making my way into the toilet Eccentric Ed *hadn't* just used. "You don't have to praise Rambo every day of your life, you can take a day off! He won't mind, I promise you!" I shouted after having shut the toilet door.

Relieved of some of my internal gas, plus a good deal more – no description required, I think – and reloaded with a much more useful butane/propane gas mix, albeit in a metal canister, I walked back to my swim and set out my three traps. Rob and Eccentric Ed had already departed in their cars to choose a swim by the time I had emerged from the toilet, so I had relocked the combination padlock through its hasp and staple on my way out of the functional wooden clubhouse. A thought had struck me it might be time for a change of combinations on all the padlocks and I decided to mention it to Rambo at some later point.

Once I was back in full fishing mode, I texted Rambo about a change of combinations. Almost immediately he texted back and said he didn't want to, explaining such actions might be misinterpreted. I saw his point and told him to forget I had mentioned it. As far as the membership was concerned the poaching charade was over and it had only been a figment of our over-paranoid imaginations.

The day passed without a bite and I whittled away at time by checking my BMC Group Chat, listening to Five Live and reading the newspaper I had brought with me. No contact from Rambo meant he was also struggling to entice a take – as a horse racing analogy the going on The Pit could definitely be described as 'slow and heavy'. My evening meal was cooked and eaten with nothing so much as a single beep from my Delkims to disrupt it and the hours of darkness slipped by equally uninterrupted, save only for the need to relieve my bladder. Twice.

Prime morning bite-time thankfully lived up to its headline billing and my left-hand rod pottered off on a casual, slow-moving run shortly after seven. Relieved to finally get some action, I was out of the bivvy like a ferret on amphetamines going down a steeply inclined and internally greased drainpipe to hit the take. Everything about the ensuing battle was slow and heavy, exactly as I had described the session so far, only this time 'slow and heavy' equated to something good and not a clapped out, slaughterhouse-bound nag struggling through deep mud into a gale-force headwind. Twenty minutes later I had visual confirmation of how good, as I regarded the broad shouldered carp in my landing net. The fish looked to be an upper fifty, so I left it safely in the net and went to get my phone from my bivvy to ring Rambo for photographic assistance. My phone had a new WhatsApp message showing so I quickly had a look and saw it had come directly from my Higher Associate.

'BMC roadshows to start in two weeks' time. Meet some of the Higher Associates in person. New press releases to coincide with major BMC initiative. Details to follow shortly.'

At last, things were moving and not just on the carp catching front. It turned out the BMC *did* do roadshows, as I had once asked myself. Could this be our chance to find out something of use? I hoped so. I didn't want Rambo's guilt to last a day longer than was necessary.

# Chapter 13

Perhaps not since the time Rambo had turned up at Pup's wedding dressed in a British Army camouflage morning suit, complete with dark olive green waistcoat and camouflage tie, had I been so shocked at his dress code. Rambo was wearing Realtree, and the sight of it was like having two daggers plunged into my eyeballs. It wasn't only the Terminator with Tackle who had moved over to the sartorial dark side, in true Mini-Me style so had Sylvester. As the pair of them walked up Rambo's drive to get in my van, I felt my grip on reality loosen further as I spotted BMC badges sewn on to the left breasts of their outfits.

"Realtree!" I gasped as they both got in. "I thought you hated Realtree?" I asked Rambo directly.

"Oh, I do, boy. Loathe it. But on some missions you have to go undercover. That's why me and Sylvester are in disguise," Rambo explained, shutting the van's passenger door.

"You are kidding?" I said, pulling off down the road.

"It's pretty hard to disguise me, physically speaking, but inside here," Rambo said tapping his head with a massive digit, "I feel as if it isn't me. Not dressed like this. It'll help me put on my act. Tonight, Realtree can be my mask."

I could sort of see what Rambo was getting at, but only sort of. The three of us were on our way to Southend, of all places, specifically to a pub called the Pig and Gristle. It was here, eight o'clock start, where our local area BMC roadshow meeting was to take place. The BMC had organised a nationwide series of meetings to coincide with the two-page press release which had appeared in last week's Angling Times and this week's Angler's Mail and Carp-Talk. According to the BMC – now supposedly boasting an impressive membership of nearly five thousand – it had decided it was time to go mainstream and relay their mission to the entire angling world. The articles appearing in the three weeklies hadn't been based on a question and answer format, only on a BMC statement – a one way, unquestioned press release issued to cover the BMC's start up and its viewpoint on all things carpy.

In these three very similar articles – each one slightly tweaked to give an air of exclusivity to each publication – the BMC had explained how a group of ordinary anglers had become disenchanted with the current modern carp fishing scene and had set up a new organisation in an attempt to counteract it. The group had singled out the commercialisation of carp fishing as the principal cause as to why it had 'lost its soul' and had made the cleansing of it as their core directive. Initially, the group had drawn up a wish list of what it hoped to achieve and had then moved on to how best attain it. Having no money or backing to speak of, the group, all 'very experienced, but unknown anglers', had hit upon the idea of a one-off payment for life membership of their new organisation; the Black Mirror Cult. It was a name they thought evocative and capable of capturing attention and they hoped the use of modern technology, as a cheap format for contacting members, would appeal across the generations.

The article further explained that wanting to build the Black Mirror Cult from a grassroots level upwards, the organisation set to its task of building its membership through the hard work of friends invited to join the cause. Gradually, by word of mouth, the Black Mirror Cult had grown, its one-off payment for lifetime membership, the promise of personal carping advice, its etiquette guide and its anti-commercial agenda proving to be a winning combination. Communicating to its members by the use of WhatsApp and encouraging them to help spread the word, numbers exploded as a tipping point was reached and membership surged exponentially. 'Having reached a point far beyond the BMC's original hopes and aspirations, it was time to go mainstream', the press release explained. 'The BMC has realised our rise in membership numbers now gives us a mandate to take things on to the next level.'

The press release reiterated what I, as a member, already knew the BMC stood for and where its future intentions lay, particularly regards to becoming the go-to organisation for reviewing carp fishing equipment. One section read; 'Any company selling anything to do with carp fishing, provided it is useful, well made and realistically priced, will have nothing to fear from the BMC. Many UK carp companies have proved over the years to be innovative and forward thinking, supplying many essential pieces of kit to thousands of anglers and the BMC review system will undoubtedly reflect the contribution these companies have made.' Another bit read; 'Our review system, based solely on unbiased non-commercial membership opinion, will not only be of the highest integrity, but will also come with the quality assurance of belonging to the largest carp fishing organisation in the country. An organisation determined to uphold the wishes and hopes of real anglers everywhere.'

What the press release hadn't told me, and it was the most important bit as far as I was concerned, was who these inaugural members were. What little that had been mentioned tied in with what Wayne had said, but only on the sketchiest of details, and to my disappointment the original founders had remained unnamed.

On its etiquette guide the BMC had this to say; 'The BMC does not wish to interfere with individual fishery rules. Specific rules laid down by clubs, syndicates and fishery owners are there to be enforced on individual waters as the ruling body/person sees fit. The BMC's etiquette guide has a far more generalised remit, one based on conduct, decorum and an upstanding carp fishing mentality. Any BMC member caught not adhering to its etiquette guide will be banned for life. This may seem Draconian but any angler unable or unwilling to adhere to the etiquette guide is not an angler capable of fitting into the BMC's vision for the future.'

Harsh words indeed. It seemed the BMC had a penchant for issuing lifetime bans even if the due process of handing one out had yet to be explained. I had seen it more as posturing, a little bit of melodrama intended to underline a point, as much as anything.

The BMC had listed a bullet point piece to clarify their etiquette guide, top of the list of which was the use of carp captures to promote commercial products – an act they described as 'unethical'. The other bullet points concerned respect for other anglers, carp and the environment; tackle and bait safety, including rigs; bankside behaviour and other generalities which could easily have been lifted from the Angling Trust Code of Conduct – those parts expressly relating to carp-only anglers, that is. The press release ended by asking all like-minded 'real anglers' to join the BMC's crusade, grab hold of this once-in-a-lifetime-opportunity and help reset the world of carp fishing and make it a better place for all anglers. It gave details of the organisations new website, www.blackmirrorcult.co.uk, where a PayPal membership joining facility was now available. It also told anglers to look out for exclusive ad-free content from BMC members and unbiased reviews of all carping products coming to you soon on the nearest computer/smartphone screen.

For those completely unaware of the BMC it must have come as a bit of a shock and the internet had exploded with debate concerning the new big player on the carp scene. The BMC's membership, those who had got in on the ground floor, were quick to back it to the hilt with the belligerent air of a fan group whose unknown band had just got to number one. '#InAtTheStartAndProudOfIt' was one Twitter feed. Other BMC members went for those thinking of opposing their anti-commercial stance. '#FiftyKilosAndWait'. Sponsored anglers backfilling the best swims and waiting it out. Nice angling!' was one retweeted hundreds of times. Dissenting voices were labelled as 'Chav Anglers'. 'Pissed up and casting into my swim. Yeah, mate, I've met your type before', was one comment that stuck in my mind. 'Snag fishing to catch your way to five kilos of free bait? Disgraceful!' was another.

It had been as if all the hate of one group of anglers had been vented on to another. I had thought you could best describe it as a superior siege mentality; the BMC against the rest, with the BMC very much claiming the moral high ground. The majority of others, who were not yet BMC members, thought along the same lines and were 'glad the carping scumbags were getting a good kicking'. Hundreds had proclaimed 'they would be joining up soon.' Whatever the true reasons for their hostility, there seemed little doubt it was genuine.

Almost immediately after the press releases, a few of the smaller, more select, universally respected tackle companies had come out and backed the motives of the Black Mirror Cult, no doubt feeling they were on fairly safe ground doing so. As a counter point, despite the three weeklies who had run the BMC pieces all editorially endorsing them, they had done so with caveats, clearly not wanting to alienate their advertisers and evidently caught between a rock and a hard place. Several carp fishing holiday firms quickly nailed their colours to the mast and offered a discount for BMC members booking with them, saying BMC members epitomised the type of angler they wanted to fish their waters. Of the rest, including the really big companies, they had yet to comment on the latest carp fishing phenomenon to rear its head. The silence remained deafening from the majority of the trade as they carefully eyed the tightrope now strung out in front of them. I had imagined them dithering, anxious to see whether the BMC could hold sway over the carp fishing fraternity, what they might do next, who they might endorse and who they might disown.

In short, they were shitting themselves. And with good reason. The BMC looked as if they *were* going to be game changers and for some unfortunate companies they might yet come to represent Game Over. The carp fishing world had never seen anything like it. The buzz was absolutely enormous. ENORMUZZZZZ!

"Where's your BMC badge, then, boy?" Rambo asked me across Sylvester who was perched on the middle-seat-with-fuck-all-legroom of the three in my van.

"On my hat," I answered, gesturing towards the woollen beanie on the van's parcel shelf.

"Sew it on yourself?"

"With a baiting needle and Milward's Black Spider," I replied.

"Old school," Rambo commented.

I laughed. "Let's hope we don't get recognised tonight or that'll blow a hole in our plans. Thank Christ neither of us, or our fisheries, have a social media presence. We've never bothered and Sylvester here's too young to have Facebook, isn't that right, Sylvester?"

Rambo's son turned his head towards me. "Yeah, that's right, Uncle Matt. Nobody my age does Facebook."

"That's because it's full of middle-aged fools showing off to their friends, trying to convince them they're leading a hedonistic lifestyle," I commented. "Luckily, Luke won't be there," I said, jumping off on a tangent. "He confirmed last night. He's doing a session on The Lake instead. He can't stop catching. He's had twelve fish so far. I bet they don't call him Unlucky Lukie anymore."

"Fair play to him," Rambo said. "Let's just hope he hasn't sold his soul to the devil to catch those fish."

The Pig and Gristle's car park was rammed. There wasn't a single space left and I had to trawl around the neighbouring back streets for ages before I could find a place to park, one located a good ten minutes' walk away. Locking the van and now late, the three of us legged it back to the pub and entered into a lounge room packed with BMC members. Trying to get a drink from the bar – full fat coke for Sylvester, effervescent fifty-teaspoons-of-sugar-equivalent lemonade for me, premium unleaded for Rambo – reminded me of when I used to keep maggots in a bait box. Every fucker crawling over the top of every other fucker in a witless attempt to get anywhere other than the minimal personal space they currently occupied. Having finally got a drink in our hand, in a plastic cup, served to us by a bewildered youth sporting strimmer-cut hair in a Slipknot T-shirt, we stood leaning against a side wall to the 'stage'. The wall looked as if it had last been decorated in the sixties. *Eighteen* sixty, that is.

The bulk of the room, to within a couple of yards of three walls and the tiny stage at the front, was filled with lines of chairs previously laid out by someone suffering from severe myopia. These wavy lines of school-assembly-style plastic chairs were occupied by arses more accustomed to the unadulterated luxury of padded bedchairs and settees plonked square-on to flat screen televisions. Consequently, it was quite gratifying to see so many of the seat occupiers regularly squirm with the discomfort caused by the unyielding moulded plastic. A seating arrangement they had no doubt smugly commandeered by virtue of not only arriving on time, but in some cases, by actually making the effort to get there early.

If I believed in God, these are the sort of things that would make me think he did indeed move in mysterious ways.

Better off out of it, we stood and leant and waited and sipped our drinks – there was no fucking way I was queuing for another – and at seven minutes past nine exactly, a bloke came out on to the stage with a microphone and, speaking into it like it was a pipe bomb about to go off in his face, asked if he could be heard at the back. The back said it could hear, but the bloke with the microphone couldn't hear the back, so, stiltedly, he asked again. This time someone *shouted* from the back they *could* hear and finally, just as I was on the point of asking Rambo to punch somebody in the face out of sheer frustration, the BMC roadshow was off and running.

The first twenty or so minutes proved to be a basic preamble through the history of the BMC, its core beliefs and a mutual back slapping exercise for all concerned – for the BMC for making it to where it now was and for us, the membership, for putting them there. Another ten minutes or so was spent outlining the next steps, the plans for the future and showcasing the new website, the content it was going to host and the new online signing up facility. Once this was done the microphone was passed over to a Higher Associate named, Simon, who explained something about the exulted position he held.

"Thanks to Vic for getting the show underway. Much appreciated. A small hand, please! [ripple of applause]. Good evening everybody, many thanks for coming. My name is, Simon, and I'm one of the BMC's Higher Associates. I'm one of the guys who tries to help you with your carp fishing problems within your Group Chat cells. At the moment, I'm looking after a few hundred of you, fielding your questions and hopefully helping you put a few more fish on the bank. It's been fantastically interesting reading your questions and I'm sure it's made me a better angler through having to try and answer them. Obviously, I don't proclaim to have all the right answers all of the time, but I will always do my best to help out wherever I can. The thing you must always bear in mind is whether what I tell you significantly helps or not, all the advice I give will always be totally free from any commercial bias. As you all know, the BMC are *not* trying to sell you anything.

I think for many of us, and I'm not just talking about carp fishing here, one of the things that is really hard to get hold of nowadays is honest, trustworthy advice. All of the old institutions we thought we could trust, like the government, the utilities, the banks and the household name companies, have let us down. Even our local tradesmen, our plumbers, electricians and mechanics, are often economical with the truth when it comes to advising us on whether our boiler can be repaired, if we need a rewire or not and what's gone wrong with our car. Right across all walks of life we feel like lambs to the slaughter when we ask for professional help with the decisions we have to make. History has proved the financial institutions, big business, the utilities, *small* business and, as has recently appeared in the news, even charities have been taking us for mugs. We've been ripped off here, misinformed there and mis-sold somewhere else. Our loyalty has been taken advantage of when we've renewed with insurance companies and we've been lied to by successive governments, and their opposition, whose individual members, let us not forget, went to the highest court in the land in a vain attempt to stop us learning the truth about MPs' expenses. We've *all* paid a heavy price for casino banking. How many of those responsible have paid a *single* penny? Comparison websites not comparing everyone equally. Independent bloggers in the pay of big business. Pension companies ripping you off when you don't understand the new rules. Energy companies quick to put the price up, but always slow to bring it down. Seemingly, *every* business, *everywhere*, trying to take a chunk out of you by not telling you the truth. You, my fellow carp anglers, might well feel trapped in a corner with no one to turn to. And with good reason.

Unfortunately, the BMC can't change much of that, but what we can change is one tiny bit of your world. The one bit of your world were you go to escape the other part of it. The tiny escapist world of carp fishing. The BMC have sworn to do away with all the bullshit getting put on you in your escapist world and to make it different from how you are treated in the rest of it. We won't take you for a ride. We won't try and sell you something every time you ask a question. We are here to look out for you because it's *you*, you who will look out for yourselves. If something is good, tell everyone about it. If it's rubbish, tell them that as well. Don't get sucked in by all the blurb and hype, turn to the Black Mirror Cult to find out if it's the real deal or not.

Let's, together, try to make our carp fishing world different from the rest of our lives. Let the BMC become the sanctity of our carp fishing lives. Let's make carp fishing a sport free from the greed of commercialisation and free from the poor, inconsiderate behaviour that perpetuates our modern society. Let's fish with style, with consideration for others, even when we're blanking, *especially* when we're blanking, and make sure our time on the bank is a pleasure for all concerned." Simon paused. "Thanks for listening, guys. Thank you very much. *The BMC*!" Simon finished, emphatically punching a fist into the air.

I clapped hard. Sylvester clapped hard. So did Rambo. And so did everyone else present. I think the expression is 'we raised the roof'.

"Okay, gents," original microphone man stated, trying to bring the applause to an end. "Thank you, Simon. Thank you very much for your passionate speech. Great stuff! We're going to take a quick break now, get yourselves a drink at the bar if you want one, and after the interval we'll have a slide show where Simon will talk us through some of the special carp the Higher Associates and the founder members have managed to tempt over the years. Cheers everybody. We'll see you all in a bit."

"Well," I said to Rambo. "What did you make of it?"

Rambo flexed his shoulders. "Impressive speech. Couldn't knock it."

"What did you think, Sylvester?"

"I didn't get all of it, but the bits about carp fishing were cool."

"Yeah, it was good," I conceded. "I came in thinking what a shithole the place was and ended up clapping like a demented seal eyeing up a bucket of mackerel during feeding time at the zoo."

"So why aren't you balancing a ball on the end of your nose?" Rambo enquired.

"Because that'd be animal cruelty," I assured him.

"Want another drink? I think *I* need one," my fishing buddy asked me.

I pulled an angst-ridden face after glancing at a bar area resembling a rugby maul during a hundred and fifty-a-side match .

"Don't worry, boy. *I'll* go and get them. You drove."

"Go on, then," I said, tempted by Rambo's generous offer. "I'll have another lemonade. I might be able to neck it before the diabetes kicks in and all my teeth fall out."

"Never let it be said your Uncle Matt is anything other than a hardened drinker," Rambo said to Sylvester. "Another coke for you, son?" Sylvester nodded. "I'll go, you stay and guard him. Make sure no one beats him up and nicks his wallet, or more importantly, his van keys. It's a hell of a walk home, otherwise."

"Sure thing, Dad," Sylvester replied.

As Rambo disappeared into the camo-fest melee orbiting the bar, I turned to Sylvester.

"Are you guarding me with your gun?" I asked.

"What, the orange one?"

"No. The real one."

Sylvester's face turned sulky. "Dad wouldn't let me bring it."

"Oh, well. At least he's a parent who knows when to say 'no'," I said, tongue in cheek.

"He's got *his* one," Sylvester complained.

"I don't doubt it," I said, unruffled. "You never know when you might need to convert some fucker into a nine millimetre-holed colander."

"Mum says Dad shouldn't swear in front of me. I'm guessing it includes you as well. I'm only ten," Sylvester said, petulantly.

"Look, don't get the hump with me just because you haven't got your Glock with you," I whispered in Sylvester's ear.

"Sorry, Uncle Matt," he apologised, gazing down at his black army boots.

Once the slideshow had started, I was quite surprised at how quickly the butterflies kicked in – although I suppose it could have been the lemonade rotting through my stomach lining. This was the crux of why we had travelled the distance we had. Before we had left, I had spent a few hours going through all the photos and paintings of newly-caught forty pound fish in order to refresh my memory. If one of the big girls popped up on the slide show, I wanted to recognise it straightaway.

Fish after fish photo went by with Simon giving us the background detail of each capture as it appeared on the large white projection screen set up on the stage. Some of the first few carp shown looked to have been caught as long ago as the seventies, judging by some of the collars on the shirts and the flared trousers worn by the anglers involved. Most of these fish were low twenties and I wondered if Sylvester had wondered why anyone would bother to showcase fish of that size.

Rambo must have been reading my mind with some kind of Delkim transmitter technology because I heard him say to Sylvester, "They were big fish back in those times, Sylvester. Might not seem it today, but back then they were monsters!"

Most of these old fish were caught by a couple of Higher Associates, but as we moved on through other younger Higher Associates, slides of a very young Simon were offered up for our perusal. Heading on further, as Simon aged in speeded up jumps in time with every new frame, so the fish got bigger. I thought myself lucky to be at the stage of my carp fishing when this same dynamic still applied to me as, presumably, there must come a time in any carp angler's life when it starts to go the other way. As you get older, I surmised, you might naturally have to regress to targeting smaller fish the more infirmed and unable to make the physical commitment you became.

Forty minutes into the slideshow saw Simon put up a photo of an upper thirty, caught by one of the founder members named, Joe. This was the first trophy shot not of a Higher Associate and I felt myself start to get incredibly tense. Around fifteen slides in and Joe was replaced by Ted and twenty slides further on by a guy named Brandon. Early Brandon was an ordinary looking bloke, older Brandon was completely different. Somewhere in his early twenties, Brandon had spent as much time in the gym as on the bank, probably injecting steroids in the toilets at the same time, and had bulked up big time. Gone was the everyman physique and in came the massive guns, ripped torso, bulging bull-like neck and the tight T-shirts trying to both contain and display the new Mr Universe look. Predictably, over the last handful of slides, came the tattoos – a Polynesian tribal armband on the left bicep and a full sleeve on the right arm. Even Simon felt the need to comment on Brandon's new body.

"This forty-three pound mirror, caught in two thousand and ten by Brandon, is a really nice scaly mirror. Unfortunately for Brandon, it doesn't look as big as some of his earlier fish because he'd been hitting the gym so hard! If you want fish to look big, be a seven-stone weakling and hold them out to the camera!" he joked. "Moving on, this next fish is a right creature, a huge upper sixty caught in France only last year."

The slide came up and a topless and tanned Brandon flashed his new tats and his pecs alongside those of the carp's – pectoral fins not tattoos. The fish was massive and so was he. It was in that instance I knew, just knew, Brandon was the one who had poached The Pit. I don't know why, it wasn't a vision thing, it was more the air of inevitability about it. That ultimately it would all boil down to Rambo getting pitched into a confrontation with the young muscle-bound BMC founder member capable of holding up a sixty like it was a low double.

"That's him," I said.

"What, boy?" Rambo asked, a little bemused..

"He's going to be the shithead who poached The Pit," I said. "It *has* to be. Sod's Law dictates."

"This next fish is incredible," Simon said, cutting across my prophetic ramblings. "A genuine UK born and bred sixty from a no publicity water in the south of England,"

A photo of Brandon, in the dark, taken with a flash, was projected up on to the white screen to murmurs of approval. I recognised the fish immediately. It was Pugwash. An old, original mirror named as a first-caught forty getting on for nearly twenty years ago by ex-member Sniffer. He had also caught and named Pugwash's Mate and The Black Pig, all thanks to his childish infatuation with the cardboard cut-out, live-action series broadcast on the BBC in the seventies. Rambo's head spun round to face me, his eyes burning with indignation. He had recognised it too.

"Sixty-three pounds eleven ounces of perfect UK carp," Simon continued, seemingly oblivious to the treachery he was condoning. "As you can see, the fish was caught in the dark, only a month or so ago actually, and the photo isn't as good as it might be. But Brandon being Brandon, certainly didn't want to sack such a beast just to get a better photo in daylight. As I don't need to tell you, fish care *always* comes first, so well done to him for not succumbing to temptation with a UK PB, for photographing the fish in the dark and getting it straight back."

If I had needed to steam some shrink tubing to create a more aggressive hook angle on one of my hooklengths, I could have done it by holding it up to either one of Rambo's ears. Rambo was staring at the photo of Brandon, locking on to it like a heat-seeking missile, so intently committing to memory the face that must be destroyed, I wondered whether he might fire off a few rounds at it for practice.

"Told you," I said, joylessly.

"The fucking cunt!" Rambo said hoarsely under his breath.

Sylvester, now apparently no longer bothered by choice language, had latched on to his father's nuclear-power-station-output levels of pent-up destructive energy.

"Are you going to get him, Dad?" he asked, looking up at his father, his body language bristling with hope, anticipation and glee.

"Oh, I'm going to get him all right," he answered. "And I'm going to get whoever was on the camera as well."

My eyes lurched from Rambo to the slide of Brandon as it disappeared and a brightly lit white screen replaced it. Somewhere on Mars, Simon was wrapping things up.

"Yes! It wasn't a self-take. Someone else *was* there with him!" I exclaimed. "And what's with all the bollocks about it being a no publicity water?"

"It all stinks, Matt," Rambo rumbled like Mount Vesuvius, circa AD 79, minutes before the big pop. "Something very rotten is going on. And we," he flicked his wild eyes across mine and Sylvester's, "are *going* to find out exactly what."

On reflection, perhaps it had been the Realtree that had done it for him. Perhaps wearing the Godforsaken outfit with its little BMC badge had allowed him to pretend to be something he wasn't. Maybe it had afforded him the mask he needed to play out the role required of him. Certainly I had never seen Rambo act like it before. It had been quite disconcerting, more so for Sylvester, until the lad had quickly cottoned on and realised what his dad was up to.

Waiting for our chance to catch up with Simon, after the crowd had thinned out and most had gone home, Rambo had gone over to chat to him and had been all over him like the proverbial rash/cheap suit.

"Oh, wow, Simon. What a fantastic evening! My son and I were enthralled," Rambo had gushed in a slightly camp voice, putting his arm around his son and cuddling him to his side. "It's absolutely fantastic what you guys are doing. Just what carp fishing needs, a bit of decency and honesty."

"Thank you very much," Simon had responded.

"We loved the slide show, didn't we, Jacob?" Rambo had asked giving Sylvester an extra hard squeeze.

"Yeah. It was well good," Sylvester had breathlessly answered.

"How old is your, son?" Simon had asked.

"Nearly eleven. It's his birthday soon."

"And you're a keen carp angler, Jacob?"

"Yeah! I love going fishing. I spend all my pocket money on tackle!" Sylvester had gushed, getting the hang of it.

"I think you must be one of our youngest members," Simon had observed. "Good to get them young," he had opined.

"Oh, definitely!" Rambo had agreed. "The kids *are* our future," he had said, earnestly.

Standing a couple of yards away, I had wondered how Rambo had kept a straight face when coming out with such a hackneyed pearl of wisdom.

"Brandon's UK PB was immense!" Sylvester had said, getting right into character.

"What a fish!" Rambo had agreed. "I won't embarrass you, or put you on the spot, by asking where he caught it because I know you said it was strictly a no publicity water," Rambo had said, gently touching Simon's arm. "But what a fish!"

Simon had laughed. "You could have asked, but the truth is I don't know myself. I appreciate the gesture, though."

"Thank you… Simon, I know this is a bit odd, but is there any way we could meet Brandon. Jacob would be absolutely thrilled to meet a founder of the BMC and it *is* his birthday soon."

Simon's face had wrinkled with awkwardness. "He's very busy at the moment, as you can imagine."

"Oh, I'm sure he is. I fully understand," Rambo had said waving a hand. "I just thought there might be a publicity angle in there for the BMC. Show how their message is getting through to the young… and the not so young!" Rambo had giggled, self-deprecatingly. "We'd really love to help. The BMC means everything to us."

"That's a good point," Simon had said, scratching his chin. "If I could organise a day's fishing for you two, say, take some publicity shots for the new website, it could work. I'm only thinking aloud here, possibly you could bring your partner along."

"I haven't got one. My brother's over there, though," Rambo had said, pointing flamboyantly at me. He had then put both of his massive hands over Sylvester's ears. "He's adopted," he had mouthed to Simon. "I'm bringing him up on my own. A day's fishing with Brandon would be wonderful. He hasn't got many friends."

"Well… okay. Does your brother fish?" Simon had asked, flustered.

"Eric loves his fishing. We both do. We often go as a threesome."

"Let me ask the question," Simon had said. "It could be a good item for the BMC. What's your mobile… er?"

"George. George Watson."

"I'll do my best, George," Simon had said tapping Rambo's number into his phone. "I'll be in touch. I can't promise anything, obviously."

Rambo had held up a conciliatory paw. "Of course. I fully understand."

"Your *brother*!" I said as we walked back to the van. "Do I look like your brother?"

"There's always a runt in the litter, boy," Rambo answered. "And I *was* making it up as I went along."

"Do you think it'll work?"

"Doubt it. If it does, it'll save us an awful lot of effort tracking the bastard down."

"Fingers crossed, then," I said, making the sign that accompanied the call of 'fainites' in my school playground days. "What's it like to be adopted, Sylvester?" I said, turning to Rambo's son.

"It doesn't make any difference," Sylvester said, huffily. "I still don't get to go out with my gun."

# Chapter 14

"Get all the gear in the back of Uncle Matt's van," Rambo instructed Sylvester. "We can't be late."

"Ok, Dad," Sylvester replied, carrying a bivvy holdall out of the garage and up to the open rear doors of my trusty fishing steed.

"Just pile it all in on top of my stuff as far forward as you can get it," I suggested. "Just mind the rod tips."

Rods. Rods had been a problem.

"I can't believe you've pulled this off," I said to Rambo. "What are the chances?"

"You know what swung it in the end? Fucking unbelievable, boy!"

"No," I said, laughing.

"Saying Sylvester was adopted! A throwaway line when I was winging it turned out to be the vital piece in the jigsaw."

"How come?" I asked, screwing up my nose.

"Brandon's adopted. He empathised with 'Jacob's' plight. That's why we got the invite." Rambo stopped at the rear of the van, a rod holdall in each hand. "Biggest mistake of his life," he added, grimly.

I nodded in agreement while wondering if it had ever crossed Rambo's mind, should it come down to 'Fisticuffs in Frederick Street', he was giving Brandon a good fifteen years' age advantage. And that was before considering the intensively-free-weights-trained, steroids-boosted muscle-bound nature of the body in question.

"He's a powerful looking guy," I ventured.

"Pah!" Rambo scoffed. "Fucking poseur. Being able to bench press a shit load of static metal doesn't mean fuck all to me, boy. Fuck. All," Rambo reiterated as he put the rod holdalls in the van and returned to the garage for more gear.

That's cleared that up, then, I thought. In any case, I suddenly remembered, Rambo always had the Glock. Good old, Glocky. Always there for us when the straits were at their most dire.

"How long do you think it'll take to get there, Uncle Matt?" Sylvester asked, now lugging a giant rucksack up the drive, one physically swamping him.

"Around two and a half hours. Depending on how busy the M25 and the M11 are."

"Dad says were going to the syndicate water Brandon's in."

"Apparently so," I confirmed. "I've never heard of it, but then again I wouldn't have, it being so far away. It's situated to the north of Cambridge, not far from some other well-known waters nearby called St Ives and Fen Drayton." I gave Sylvester my most serious look having finished the geography lesson. "Now, you have got the right rods with you, haven't you?"

"Yeah," Sylvester confirmed, somewhat disconsolately.

"You'll have plenty of time to use your new ones," I consoled him before snapping, "What's my name? Go!"

"Uncle *Eric*," Sylvester replied, in a 'Duh! What do you think, it is?' tone.

"And yours?"

"Jacob."

"And your Dad's name."

"*Dad*," Sylvester answered with sarcasm.

"George Watson," I corrected in a stiff schoolmaster tone. "I know this might seem a bit mental," I said, softening my tone, "but it's so easy to slip up if you don't keep thinking about it. Especially when we're with them. You know how important it is."

"Do I. Dad's been hyper." A big grin spread across Sylvester's young face, replacing his earlier grumpy demeanour, partially caused by our six o'clock morning start time, and more definitely by the fact he wouldn't be using his brand new bespoke fishing rods. "I bet it's going to kick off with him and Brandon. Least I hope so. I want to watch Dad flatten him."

"Yeah, well, be that as it may, you have to carry on sucking up to him. Like with Simon at the roadshow. We've got a lot to find out before any warfare can start."

"Sure. No worries, Uncle Matt. I mean, Eric," Sylvester quickly corrected. "Sorry."

I put on my 'told you so' face. "Put the rucksack in the back and then go and get your dad. It's time we were leaving," I told Sylvester, first glancing at my watch and then down towards the blackness of Rambo's open garage.

I walked round to the driver's door and got in, wondering if I was getting a bit long in the tooth for all this hidden agenda, cloak and dagger stuff. Three of us keeping up the façade of pretending to be something we weren't, for a forty-eight hour carp fishing session on Brandon's home patch, wasn't going to be a cakewalk. One verbal slip up, one misjudged comment and the whole deceit would come crashing down around us like a bivvy of cards. We couldn't let it happen. We had one take at this. One chance to get to the bottom of the Black Mirror Cult.

"Keep calm, 'Eric'," I said quietly to myself. "And pull yourself together. It'll be just like the old times."

Obeying my own orders, I retrieved the sat-nav from the glove compartment, licked the plastic suction device and fixed it to the windscreen. I had barely enough time to turn it on, wait for it to load and set the destination postcode before I heard the van's rear doors being slammed shut through the steel bulkhead. The loadmaster was done. We were fully laden, the van was down to its plimsoll line and it was time to set sail. Seconds later Sylvester jumped in followed shortly by Rambo. All aboard.

"Okay, bruv. We're ready to roll. Hit the road!"

"Just out of interest," I started, cranking over the diesel engine, "which one of us is Watson senior?"

"Even though I look much younger, I think it ought to be me. By three years, if it crops up."

"What about me? My backstory. Am I married?" I asked, ignoring Rambo's jibe about me looking older.

"Only to your right hand, internet porn and carp fishing," Rambo answered. "You work in B&Q's, live in a flat on your own and you last had sex with a woman in nineteen ninety-seven."

"Don't make it sound too glamorous," I insisted, deadpan. "Or I might start wishing it was for real."

"A small price to pay for having me as a brother," Rambo grinned.

"You're loving all this, aren't you! The conflict. The possibility of battering Brandon to a bloody pulp and finding out the truth about the BMC," I asked, as much out of admiration as anything. Rambo had never dodged trouble. Not once in all the years I had known him.

"I'll admit it does have its appeal. Of righting the wrong that took part on my watch," Rambo agreed. "Standards, you see. I fell below my own and this is where they start to get knocked back into shape. *Plus*," Rambo continued, "I do have a funny feeling there's more to this than meets the eye. And I *need* to know who took the photo."

"Let's hope we can find out," I said. "Without anyone dying. Again."

I saw Rambo's eyes drop down to the BMC badge on his Realtree coat and knew he was packing a Glock. Sylvester was already away with the fairies on his phone, so I couldn't tell if he had been allowed to bring his. A possible thirty-four bullets' worth of mayhem between them and what did I have as back up? A pair of braid scissors, a few baiting needles and a lighter doubling up as flame thrower for killing slow-moving insects.

On the whole, it was probably better that way.

Rods. Rods had been a problem.

And all because the three of us were such tackle tarts we had our names on our current sets. Not an ideal situation given the nature of the deceitful session we were to embark on. This giveaway attribution aspect to our collective casting tools had meant a panicky rummage through my and Rambo's rod back catalogue in an attempt to find three pairs possessing moniker-free butt sections. In the darkest crevice of my garage, I had found an old pair of Terry Eustace pound and three-quarter test curve carbon carp rods – a Sportex blank – made shortly after the end of World War II. Rambo, equally as much a magpie, hooked out four Daiwa Amorphous rods from his attic carbon dating back to six hours after the first moon landing. Problem solved, we had thought, only to realise, on closer inspection, it hadn't been.

The trouble was, even if I was exaggerating the point, all these rods looked totally out of kilter when set against the rest of our modern expensive equipment. The rods

151

were anachronisms and stood out from the rest of our kit like a white Casio G-Shock on the wrist of a Dickensian TV character. To have used them would have raised too many eyebrows, especially if we found ourselves amongst true carp fishing aficionados. We had been in big trouble, with less than ten days to go before our trip to Brandon's two-rod limit syndicate water, and the race had been on to solve the rod issue. I coined it, 'The Greater Great Rod Race' (with apologies to Matt and Mick).

A mini Eureka moment, I had completely forgotten about them, saw me mugging Pup's rod holdall I had put in my garage the day he had brought Hobbes round. Inside it were four Grey's Prodigy GT3s in a two and three quarter pound test curve format, which I gladly borrowed without the owner's consent. Luckily, the ex-boiliemeister hadn't had his name put on them and two of us, Rambo and Sylvester seemed most logical, were now sorted. With nowhere left to turn, I had gone on Ebay and bought a couple of newish second hand Harrison Ballistas for myself, making the excuse to Sophie they would do a job for Adam when he was old enough to start carping.

"All the fishing tackle you've got, Matthew, and you still haven't got enough," Sophie had said. "It *is* a disease, you know. Where did you say you bought them? Ebola?"

"E*bay*," I had said, countering her sarcasm. "I got my asthma and psychological issues from Ebola. They had a buy-one-get-one-free deal going."

A mass swapping of reels on to the new old rods had taken place in two garages and a re-tackling, re-rigging and replacing in rod holdalls. Our usual sets were left standing naked in each garage, wondering what they had done wrong to deserve such brutal rejection.

"I wonder if he'll use the dark pink bait?" Rambo asked, shortly after we had left his driveway.

"I expect so," I replied.

"It's going to be quite a battle to see who comes out on top, catch-wise," Rambo commented. "His bait is good, ours is better, but he's playing at home. Local knowledge is a powerful weapon."

"Are we actually looking to try and out-catch him and whoever else is there?" I asked.

"Too right we are!" Rambo responded. "And by the more fish the better. After this weekend I don't want Brandon to know whether his arsehole has been punched or bored… On every level."

"Total annihilation and total fishing *humiliation*," I suggested.

"Ideally." Rambo produced a Mars bar from his pocket and started unwrapping it. "Sylvester's the key, I reckon. Brandon's empathy and common ground with him is Sylvester's 'in'. I suspect he'll be able to get closer to him than either of us and it could be useful. I've given you a full brief, haven't I?" Rambo asked his son, who was so engaged with the phone held inches under his nose he never heard. Rambo snatched it from Sylvester's grip with his non-Mars-bar-holding hand. "*Listen* to what I'm saying, Sylvester," he barked. "This is more important than you mucking around on your phone. You've got to *learn* to take orders. That's how it works, young man. The commanding officer issues the orders and *you* carry them out. Got it?"

"Sorry, Dad."

"You're very important to this mission's success. You know that, don't you? They'll be no time for reading a book and 'chilling', as you call it. You'll need to be on the case twenty-four seven." Sylvester nodded and Rambo ruffled his spiky blond hair. "Good lad. Remember everything I told you, carry it out as I told you and everything will be fine."

"What about me?" I asked, not wanting to be left out. "What are my orders?"

Rambo took a chunk out of the Mars bar and pouched the ball of nougat and chocolate in a stubbly cheek. "You just concentrate on catching as many fish as you can and remembering to be Eric. If you manage anything else on top it'll be a bonus."

"Thanks," I said, acerbically.

"At least this has got you out of that dingy flat of yours."

"And a weekend shift at B&Q's," I added.

"That's good, little brother. Real good."

"Why, thank you, George," I said, grinning. "Praise from my older brother is like praise from no one else."

The journey to Brandon's syndicate water proved to be a cinch as both motorways and the Dartford Crossing were free moving all the way. We stuck to the sat-nav's predicted arrival time more or less to the minute and once we were only ten minutes or so away, Rambo phoned Simon to say we were almost there. The access to the six acre water close to the Great Ouse was off a small road via a gated entrance. As we drove through the open gate there were a couple of cars parked the other side and I saw Simon leaning against one chatting to the unmistakable figure of Brandon. Waving enthusiastically and pulling up alongside, the three of us got out the van and went and shook hands with our hosts.

"I'm Eric," I said pumping Brandon's hand and eyeing the tattooed muscular forearm attached to it.

"Hi, Eric. Good to meet you," Brandon replied.

"Simon. Good to see you again," I said to the genial Higher Associate as Rambo and Sylvester pressed flesh with Brandon.

With the introductions done, Brandon took the lead. "Welcome to my syndicate water fellow Cultists and especially to you, young Jacob. I've pulled a few strings with the other members and we've got the place to ourselves for the whole weekend. Some of the others might pop by to say hello, but it'll only be the five of us fishing. Simon, here, will be on the camera to take some photos, hopefully of you Cultists with a few fish, and one of us will write up an account of the weekend and it'll go on the new website in a week or two. You're going to be famous, Jacob. The youngest BMC member to date and you get to fish with me, a founder member."

Sylvester spun in wide-eyed delight to his supposedly non-biological father and said, "Wow! Cool!"

The lad's good, I thought. Maybe Steffi was right and he could do something more artistic with his GoPro. Like acting in his own films.

"Thanks, Brandon," Rambo said in the strange 'George' voice. "We've *so* been looking forward to this."

"No worries. Let's go and have a look around the lake and choose some swims. I'll give you the lowdown."

As we wandered off, Sylvester quickly inserting himself alongside Brandon, Rambo held back and I slowed my walk to get close to him.

"Pictures on their website," he whispered. "If a Pit member was involved then our cover's blown the minute he sees them."

That was a certainty for sure and I felt troubled at another new possibility I had just considered. Any Pit member involved with the poaching would surely have warned Brandon about Rambo and mentioned his formidable appearance and attitude. Yet here we were. I could only guess a vague description combined with our current 'disguises' meant no alarm bells had been raised so far. The other factor in our favour, by declaring the 'baits in the margin affair' to be a complete mix-up, was our possible Pit poaching provider may have lowered his guard and become less concerned with the case apparently closed. Even so, with this new time constraint, things were definitely more on a knife's edge now. The only alternative left to consider was someone other than a Pit member, an unknown outsider, had wielded the camera. My gut feeling, as I walked alongside Rambo, was we couldn't take the chance. Things had to be resolved before any pictures appeared.

Brandon's syndicate lake was a pretty enough water; roughly rhomboid in shape, had eight swims, and a stock level of over two hundred carp ranging from upper doubles to a lake record fish of forty-two pounds ten. Three of the banks had a dense growth of mature trees behind the small track running around the lake, trees which isolated the lake from the road running alongside one of the longest sides and two farmhouses on the short sides. The remaining furthest bank, running parallel to the road, backed on to flat agricultural farm land and was much more open and exposed. Only a handful of smaller individual trees grew along this bank.

The majority of the swims had small platforms to fish from with a level bivvy parking space cut out into the gently rising banks. Only the three swims on the farm land side were without platforms and bivvy cut-outs as this bank was much flatter and at a similar level to that of the water. All these swims could easily be fished with banksticks or pods pushed directly into the grassy bank.

According to Brandon, Rustle Lake was fairly devoid of features. I could see with my own eyes there weren't any islands – I'm very observant when it comes to that type of thing – but according to our host there was little depth variation, something not so obvious, even to a sharp observer like myself, without resorting to a quick thrash and foam of the water's surface with a marker rod. Margins were relatively deep, around seven foot, and the bottom tapered down to a pretty universal ten foot of water through the middle. Weed was fairly sparse at anytime of the year – we were now in May so what little growth that might develop hadn't materialised yet – there were no lilies and only a couple of swims offered an overhanging tree in the margins. My initial take on the place, in terms of tactics, was it lent itself to fishing over a smallish bed of baits at short and medium range to cover what little depth differential there was. As for hot spots, I supposed there were a couple of swims which produced more fish than the others, but having walked around it only once, I would have been hard pushed to say which ones they were. Nothing screamed out at me, if I was honest.

Brandon saved us the bother of agonising over where to fish and decided to put Sylvester into 'Willow Tree', 'the banker swim' as he termed it, with himself and Rambo on either side in 'The Cut' and 'First Swim' respectively. These three swims were on the road side of Rustle Lake and on Simon's suggestion he and I plumped to fish two swims on the opposite flat bank. Myself in 'Pancake' and Simon two swims down in 'Mink Trap'. These two swims were at either end of the bank and offered one rod's margin fishing down both of the shorter side banks. A tactic made more appealing thanks to us knowing both of the swims on each of these two side banks were not going to be occupied. Fishing the far flat bank opposite Rambo, Sylvester and Brandon suited me down to the ground. I was out of the way round there and felt I might be able to relax a little while Rambo and Son got on with the firm's business of digging out classified info. Always the superhero, me.

Having completed the once around, engaging in small talk as we did, it was time to load up our barrows and haul our gear to our swims. Brandon made a great show of piling up his barrow to the height of a small block of flats and, with biceps bulging in the obligatory tight T-shirt, of powering off four-litre V12 style around the lake. Rambo, on the other hand, took two trips at a very steady pace complaining he 'wasn't as fit as he used to be'. I did the same, the only difference being I was doing it for real.

Pushing my barrow the opposite way round the lake to my fishing buddy, I marvelled at Rambo's ability to cede Alpha male status to Brandon, something I reckoned he had never done to anyone before in his life. In letting the steroid-enhanced BMC founder member take the lead, and by underplaying his own hand, Rambo was bluffing in a game of poker. Only when Rambo had the knowledge he required would he flick over his cards to show a royal flush. Then look out. All hell would break loose.

Once I had all my gear in position, I started erecting my EuroDome in Pancake, which was the first swim you came to out of the pair Simon and I were fishing when walking anti-clockwise from where the vehicles were parked. Going back clockwise from myself, the order of anglers was; Rambo, Sylvester, Brandon and, almost full circle, Simon. Starting to slip into 'fishing head on' mode as I popped up the dome,

I recognised if it hadn't been for the true nature of why we were here, I would have been excited at the prospect of fishing a new water. Running The Pit and The Lake and fishing them exclusively was the only minor negative attributable to my carp fishing way of life. The 'new water' buzz was the only thing lacking in it. In truth, it was a very small price to pay for having unlimited access to two such wonderful waters, but setting up on a brand new venue, the challenges of working out the jigsaw still box fresh, a little hint of the unknown present, was a pleasant diversion. One that could have been savoured if I wasn't so on tenterhooks.

By early afternoon I was ready to cast out. Simon had left me in peace to set up at my own pace as he too had prepared and I thought it only polite to pop along and see him before casting out. Simon was baiting up with a catapult as I arrived in his swim and he told where he was going to be fishing and why. He passed on a few tips about Pancake as he put in around a hundred boilies which were most definitely not dark pink in colour. Brandon clearly wasn't the sharing kind.

"What's a good catch rate for a forty-eight hour session?" I asked.

"Two fish a day is good. It's not a hard water, not at this time of year. They're usually feeding pretty consistently by now, not unless the weather is doing something awful. Spawning is usually only three to four weeks from now and the fish should be starting to get on the munch soon," he told me.

"Are we worse off round this bank compared to the others or doesn't it make much difference?"

"Not really. Jacob's swim, Willow Tree, is very reliable. The margin tree spot Brandon showed him produces a hell of a lot of fish and he will have told him to always have a bait on the spot. That still holds good if fish are showing elsewhere in the swim."

"I see," I said. "I hope Jacob was listening carefully." Trying to keep things light and airy I moved on to a different subject. "How long have you been friends with Brandon, then, Simon?"

"Since I got in this syndicate three years ago. I hadn't met him before."

"What made him think about starting up something like the Black Mirror Cult? It's quite a radical thing to come up with."

Simon shrugged. "I don't really know, Eric. One day, last year sometime, he told me him and a few others had had this idea to start up an organisation with the idea to change carp fishing for the better. He said they were going to give it their best shot and have a go at trying to make it happen. I'd come recommended by another syndicate member when I'd initially joined and once the BMC had got going, Brandon asked if I would be interested in becoming a Higher Associate. He'd already explained to me what the BMC stood for and I was all for it. I thought it was a great idea. He said he really respected me as an angler and a person, now he'd seen me fishing, and thought I could do the job required of a Higher Associate. I was flattered and agreed straightaway because I believed in what he was doing. Still do, it goes without saying. Carp fishing has become a bit of a circus, definitely a bit too commercial, and I liked the etiquette side of the BMC's message as much as anything."

"I hope you don't mind me asking, but do you get paid anything for doing it. It must be very time consuming fielding questions from, how many was it? Two or three hundred Black Mirror Cult members?"

Simon laughed. "It's more like four hundred now. They cover my expenses and give me a monthly salary out of the membership fee, if you can call it a salary. Let's put it this way, I'm not doing it for the money!"

"No, sorry, I never meant to suggest you were. It's a big commitment, that's all, and I just wondered."

"I believe in the BMC," Simon said, soberly. "And so do all the other Higher Associates I've met. I love carp fishing, it's a massive part of my life and I'm proud to be part of something I truly believe can make a difference. I don't want kids like Jacob to grow up fishing ridiculous rubbish-strewn puddles full of identical carp with anglers doing exactly what they want, casting here, there and everywhere, completely oblivious to how they should behave and conduct themselves. I don't want them thinking the be-all and end-all of carp fishing is to get into a magazine with a bloated fish and become a sponsored angler. It's not about that. It's about going fishing in a nice environment, anglers respecting each other and enjoying all the fish they catch, whatever their size. It's about having a bit of 'me' time on the bank, away from work and, I admit, from families as well. It's about escaping to a world of you and nature and the game of trying to outwit a carp and catch it. And doing it within a set of rules allowing others to do the same."

"Very eloquently put, Simon," I said, genuinely impressed. "I can see why Brandon wanted you as a Higher Associate." Simon nodded and smiled his appreciation of my comment. "I'm going to go and cast out if it's all right by you. What I wanted to know and what I intended to ask before getting side-tracked was, can I sack a fish if I get one and come and get you to photograph it?"

"No problem. The margins are deep here. We don't mind the sacking of fish for short periods."

"Great. Give me a shout if you get one. I want to see a Rustle Lake carp!"

"Will do, Eric. Good luck!"

"If I haven't caught one by tomorrow morning I'll be WhatsApping you to ask why. Even if you're not my Higher Associate!" I joked, regurgitating it from the last time I had cracked it to Rambo, as I turned and left.

Walking back to my swim, I would have bet my life on Simon's sincerity. Rambo's theory of there being more to the BMC than meets the eye seemed harder to justify after my short, but very insightful, chat to Simon. At least I felt as if I had started to make a small contribution to joining up the dots making up one page of the Black Mirror Cult's picture book.

Back in Pancake, I had a decision to make. To follow Simon's advice or fish the swim as I saw it, the reality being there wasn't an awful lot of difference between the two. In the end, I plumped for fishing the areas Simon suggested, but went one rod on a bottom bait and one on a tight-to-the-deck pop-up. I thought it worth the gamble, despite both Brandon and Simon saying bottom baits were generally best due to the nature of the clear bottom. I was feeling super confident going this route because I had used similar tactics on both The Lake and The Pit earlier in the year to good effect.

Half an hour later, I had a bottom bait in seven foot of water a couple of rod lengths out from the side bank, forty yards down to my left, and a pop-up fished in nine foot of water, the deepest I could find, fifty yards straight out in front of me. I had catapulted out around fifteen pouchfuls of our exclusive, revolutionary, indented, dirty brown bottom bait boilies, at three baits a pop, spreading them over an area approximately seven to eight yards square with a slight concentration over the hook bait. With my part done and the traps set, I sat back and waited for Pup's boilie to produce the magic of which I knew it was capable and decided to phone 'George'. (We had all gone to the trouble of changing each other's contact details on our phones in case a worst case scenario should arise.)

Rambo was obviously alone because he answered in his normal voice, if quietly. "All right, boy? How's it going?"

"Good. All set up and ready for action," I told him. "I've decided to fish one and one. Bottom bait and pop-up, ring the changes a tiny bit. I also had an interesting chat with Simon about the BMC."

"Go on," Rambo urged.

"I would bet all my fishing gear, and yours come to that, which is *more* frightening considering what you might do to me if I lost it in a wager, Simon is a one hundred per cent straight guy. And I'm not talking sexuality here," I said, before retelling the conversation verbatim I'd had earlier.

"That's interesting. I thought he came over as a genuine type of bloke at the roadshow, too."

"Have you found anything out?"

"No. Early days yet. I'm letting Sylvester do all the talking and keeping myself to myself. It's always been the game plan and I'm sticking with it until it gets to the point, if we don't get anywhere, where I'll have to throw caution to the wind."

"You think there's something else going on, don't you? Aside from Brandon poaching The Pit."

"I do, boy," Rambo confirmed.

"Why?" I asked, baffled. "Everything the BMC has said, everything the BMC stands for is fine by us, isn't it? You might say it's a little too 'holier-than-thou', but that's only being pernickety."

"On the face of it, yeah, we all agree with the BMC's general take on things" Rambo agreed. "But why would a founder member of an organisation, supposedly devoted to a carp fishing etiquette based on decency and respect, poach a water? They might encourage their membership to put in the hard yards, but poaching a water is something different altogether."

"To look good in a slide show?" I suggested. "To up a UK PB? To give yourself more credibility when you're a founder member of a carp fishing organisation? A 'show us your medals' thing? Or, looking at it from another angle, maybe the BMC do see us as a greedy commercial water and therefore fair game for any atrocity."

"Even if it steps over *two* lines you've drawn in your own manifesto? The carp etiquette line and the use of a carp capture as a promotional tool being an unethical act. I don't buy it, boy. If you're trying to set an example for others to follow you can't go poaching a water and then brag about the fish you caught. I reckon that's why Simon doesn't know where Brandon caught his, *our*, fish from. Brandon knows Simon, and maybe the other Higher Associates, wouldn't approve so he's kept it hush-hush. Something's rotten, Matt, rotten to the core. The rest of the apple might be fine, the Simon's of the BMC everybody can see and take bite of, but I'm convinced there's a fucking great maggot hidden in the middle. Hidden from everybody, Higher associates included, if what you say about Simon is right."

"So, what's the maggot up to?" I asked, carrying on with Rambo's fruit analogy.

I heard Rambo grunt in frustration. "That's what I don't know and hope to find out. Jesus! I've got so *much* anger, Matt, it's killing me bottling it up and acting as weak as dishwater. Being *fucking* George. Wearing *fucking* Realtree."

I had to suppress the amusement in my voice. "Now, you hang on in there, George. I know how tough it's been bringing that poor boy up on your own, what with his real parents not wanting him. And I know Mum and Dad, God rest their souls, always loved me more than you and it can't have helped when we were younger. But as George Senior, God rest his soul, always tried to tell you, you can't give in to your temper. You've got to see it through and not lose your rag. Like I do. Every day at B&Q's. Even when I'm losing the will to live and it's only half past nine in the morning and some cretin's just asked me what size compression fittings they need to fit fifteen millimetre copper tube. I breathe in deep and slow and make it through the day without blowing up, whether I'm on Heating and Insulation, Outdoor and Garden, Flooring and Tiling…"

"Eric," Rambo butted in. "You might be my only sibling, but don't make me come round and push your landing net handle right up your arse, spreader block first."

"See," I said. "That there. *That's* why Mum and Dad, God rest their souls, loved me more than you. You always take things one step too far. 'Spreader block first'. *Really*, George? I ask you. Where's all the love for your little brother gone?"

# Chapter 15

Three hours. That's all it took. Pop-up up and away! After a straightforward and brief skirmish, I sacked the culprit, an upper double common, and legged it down the bank to get Simon. Was I feeling chipper about catching one so quick? You bet I was.

"That didn't take long," Simon remarked, once I had told him. "Well done!"

The pair of us returned to my swim, Simon facilitated the David Bailey side of things, and I returned my first new-water capture for more years than I cared to remember.

"Where did you pick it up, Eric?" Simon asked.

"I'll show you," I replied, grabbing the Ballista propped up against my dome, thinking how soon the tables had turned, thanks to one solitary capture.

I cast the pop-up out, guessing the distance, but aiming against a particular tree I had memorised on the far margin to the right of Rambo's swim. I feathered the cast down and felt a satisfying 'donk'. Perfect. Setting the rod back on my rod rests, my marker, a piece of blue electrical insulation tape, pleasingly ended up between the second and third rod ring. Good enough. I was smouldering, if not quite on fire! My cast was on the money in both length and direction thanks to the nature of the area I was fishing; this type of lake bottom didn't require an inch-perfect pedantic approach. Quickly grabbing my catapult, I fired out my baits towards the centre of the still visible ripples caused by the cast. Once the first three baits were in, I slipped into a rhythm of baiting up in a similar pattern as before. With seventy odd baits dispatched, I tightened up and set my hanger indicator and restored the volume on my Delkim to the setting '3'. Loud enough without being overtly ostentatious and overbearing. In a few hours I would switch to receiver alert for the night time.

"There," I said, walking back to where Simon was standing. "That's pretty much where I had the take from and what I did the first time. There's nothing much out there apart from nine foot of water. The bottom seems completely clear."

I could sense Simon slowly re-evaluating me as a carp angler. "And on a pop-up?"

"I've done well on the rig this year, not that it's anything special, and decided to stick with it. The other rod's on a bottom bait," I added, hinting I hadn't completely ignored Simon's guidance.

"It certainly worked."

The words had slipped out of Simon's lips by all of two seconds when my margin rod rattled off on a blistering take, one yanking the Ballista's tip round sharply to the left. Scuttling to the rod as quickly as possible, I hit the run and felt the rod pull over into a manifestly bigger fish than the previous one. Applying side-strain with as much style as possible, I hoped Simon couldn't see what I felt – the slight unease of using unfamiliar tackle. The Ballistas were more powerful than my old Slims and different again from the Torrix rods I used on The Pit. Consequently, I didn't feel quite so in tune with them – it was my first use of them – as I would have done using my other sets. Heroically, like the true trooper I am, I pushed this minor disadvantage to the back of my mind and concentrated on taking the opportunity to establish a two-goal advantage. Not that it was a competition or anything, despite Rambo having insisted it was.

Simon appeared at my side with the net. "I don't believe it," he said. "Jacob's into a fish as well!"

Lifting my eyes from where my line was cutting into the water, I peered across the lake to see Sylvester in the throes of playing a fish and the huge bulk of Brandon trotting along the bank to help him. Significantly, Rambo was still by his rods, sticking to his game plan.

"It's all happening!" I said, excitedly, briefly wondering how Sylvester would deal with playing a fish on Pup's rods.

"It sure is," Simon responded. "For you guys," he added, self-deprecatingly.

The fish I had hooked put up a dogged resistance and it took me a fair few minutes to get it up the side bank and across in front of my swim. Once there, with it already on the surface thanks to my having worked it back over forty yards, it was merely a case of keeping calm and carrying on. (Someone should paraphrase that and put it on a coffee mug, they'd make a fortune.) I could see the fish was a mirror and it looked an upper twenty, if not a thirty, and I put forward this weight hypothesis shortly before Simon netted it. Once the carp was safely on my unhooking mat, I had further confidence in my previous assumption.

"It does look like it's a thirty," I pronounced. "Thirty-two, thirty-three, something around there."

My Reuben Heaton scales thankfully confirmed thirty-three pounds and six ounces and Simon photographed me holding a really nice looking dark grey mirror, one with a cluster of star-burst scales near to its wrist.

"It's a well-known fish," Simon told me as he fired off my Eos. "'The Grey One' it's called. It doesn't get caught often. You've done exceptionally well to catch a fish like that within a few hours. Quite a few of the syndicate lads who have been on here for years haven't managed to catch it."

I laughed as I carefully laid the fish back on to my unhooking mat. "It's the luck of the draw and carp fishing all over! It is what it is and can easily make fools of us. How many times do you hear of a new angler on a water pulling out one of its most sought after prizes?"

Simon's phone started to ring before he had chance to answer my verbal musings.

"Brandon," he commented, looking at the screen. "Hello, mate. How's it going?... Crikey! That's a result... Nineteen common and The Grey One at thirty-three six...

I know!... Yep. Okay, mate... Yep. Bye. Bye." Simon put his phone back in his pocket and looked over to me. "Young Jacob's had a thirty-six twelve common! It's the biggest one in the lake!"

"Brilliant! He'll be well chuffed!" I gushed.

"Brandon said he's never seen a kid so good at angling. He says he's very accomplished for someone so young. His casting, his bait application, playing that big fish and holding it for the camera, all of it's been textbook according to Brandon. Reading between the lines, I think he's a bit gobsmacked!"

"George *has* taught him well. I'll admit to him being a very good angler and a patient teacher, even if he is my brother," I said, smiling.

"Well, it's fantastic to see a young BMC member doing so well. Brandon's got some great photos for the website." Simon pulled out his phone, looked at it again and grimaced. "I've got to head back and do some work, I'm afraid, Eric. I've got over twenty members' questions to answer. So if you're okay...?"

"You crack on, Simon. I don't want to hold up the work of the BMC."

"I've got an article to write for Carpworld as well," Simon told me. "For the July issue. They wanted something as soon as possible after we went in Carp-Talk. There might be a chance we could use Jacob's photo with the common to go in with it. I'll have to get Brandon to see what the other founder members think."

"Excellent. Everything's starting to take off, isn't it?"

"Yeah," Simon agreed. "Brandon's dream is happening. The Black Mirror Cult is on its way and I'm playing my part at the very centre of it. It's a bit hard to believe when I stop and think about it." Simon looked a little watery eyed as he paused. "I'll see you tomorrow morning, Eric. If you get anything in the night, come and get me."

"Likewise," I reciprocated.

Watching Simon walk back to his swim, I was totally convinced he hadn't a clue about the maggot at the heart of the BMC – if indeed there was one.

By ten, I had turned in and was lying snuggled up in my bag, enveloped in the still darkness of the night. I'd had no more action apart from a single beep on my right-hand rod some time earlier that may or may not have been a liner. The last half hour in the bag had been spent scrolling through my BMC Group Chat, simply to keep abreast of things, although I hadn't bothered to contribute any messages. In fact, all three of us had been specifically asked by Brandon not to mention us fishing with him and Simon, citing the issue of setting a precedent. 'I've done this for Jacob,' he had said. 'I can't do it for other BMC members, I simply haven't the time.' I had thought it a reasonable request and it had only underlined how fortunate we had been with Rambo's throwaway adoption line. Without it, the gates to the BMC's inner sanctum would never have swung open. To me, it also said something about Brandon – underneath his bulging left pectoral muscle there must have been something going on. Not that Rambo had agreed, he was far too centred on Brandon's Pit poaching antics to cut him any slack.

Yesterday's Daily Directive had read, 'OMG the BMC, making carping better'.

The one before had said, '666 – the number of the beast. BMC – the letters of the best'. These latest directives did reflect the general consensus of my cell group, and all the others I suspected. Everyone seemed proud of the BMC, and to be associated with them, especially now they had broken into the mainstream and their message had remained unequivocally spot on. Sure, there was a certain hint of smugness and elitism exuded by those who had been members for several months, but generally speaking everyone seemed happy the BMC was opening up to more and more anglers. The common theme of so many of the messages I had read was, 'power in numbers'. Most thought a BMC agenda was now a real probability, given the vast amount of fresh publicity coming the Cult's way and the assumed associated proportional membership rise.

Feeling a bit droopy from spending too long looking at the screen on my phone, I took off my reading glasses, put them on top of my terminal tackle box and reached out and popped the phone into one of the dome's internal pockets adjacent to my pillow. Five minutes later the bloody thing rang and I groped in the partially phone-screen-lit gloom to grab it. It was Pup.

"How's Hobbes?" the ex-boiliemeister asked, employing his usual guilt-ridden conversation starter.

"Good as gold," I assured him.

"Things have taken off over here," Pup gabbled, his words spewing out quickly as he moved the conversation along to what he really wanted to talk about. "We've had our first big order. And on a pro forma invoice."

"Big order? And what the hell is a pro forma invoice?" I asked, confused, my usual default mode for interPup exchanges.

"Daisy's *business*! The one I've been pouring my cash into? The one I've been telling you about *every* time we've spoken?" Pup blustered. "The reason why I rented my house out to get the cash flow enabling me to live here while I invested my life's savings into *Daisy's business*? Remember?"

"Oh, yeah. Sorry. Not with it. I was fast asleep in my bivvy," I lied.

"Well there's a surprise," Pup commented, caustically. "You asleep in a bivvy."

"It's not like normal. We're on a secret mission," I confided.

"Is that what you're now calling 'going carp fishing'?" Pup asked, his voice sneering and his tone derogatory.

"No. We really are on a secret mission..."

"*Fifty* fucking grand!" Pup boldly stated. "And on an upfront payment for the goods! *That's* the value of the big order and *that's* what a pro forma invoice means. Mullah first, goods after! Daisy's paid me back all the money she's borrowed already. *And* paid me my half of the profit. Six K! Six *thousand* quid! That's seven hundred and fifty kilos of bait at eight quid a kilo," Pup pointed out. "Fuck having to roll it!"

I was listening intently now. "You're making money?" I asked, unable to keep the shock out of my voice. "*And* she's paid you back everything you've lent her."

163

"Yeah. Every penny. Plus six *thousand* quid! My cut of the profit! On one order! And I'm fucking her. And she likes it," Pup gloated.

"That's… that's…"

"*Surprising?*" Pup offered.

"No. That's amazing. Fantastic…"

"Fuck off, Matt," Pup heckled down the phone. "I know you thought I was going to get shafted. I bet you said to Rambo I'd be back home in six months without a penny to my name. I bet you said that, didn't you?" Pup insisted.

"No!"

"Liar!"

"It was *three* months," I grudgingly admitted.

"I *fucking* knew it! Thanks for all the faith you showed in me. "

"It wasn't like that," I protested. "We weren't being horrible, we were *worried* about you. That's all. You've had some rough dealings with women in the past and we didn't want you to get fucked over again. And, okay, me and Rambo *did* think you would get ripped off. We'll hold our hands up to that. You have to admit, from our viewpoint, it did all sound a bit shady. But… But nothing is more pleasing for me to hear than we were wrong. I'm chuffed for you it's working out so great. For both of you. Business wise *and* on a personal level." Pup had stopped ranting and cutting in by now, so I pushed on. "I still helped, didn't I? Took on Hobbes and done my bit with the house."

"Yeah. You did," Pup conceded. "I was acting a bit hyper because I'm so excited with how well it's going," he confessed. "I was crowing. Sorry."

"That's okay, mate. You're entitled to. You've *earned* the right. Good for you. I'm really pleased. When you make your first million you can buy me a Porsche!"

"Ha!" Pup laughed. "I'll tell you what, you can keep my fishing gear and the bait-making stuff for nothing. How's that sound?"

"Okay, thanks. Ah… Rambo and Sylvester are already using your rods this session," I owned up.

"Are they? Why's that?" Pup asked, a little startled.

"It's a long, long story. When you come back to see Hobbes, you can come in, have a cup of tea, he can sit on your lap while Daisy sits with Sophie in the garden and I'll tell you the whole shebang."

"Fair enough. In any case, I don't care if they're using them," Pup said, unconcerned.

Now Pup was on a level keel, emotionally speaking, there was something I had to know. "Pu… Peter. Now it's going so well and it's out there and working and you're earning money from it, can I ask you what business you're in? Surely you can tell me now."

There was a pause. "No problem. You can ask what the business is."

I waited for Pup to tell me and when he wasn't forthcoming, I guessed he had been talking literally.

164

"What's the business you two are in?" I asked, stiltedly.

"Murano glass dildos," Pup replied.

"Eh?"

"Murano glass dildos. Top end, high quality, distinctive sex toys," Pup reiterated. "Daisy designs them and road tests them, if you know what I mean. The Yanks can't get enough of them and are snapping them up. Some of those rich Beverly Hills women are buying two or three each! A famous film star got hold of one, Tweeted it and everything went into meltdown! Daisy packed her teaching job in the following day there were so many orders. The Germans are keen as well. No one does fetish like the Krauts. We've now got wholesalers and distribution set up in both countries so we can sell in bulk. New enquiries are flooding in every day. Me and Daisy decided we would get hitched after we celebrate the sale of our first hundred thousand units."

"When will that be?" I asked, bemused at the torrent of information Pup was spewing out.

"Probably around August. I'm sorting out a provisional date for the wedding boat on Monday."

"Not a tandem?"

"A tandem! What the fuck is it about you and tandems?" Pup shrieked.

"I meant tugboat... trawler... sorry. No. Talking shit. I had an early start," I bumbled.

"You, Rambo and your other halves will naturally get an invite to the wedding. I think I can run to paying for your flights and accommodation," Pup gestured magnanimously having speedily calmed down.

"Wow! Thanks," I said, stunned. "That'd be fantastic. The others will be absolutely thrilled when I tell them. A paid trip to Venice!" I said, virtually to myself, finding it hard to comprehend the new world in which Pup found himself.

"No worries. I want the pair of you there and I want one of you to be my best man... Well, I want *you*, Matt, to be my best man. Um... perhaps *you* can break the news to Rambo, if you don't mind," Pup hesitated again and I could almost sense the cogs of his brain whirring. "Say I spun for it. Say I flipped a pound coin because I couldn't choose between the pair of you and he lost and you won. Just between you me and the gate post that's all bollocks. The real reason is because of him and Hobbes not getting on... Look, you've got to swear you'll never tell him. I don't want him going off on a jealous fit," Pup said, urgently.

"I swear," I said, thinking Rambo would hardly be offended. Most likely he would think he got the best of it. He wouldn't have to fuck around cutting and pasting a best man's speech from the internet for a start.

"Great... Hold on, Matt... Okay, love. Coming... That's Daisy. I've got to go, Matt. We're thinking of going into butt plugs and she's got a few colour schemes and shapes to run by me. Not that any of them are going anywhere near *my* arsehole," Pup quickly underlined.

"Sure," I said my head boggling. "Don't let me hold you up. Great to hear things are going so well. Bye, Peter."

"I'll be in touch shortly," Pup assured. "I'll work on the wedding details and let you know once I've something concrete. I can book the flights, hotel, all that kind of thing, at my end."

"Cheers," I said, a notion swishing into my mind. "Incidentally, will all the female guests get a complimentary Murano glass dildo," I asked, joking.

Pup thought about this for a couple of seconds. "I'll see what Daisy thinks. You know, it might actually be quite a nice gesture. Have them individually gift wrapped and handed out before the marriage ceremony. You could always display it as an ornament at home if you didn't want to employ it for its primary function. The Ten Inch Contoured in Blue Algae would look great on a coffee table... Yes, food for thought. I'll catch you later."

I tried to sleep, but I couldn't, what with everything Pup had said going around and around inside my brain like a centrifugally directed marble in an empty biscuit tin. I Googled 'Murano glass', so I at least understood part of the story, and then tried to get my head down. At first it was difficult to dismiss the image of a large, blue, phallic glass dildo set atop my living room's coffee table, but eventually tiredness won and I dropped off. An hour later I was awake again. Rambo had roused me by phoning to tell me he'd had one. A low twenty mirror Sylvester had already photographed.

"Well done, mate," I slurred, my head pounding.

"Thanks, boy. We've had four now and they haven't had a fish," Rambo said with gleeful relish. "For the record, Brandon's using his dark pink bait. Sylvester got hold of a couple and palmed them to me. Definitely the same bait."

"Has Sylvester come up with anything else?" I enquired, my head gradually clearing.

"Unfortunately, not much. He says Brandon's on his phone a lot and has to keep charging it with a power pack. The trouble is he's very careful. If he's with Sylvester and it rings, he always walks off and has the conversation out of earshot. Apparently, the only thing he does equally as much as talk on his phone is eat. Eggs, milk, lots of cooked chicken, he's shoving a shit load of calories down his neck."

"Fuelling his body for more gym work?"

"Without question. Sylvester says at times he's been talking to him and all of a sudden Brandon will drop down and knock out fifty press-ups. And he's got a set of dumbells in his bivvy so he can do bicep curls. Guess he's trying to bulk up on the bank, or at least maintain it. It makes me laugh, boy. He's typical of a lot of those sorts," Rambo said scornfully. "All upper body and guns and forget about the legs. Brandon's nowhere near as big from the waist down. Anyhow, what about you and Simon?"

I told Rambo how Simon had related Brandon's appraisal of Sylvester's angling skills and my thoughts on the Higher Associate's honesty and his belief in the BMC.

"If it has got a rotten core, I'm positive he's not party to it."

"Or he's outdoing all of us in the acting stakes."

"If he is, he's bloody good... Oh, and Pup's phoned as well," I went on. "Mental as usual, but it seems like, contrary to all expectation, it's working out for him and Daisy. Big time." I quickly retold the conversation I'd had with our ex-boiliemeister.

Rambo's reaction was similar to mine. "That's a bit of a turn up for the books. I didn't see that one coming, boy, I have to admit. Still, good for him and a free trip to Venice might be an interesting bonus. One thing I do know is once we've finished here we'll put his rods back with the rest of his kit and mothball it. Just in case he ever wants to start fishing again. Even if it is in Italy."

"Good idea," I concurred. The world was littered with carp anglers who had sold/disposed of their tackle only to later regret it. "What's the game plan for tomorrow?"

"Same as. We carry on with the softly softy approach and see where it takes us. Sylvester says Brandon's planning a barbecue tomorrow night so that might present an opportunity."

"An opportunity for what?" I asked.

"Not sure yet. I'm working on it. See you tomorrow, boy."

"Will do. Bye, Rambo."

I hung up. Sleep! *Now*, my brain insisted, you must have some sleep now. I closed my eyes and thankfully it came quickly.

The best kind of alarm clock in the world woke me up. Frantically disentangling myself from my bag, I swung my legs out and rammed my feet into my loosely laced, ready-for-a-run-in-the-middle-of-the-night trainers and staggered, wide-eyed and adrenalin-engorged, out into a bright new day towards my spool spinning right-hand rod. The shock and excitement of getting dragged from behind the wall of sleep by a belting run never gets old – it's just a shame we have to!

After having played the fish for several minutes, I felt a presence behind me. One that spoke.

"All right, Eric? In again?" said a slightly breathless voice.

I rotated my head, owl style – old, geriatric, not much movement left owl style, admittedly – and saw it was Brandon.

"Yeah," I said, contributing fully to the scintillating conversation.

"I've just had one. A twenty-three six. Thought I'd reel in and have a quick run round the lake rather than cast back out straightaway. Keep the cardiovascular levels up," the muscle-bound poacher informed me.

"Did you? Nice one," I answered, confining my comments to the non-cardiovascular components of Brandon's statement.

"George had a couple in the night and Jacob had another more or less the same time as I had mine," the block of muscle informed me. "Poor old Simon's still blanking. Maybe I ought to make you three Higher Associates instead of him!"

I strategically laughed at this gentle piss-take of Simon. "I'm sure his turn will come soon," I responded, ever the diplomat.

Brandon strolled down to the water's edge and picked up my landing net. "What bait are you using? The same as the other two?" he asked.

Under my legal rights, those stipulated in the Carp Angling Act of 1988, I could have told him to mind his own fucking business. However, we were here on his syndicate lake at his invite under false pretences and provocation wasn't our game plan, so I didn't.

"Yeah, it's our own one. Me and George make it up," I answered, which did sound a whole lot cooler than saying we had obtained it by way of barter for housing the pet and help selling the house of an ex-boiliemeister who was now a Murano glass dildo wholesaler. It also told him everything and nothing, which was fine by me.

"It's a good bait," the poor man's Arnold Schwarzenegger stated.

Yeah. Nine and a half out of ten good, I thought, "We do all right on it," I said, modestly.

"Looks a decent fish," Brandon said, as my hooked adversary rolled on the surface.

"Yeah. You've got a nice head of carp in here. The grey fish I had was a cracker," I said, happy to be off the subject of bait.

I was pleased with my line. A little bit of ego massaging normally never goes amiss when playing subservient roles. Brandon nodded in response saying nothing else and I clammed up too, concentrating on playing the fish.

The latter stages of the fight were routine and after another five minutes of verbal silence, side-strain and gentle pumping, Brandon slipped the net under an upper twenty mirror, lifted it clear of the water and placed it on my unhooking mat. Before I had chance to react he unhooked the fish, checked out my rig and then pulled off my pop-up, pinching it between his thumb and index finger as he held it up to his nose and sniffed. What a fucking liberty! BMC carping etiquette, my arse!

"Nice smell. Very carpy, Eric," he said. "Does anyone else use this bait or is it just you three?"

Shocked at Brandon's blatant invasion of my personal carp fishing privacy, I now found myself desperately trying to think myself out of the jam I was in. Had Brandon recognised our bait or was it only my paranoia talking? Not knowing for sure whether anyone, including the possibility that Brandon himself, had taken a few of our exclusive, revolutionary, indented, dirty brown bottom bait boilies meant I was groping blindly in the dark. I cursed inwardly. I *should* have counted all my boilies out and then counted them all back in on that night.

"I think George lets a few of his mates use it. He was the one who came up with the recipe. It's up to him who he gives it to," I said, thinking widening the scope of the bait's usage clouded things as best I could hope.

"Sure," Brandon said with understanding. "I'll get Simon along to photograph this fish for you. I need to crack on... Oh, I've organised a barbecue for tonight. In Jacob's swim so he can carry on fishing. The rest of us can reel in and we'll have a social. I've got a few bottles of wine and loads of sausages, beef burgers and chicken breasts coming. Come round at six this evening."

"Lovely. Thanks, Brandon, I'll look forward to it."

"No problem," Brandon said, turning and jogging off towards Simon's swim.

I watched him go. In amongst the anger and resentment I was experiencing, I noticed Rambo had been right. Brandon's upper body was disproportionate to his lower one. His legs *were* considerably less massive than the rest of him. Unfortunately, recognising Brandon had compromised his leg workout routines in favour of his upper body did little to placate me. I helplessly stood in my swim, unsure of whether our cover was blown or not, waiting for Simon to appear and photograph a fish I now no longer had much interest in.

Rambo must have been watching all of this from his swim because as soon as Simon had gone back to his bivvy after the brief photographic session (I had assumed he had returned quickly because he hadn't wound in and *wanted* to catch, for his own ego's sake), he phoned me.

"News from Sylvester," he said, his voice full of anger.

What? What's happened," I said, picking up the inflection in my best friend's voice.

"When muscleboy was out parading around the lake, Sylvester took a chance and nipped into his bivvy. Guess what he found in his rig box?"

My guts started to churn in an instant. I knew what the young lad had uncovered.

"Not The Carper's super trick rig?" I answered, my knees weakening.

"In one, Matt. The fuckers! Either Brandon or the guy on the camera must have gone in your bivvy, photographed it and they've since made up their own version. Sylvester said whoever tied it has used different components from the ones we use, but essentially it's the same rig. The chances of Brandon developing it off his own back, knowing he's poached The Pit and after what you felt when you went back to your bivvy, are way too long to be possible. Even The Bookie might offer you a few hundred to one on that scenario. The strange thing is Brandon hasn't been fishing it."

"Nor have we. Probably for the same reasons as him," I replied.

"Yeah. Good point, boy."

Starting to feel angry myself, I told Rambo of the fiasco involving Brandon and my pop-up and the possibility our bait might have been recognised as the one stolen from my bivvy.

"If someone went in my bivvy, there's every chance they took a few boilies as well," I said, my heart sinking.

Rambo was outraged. "Sylvester said once you two had caught those first three fish, Brandon became very interested in our bait, constantly taking little looks at it when Sylvester was casting out and baiting up. Not that he tried anything as barefaced as he did with you. Fucking cheek!" Rambo exclaimed, angry. "We should have turned up with bags of readymades, cast out with our bail arms closed, thrashed the water to a foam and recast every hour and a half and acted like right Noddies.

With hindsight, I think we might have shot ourselves in the foot, boy, bringing our bait and catching so many. It's my fault. I was too focussed on kicking their arses catch-wise."

"So you think Brandon might know who we are?"

"No. I don't think so," Rambo answered, positively. "Sylvester said Brandon only became interested in our bait once we started catching fish. Brandon's attitude to Sylvester himself hasn't changed at all. Now I know *he* might be a good actor, too, but I'm still convinced he hasn't linked us to The Pit. We might not have turned out how he initially thought we would, we've probably come across as much better anglers than he imagined, but I'm sure he still thinks we are who we say we are. I reckon he took the action he did with you just now because he's longing to find out as much as he can about a bait that's outfishing his own very good one. I doubt he gets outfished often. Us kicking his arse when we're on a totally new water might have tipped him over the edge. Sylvester says there's no doubting Brandon's a very driven and motivated man. I mean, come on. Pumping weights, doing press-ups and running round the fucking lake? That's not normal. Maybe the body image thing and starting off the BMC are all part and parcel of what's going on in his head."

"The need to prove himself?"

"I think so, boy. He had a tough start in life and it obviously meant enough to him to want to do something for Sylvester, because he thought he'd suffered similarly. His tough start might be the thing that drives him. The thing driving the maggot."

"You and the maggot," I said.

"We'll see," Rambo replied, conviction in his voice.

170

# Chapter 16

Losing something as potent as The Carper's super trick rig, thanks to a bivvy break-in, weighed heavily on me as I continued to fish throughout the day. In the warm sun I sat and festered, brooding over the injustice of losing control of a rig we had chanced upon the night The Carper had been mown down by machinegun fire and we had landed The Seventy. Despite Pup having assured me it would be incredibly difficult to analyse our exclusive, revolutionary, indented, dirty brown bottom bait boilie, it still felt as if all our fishing edges had been compromised. And what a way to lose out after all the years of jealously guarding and protecting them – to a bloody bivvy burglary. It seemed almost ironic, after all the lengths we had gone to in keeping our edges safe, to be undone by the most simple of crimes. I mean, you hardly needed to be an evil genius to be an effective bivvy thief. You didn't need the in-depth knowledge of a master criminal, the nous of a dynamite/tunnel king or even the right tools, like a fucking great Gorilla Bar, a Hilti and diamond tipped core drill (see Hatton Garden safe deposit burglary) or a set of skeleton keys; all you needed was to have sussed the right way to move a zip to undo it.

What you also needed – the common thread in all breaking and entry cases, however sophisticated or otherwise – was the sheer audacity to do it. Undoing my bivvy's zip, any zip on any bivvy for that matter, effectively broke the seal of trust all anglers ought to have with each other. One they should be able to take for granted without the remotest fear of it ever being violated. Yet someone had broken that trust, on *our* water – twist the knife, sprinkle salt on the wound – and, gallingly, we still didn't know who it was.

Brandon *had* poached The Pit. Fact. The two dark pink baits were already in the margin when I had fished East Ender and it had been during that session where I had experienced the feeling of someone having been in my bivvy – an incident we now knew *had* happened. Another fact. On my next session in the same swim, some two weeks later, I had caught a fish which had excreted a lot of the dark pink bait. Yet another fact. Given this evidence, the questions springing to mind were: Had Brandon been fishing The Pit at the same time as Rambo and I? And: Did my capture of a dark-pink-bait-excreting carp mean Brandon had fished at least two sessions? As Rambo had said, either the dark pink bait had sat at the bottom of The Pit for the best part of two weeks without being eaten, or someone had put some more in. It was a good bait, so the answer seemed obvious. Brandon must have fished The Pit twice and most likely caught Pugwash on his second visit. Why risk coming back if he had caught it at the first time of asking?

To my mind, as I sat mulling things over, stewing in the juices of my wrath, I became more convinced Brandon hadn't fished The Pit at the same time as when we had been there. (Although how he had managed to fish The Pit, at any time, without being spotted was hard to fathom.) That meant somebody else must have broken into my bivvy – just call me Sherlock – a person who was evidently embroiled with Brandon and, presumably, the BMC. But how did pinching a rig and a bait fit in with the BMC's agenda – just call me confused – and what purpose did it serve? And on a more simplistic level, what was in it for them? That didn't make any sense, either.

The members on The Pit at the time of the bivvy break-in, other than Rambo and myself, were Astrological Jim and The Bookie. I was as sure as I could be neither of them would have done the dirty deed. Jim, an upstanding long-time member; The Bookie, a much newer one, with a *different* dark pink bait. Why would either of them risk their ticket and the fury of a revengeful Rambo to let someone else catch a big carp? This left me wondering who else might have been wandering around The Pit at night and chanced upon my unguarded bivvy? Nobody, you would have thought. In that case, had someone, somehow, seen me leave and gone in under the cover of darkness to steal a few baits and photograph The Carper's super trick rig? Was it a member, as Rambo thought, or a complete outsider, who had stolen the rig and bait and had helped Brandon catch and photograph his UK PB? If someone had seen me leave they would have needed to have moved fast, down the access track and through the combination-padlocked gates. Anyone could give out the combination number, I supposed, but you'd have to be familiar with The Pit to get around it efficiently in the pitch black. And what if you bumped into someone? An outsider was in bother, a member wasn't. Logically, I had to agree with Rambo – it must have been an inside job.

My thinking, having made that conclusion, sparked into a wider realisation. Randomly breaking into my bivvy, on the face of it, seemed very odd. Going in and stealing tackle, maybe, but limiting the theft to a rig concept and a couple of boilies? Yes! That was it! Whoever went in there did so for a specific reason. They knew it was *my* bivvy and they went in it to look for and take the very items they stole. They had prior knowledge of me and that had to mean they had observed me and my angling at close quarters. They knew I always caught well and might have noticed I always left my unbaited rigs in the margins when not in my swim. Perhaps they had guessed why. Definitely an inside job!

I sat there and my thoughts started to merge back into opacity. This was all well and good, but why would any member be so motivated to look in another angler's bivvy, especially if they weren't actually there and fishing? And why now? Why not last season, or any of the others before? Why now make a move for a bait an ex-boiliemeister had said would be virtually impossible to unlock and a rig they could never dare to be seen using on The Pit. No different to how Rambo and I used it, I know, yet it still didn't add up. Why was the member involved with Brandon and the BMC? Why was a founder member of the BMC breaking his own organisation's carp fishing etiquette? It all seemed so intense, so fervent, so driven, so motivated by reasons Rambo and I, frustratingly, weren't aware of.

And there we were, back full circle to Brandon and his driven personality. The more I thought about it now, the less clear it became – other than the fact I was convinced a member had been involved. I started to dream up wild unlikely scenarios to fit in with the very few solid facts I knew and then began running the membership through my head, trying to judge who was capable of such deceit. In the end, I had to give up. Nothing I could put forward and no one I could put forward, as a theory or a culpable person, seemed to hold water. There was always a problem, something didn't fit or feel right.

We had to find out more. That was the inevitable conclusion. How? Well, that was the inevitable question.

By the time Simon had caught his first fish, at just gone one in the afternoon, I'd had two more. Rambo had also picked up a couple of fish through the morning and Sylvester, making full use of his banker overhanging tree margin spot, had whipped out three. Brandon doubled his paltry total mid-afternoon as I sat drinking a cup of tea, slumped in my sitting-outside-the-bivvy-in-the-sun-during-the-day chair, hatefully watching him play it, willing the fish to drop off.

I was acutely aware of how my mood had soured and it had taken a considerable effort to be chatty to Simon and congratulate him on finally getting off the mark. The broad brush strokes of my bitterness had tarred him by association and I had been glad to get away from him and back to the solitude of my own company. I could see the barbecue was going to be horrendous, the three of us hiding our loathing with a Rizla-thin veneer of false civility and Brandon concealing whatever the fuck it was he was up to. Like a massive pus-filled boil, the occasion would need lancing and only then would all the disgusting fetid poison ooze out. As is my place in these sort of things, as it has always been, I would have no say in when this might take place. It would be Rambo holding the needle and dictating the timing of its insertion into the carping carbuncle in which we were held captive.

At half five, I began to wind in. Anxiety and anger had upped my adrenalin levels to a two-takes-at-once, naked-underwear-model-walking-in-my-swim level and I felt my whole body flutter, fidget and shake as I went about decommissioning my two rods. I wasn't a person who enjoyed confrontation and I thanked my lucky stars I had a friend who revelled in it and who, more importantly, wasn't a deluded motor-mouthed seven-stone weakling. Even so, my earlier fears concerning Brandon's youthfulness and his huge muscle-bound body still agitated me. Could Rambo match him if it came down to it? I never doubted him for a minute, but time does catch up with everyone at some point. *Everyone.* There was the Glock, but the thought of Rambo using it was frightening. Rambo might be all for the right to bear arms, and I'm not talking sleeveless tops here, but shooting someone with witnesses around wasn't a good policy. If it came to it, I foresaw a physical battle; where guns were arms and arms were appendages attached to torsos rather than weapons like guns.

I hope that's cleared that up.

"Let's hope it's not today the Terminator with Tackle gets temporally tarnished," I sardonically mumbled, as I headed off to see Simon.

The Higher Associate still had his rods out when I arrived in his swim and the look on my face must have betrayed my thoughts, which wasn't a very promising start to the evening.

"Yes. I'm dragging it out to try and get another one," the Higher Associate confessed. "You guys are making me look like an amateur!"

"I didn't think the BMC liked professional anglers," I said, a little too tartly.

"No. Of course not. It was only an expression," Simon said, back-pedalling. "What I meant was…"

"I know what you meant, Simon. I'm only yanking your hanger chain," I said, turning it into a joke I wasn't laughing at. Not on the inside, anyway.

Simon smiled and looked at his watch. "Ten more minutes?"

"Sure," I answered. "Why the hell not?"

The delayed wind in was unsuccessful. We all try it from time to time and every now and then one of us gets lucky and goes home cock-a-hoop. The majority of the time it only makes us late.

"You're late," Brandon said to Simon as we arrived in Sylvester's swim, the propane barbecue coals white hot and him eager to start cremating the food.

"Sorry," Simon apologised.

"No sweat. You're here now. There's glasses over here, Eric," Brandon said gesticulating to the items on the ground beside the propane barbecue. "There's red wine as well. Sort out what everyone wants and I'll crack on with the cooking. Oh, and there's a bottle of Coke for Jacob. I know he likes Coke." Brandon gave an embellished thumbs up to Sylvester and a little bit of sick popped up into my mouth.

Slipping into my waiter's role – talk about a multi-layered personality; I was Matt being Eric being a waiter – I took everyone's drink order and, having poured them, handed each individual their choice. When I had poured the wine and Coke into the glasses, the two bottles had oscillated wildly and I had spilt some thanks to my nervousness. Seeking to quell them, I had quaffed a full glass of wine and poured myself a refill there and then before taking everyone else their drinks. It hadn't helped much.

"To the BMC!" Brandon said, lifting up his glass of red.

"The BMC!" we all responded, lifting our own.

I had taken my place next to Rambo, the pair of us sitting on the grass of the inclined bank to the side of the cut-out where Sylvester's bivvy was parked. Simon had opted to stand and talk to Sylvester, probably to pick up some tips – he needed them – who was sitting in a stalking chair next to his rods. Brandon, his feet level with Simon's head, slaved over the barbecue parked on the narrow track running around the top of the bank. He was on the high ground, but there was nothing moral about it.

"How's it going, George?" I asked Rambo, who was idly poking the ground with a stainless steel bankstick.

"All right, thanks, Eric," he answered in his 'George' voice.

"Any idea what's happening?" I asked, quietly but pointedly.

"Nothing until I've had something to eat. I'm starving. I've only had a Mars bar since this morning."

"Fair enough," I said, going to sip my wine only to find my glass was empty. "I need a refill," I told Rambo, showing him the offending vessel.

I scrambled up the bank and grabbed one of the bottles of wine beside the barbecue and filled my glass to the brim. The bottle hardly wavered. Result!

Smoke was now billowing from the barbecue, as the grease from the sausages and beef burgers dripped through the grill on to the hot coals. As Brandon flipped a couple of the burgers with a pair of tongs, I gawped at the size of his forearms.

"How the hell did you get so big?" I asked, downing half a glass and motioning towards the massive cooking utensil wielding limb. "Your arms are fucking massive!"

Brandon gave me a self-assured smile. "A lot of hard work in the gym. Good training routines and a good diet."

"Plus a few steroids?" I suggested.

"Everyone's on steroids," Brandon said, a little rattily. "One to bulk up and then one for leaning out. You've still got to push the weights, Eric. It doesn't happen on its own."

"Yeah. I'm sure you have," I conceded. "So, what's the next step for the BMC, then, Brandon?"

Brandon nudged at a few sausages with his tongs. "Simon's doing an article for July's Carpworld. The new website's going live soon, I think photos of Jacob will be involved in both of those, and we need to get the review section up and running. That's really important. And keep growing the membership. The more of us there are, the more power and influence we'll have. We have to continue the crusade to rid carp fishing of all commercialism and give it back to real anglers."

"Nice," I said. "Just out of interest, who writes the Daily Directives? They're an interesting mix of ideas and pretty entertaining," I asked, feeling much more at ease. The wine *was* working now.

"Oh, some guy," Brandon answered, vaguely.

"A founder member?"

"No."

"So, a Higher Associate?" I persisted.

"Some guy. I'm not sure who pulled him in," Brandon said with irritation.

I bent down and picked up a fresh bottle of red, opened it and filled my glass.

"Top up?" I asked.

Brandon bent down and scooped his glass up from the ground and offered it up. I filled it for him.

"Your bait," he said, turning over six chicken breasts. "Could you give me the recipe for it?"

I felt my hackles rise, despite the wine having dissipated my earlier nervousness. "*I* couldn't. I help George make it, but I don't know everything that's in it."

Brandon shot a glance over at Rambo who was still sitting on his own. "Maybe you could have a word with him. It wouldn't go unrewarded."

"What do you mean?" I asked.

"I can see you three rising up through the BMC ranks. For a start, Jacob could be our poster boy. The face of the BMC. An aspiring, extremely gifted young angler fronting the most powerful carp fishing organisation out there. Look at him! He's perfect. So photogenic." Brandon leant in close to me. I could smell the wine on his breath and feel the draught from his six pack scrunching. "You and George, you're good anglers. You could come and fish here a few times a year for nothing and once we start the review system, you could be our top venue inspectors. Travel the country, fish for free, say it as it is. And not only in this country, abroad, too."

I feigned absorption. "Wow! All for our bait recipe?"

Brandon cocked his head. "Someone's got to do it. It might as well be you two, if we can come to an arrangement."

"I'll have a word," I said.

"You do that." Brandon looked down at the meat sizzling away on the barbecue and his face clouded. "Do you think the chicken's done?"

"Cut a bit in half," I suggested. "If it's still pink in the middle, burn it some more. They say when it's black it's done, but that's bullshit. Black on the outside and white in the middle's okay, a black and pink combination's campylobacter city, projectile vomiting and major league stomach cramps."

"Right," said Brandon, looking at me with curiosity.

Having imparted my culinary words of wisdom, I went to walk back down to Rambo, stopped, went back and picked up the wine bottle I had opened and then returned to sit by my best buddy.

Rambo eyed the wine with suspicion. "Take it easy, boy," he said, softly. "Alcohol might be the great social lubricator, but I don't need you getting pissed and making a mistake."

"I'm fine," I insisted. "I had to get enough down my neck to take the jitters away. I couldn't stop shaking earlier."

Rambo scrunched his brow. "Why?"

"Because it's all going to kick off at some indeterminate point tonight. Being with you in a situation like this is like sitting on a barrel of nitroglycerin and randomly hitting it with a club hammer."

"I shouldn't stress over it. Even *I* don't know for certain when it's going to go bang," Rambo admitted. "I'm still biding my time."

"He wants our bait," I whispered. "Says we can be BMC bigwigs if you hand over the recipe. I said I'd ask you."

Rambo's face cracked into a grin. "The prick *doesn't* know who we are. Our cover's still good!"

"I'll drink to that," I said, raising my glass to my lips.

"Grab yourselves a paper plate. We're ready to eat," Brandon declared from above a short time later.

Hungry as we all were, we didn't need a second invitation, the four of us formed an orderly queue adjacent to the barbecue – we're British, it's genetic – and Brandon handed out our grub. There wasn't only the meat he had cooked, he had brought along several bags of pre-sliced baps for the beef burgers and finger rolls for the sausages. There were condiments, too; salt and pepper, mustard, a large bottle of tomato ketchup and some brown sauce. Once we had been served, Brandon reloaded the grill with more chicken and the ground up bits of cows and pigs you're better off not knowing about and grabbed his own food. Like salivating carnivores, we tucked in – because we *were* salivating carnivores.

Party central moved to behind Sylvester's rods, the level ground easing the mountain goat stance requirement of the sloping bank. Brandon was engaged in a small talk conversation with Rambo while my buddy most likely mentally planned the Pit poaching prick's method of execution – I reckoned either by punch decapitation or swung round by the testicles until pronounced dead – while myself, Sylvester and Simon made up a conversational ménage-à-trois. I sipped away happily on my wine in between eating highly carcinogenic blackened meat inside white bread (I'll be lucky to see fifty), as Simon commenced a boring and introspective 'What I think I've done wrong this session' monologue. Sylvester, sporting a five-hundred-yard stare Roman Abramovich would have been proud of, hurried along his future diabetes by swigging Coke and eating chicken drowned in tomato ketchup.

I had tuned out Simon by his second sentence and had inexplicably started to daydream over when Sophie might re-introduce her super-sexy-stranger alter ego to me. The more I thought about it, the more vivid my fantasies became. Firstly, I imagined us having sex on Bondi Beach and then, doggy style, in the back of a taxi driven by the female co-presenter of Countdown who kept winking at me in her rear view mirror and mouthing the words 'Faster! Harder!' A sharp kick on my ankle snapped me out of it.

"I said, isn't that right, Eric?" Simon was saying to me. "A new angler on a water *can* turn the perceived way of doing things totally on their head."

"Oh, totally," I answered, lost for a different adverb at such short notice.

Sylvester gave me a filthy look. It might not have appeared so, but the prospective face of the BMC had been paying attention.

"You guys catching so well on a pop-up has been a real insight," Simon continued. "When we go back to our rods, I'm going to put on a couple for the last night."

"It's a good call," I said, deciding I had better try and get my act together.

"Resistance to change, stubbornness, ignoring the evidence of others, all these things can cost you fish," I theorised, giving it my best shot at being a carping sage.

Simon agreed. "Brandon has always said he won't come off bottom baits on here. He reckons his bait is so good, there's no need. Be interesting to see if he thinks the same after this weekend."

In one of those divine, 'scripted life moments', Sylvester's banker rod went into the mode all nuclear power station controllers dread – meltdown. All five of us elicited the classic carp angler Pavlov's Dogs response to a Banshee-ing buzzer and went to hit it. Two burgers, one piece of chicken and three glasses hit the deck before four of us realised, 'Fuck! It's not my rod'. The fifth individual, whose rod it *was*, who hadn't dropped anything thanks to placing his glass of Coke and plate of chicken carefully on his stalking chair, moved to his rod with the precision of a World War II fighter ace scrambling to his Spitfire. How the four of us cheered. How the four of us laughed at our own stupidity. How I wondered why Rambo was sneaking up to the barbecue. How I thought, 'Oh, my fucking days' as I saw him place the stainless bankstick, point first, into the coals.

"Things are hotting up," Rambo whispered covertly into the back of my head as he returned unnoticed.

"A Brandon branding," I whispered, leaning my head back and speaking from the corner of my mouth.

"Something like that," Rambo replied.

I downed what was left of my wine – I had dropped a burger – and felt my knees knock a couple of times.

I don't know if it was a sub-conscious reflex reaction on my behalf at the thought of witnessing future burning human flesh, but watching Sylvester play his latest fish proved a pleasurable piece of escapism. Perhaps those seeing a young Lionel Messi, Novac Djokovic or Lewis Hamilton driving a go kart, had experienced a similar sensation. That feeling of gratitude for being present and able to watch something out of the ordinary; of viewing a special young talent on the cusp of stardom. Now, I'm not saying playing a carp in anyway equates to being the world's best footballer, tennis player or motor racing driver, all I'm saying is, considering his age, Sylvester was awesome. As a lifetime angler, it was fantastic to watch and to appreciate such a flawless display from a boy so tender in years. Much as I had at The Lake, where I had alternated between watching Rambo watch his son play a fish and watching it for myself, this time I alternated with Brandon. With every deft movement of rod and reel, every skilled adjustment, I could see Brandon become ever more smitten with Sylvester's 'unholy angling talent'. (If you can read it in your head using the voice of Calculon from Futurama, so much the better.) A talent, to my eyes, that had visibly grown over the last six weeks or so.

Brandon displayed a little shake of the head in disbelief here and a little observational comment to Simon there. I suspected the notion of Sylvester becoming one of the defining images and personalities of the BMC was forming in Brandon's head. In a perverse way, it almost seemed a shame it was destined to implode, to come crashing down like a demolished block of flats.

"Well done, Jacob!" Brandon gushed, as he slipped the net under a completely outclassed carp.

"Thanks," Sylvester said, moving forward and peering into the net Brandon was holding in the margins.

"Let's get her out and have a look at her," Brandon said.

The three of us not involved in the capture edged back, affording Brandon and Sylvester some extra space. The muscle-bound BMC founder eased the net from the water, putting it and the carp inside, on the well-used unhooking mat lying in front of Sylvester's bivvy. Brandon efficiently cleared the landing net's mesh out of his way, unhooked the carp and held aloft Sylvester's rig.

"Your pop-up again!"

Sylvester took the rig from Brandon with his left hand and hooked it on to the butt ring of the rod he was holding with the other. Tightening up with a few turns of the reel handle he placed the rod and safely secured hook back on its rest. As he did so, his Delkim made a few beeps. No one flinched an inch this time.

"I'll get you my sling," Sylvester told Brandon.

Taking it down from a tree branch, the young maestro dunked it in the lake, wrung it out and after extracting his scales from his bivvy porch, proceeded to zero them in.

"There you are," he said, giving the sling to Brandon. "All ready to go."

Brandon transferred the fish into the sling, got off his knees and accepted the set of scales from Sylvester. The scales' hook went through the sling's cords and Brandon lifted. Muscles popped out of everywhere.

"Still reckon you can take him?" I whispered to Rambo, transfixed at the bumps and bulges in Brandon's arms and torso.

Rambo smiled. "We'll find out soon."

I studied Rambo's face. "You're looking forward to it, aren't you?" I hissed with incredulity.

"A bit," Rambo confessed. "See if I've still got what it takes. I haven't had a ruck with anyone half sensible for years, boy. They all back down without a fight. Maybe he will, too, once he realises his over-exercised body doesn't cut any ice with me."

I thought of Punched-son and Rambo's comment on how I would never win a conflict purely on the basis of an intimidating physical appearance. Looking and acting the part was one hell of an advantage, one I could never aspire to because I lacked the look and any 'surprise package' physical ability that might install trepidation. Rambo, naturally, was a different matter and had all the requisite attributes. Despite being garbed in Realtree – complete with BMC badge – and talking in a strange voice, it was obvious to me he was a trained killer even if he wasn't acting like one. Whether Brandon realised this was another matter; he was at a distinct disadvantage never having seen the Terminator with Tackle kick off.

Brando only knew the vanilla character of 'George' and when George morphed, Transformers-style, into a full on rumbling Rambo then we would see what the BMC founder was made of.

"Thirty-five eight. Nice one, Sylvester! You've had Big Tail, another one of our most sought after fish! You'll see why she got her name when you hold her up!" Brandon exulted. "Keep an eye on her while I nip and get my camera." He turned to the three of us. "If one of you guys could run a check on the barbie for me."

"I'm on it, Brandon," Rambo said, scuttling up the bank like a personal assistant ordered to get a coffee by their CEO.

I was feeling much less relaxed now, queasy almost, and as agitated as when I had wound my rods in – an amalgamation of the wine's effect on an empty stomach being neutralised by the intake of food and Rambo's declaration of the confrontation time being nigh. Trying to snap out of it and steel myself to make a contribution to the cause, I engaged Simon in chit-chat over Big Tail, in an attempt to distract him from Rambo's antics. Out the corner of my eye, I could make out Rambo turning over the sausages, burgers and chicken and, having flipped the food, wriggle the stainless steel bankstick in the barbecue's coals like it was a poker.

Brandon had speedily returned with his Nikon and once he became embroiled in photographing Big Tail, Rambo declared the next round of food would soon be ready.

"I'll put it on some plates and bring it down," Rambo said as Sylvester lifted Big Tail off his mat.

"Plain chicken for me," Brandon answered, squinting into the Nikon's viewfinder.

The light of the evening was starting to go and the Nikon's flash started to strobe away, dispensing brief chunks of intense luminescence across the edge of the Willow Tree swim. I watched, distracted by worrying thoughts, as Sylvester and Big Tail were bathed in staccato brightness.

"Grab a couple of these, Eric," Rambo said, appearing by my side with four platefuls of cholesterol carnage and one of plain chicken. "Chicken for Brandon and the rest can be for anyone."

I took the chicken offering and a beef burger/hot dog combo for myself and waited until Sylvester had completed the photo shoot and safely transferred Big Tail back into its watery home. Once this was done, I moved down to where Brandon was standing.

"There you go, Brandon," I said, handing him the paper plate possessed of poultry.

"Cheers, Eric," the latter day Charles Atlas wannabe responded.

"This one's yours, Jacob. I'll put it next to your other plate on the chair," Rambo told Sylvester who was already getting on with the job of recasting. "Simon, this one's for you."

"Thanks, George," the Higher Associate replied, taking his plate of food.

"Well, this is nice," I said, trying to sound convincing, as the four of us stood behind Sylvester's stalking chair.

"Yeah. It's good," Brandon agreed, nodding enthusiastically while upping his calorie intake for the day. "Have you had a word with your brother?" he asked.

"Yes, I have," I answered, thinking, here we go; light blue touch paper and stand well back.

"And?" Brandon responded, his attention switching to Rambo.

Rambo munched through the wad of beef burger in his mouth before replying. A deliberate act intended to keep us all on edge for a little longer.

"I'll tell you what, Brandon," Rambo proffered. "I'll give you our bait recipe, if you tell me where you caught your UK PB from."

# Chapter 17

**B**randon's face cracked into an apologetic smile. "Sorry. I can't do that, George. It's not that I don't want to tell you, it's that I can't. Like I've said before, it's a strictly no publicity water. Now, did Eric tell you what I *can* offer you in return for your bait? The venue..."

"Seriously? You *can't* tell me?" Rambo interjected. "To me it sounds like you've got something to hide, boy. I don't take kindly to people feeding me a pile of crap," Rambo announced, speaking to Brandon in his proper voice.

"What?" Brandon queried, a bit at sea from the abrupt change in Rambo's tone, both in delivery and message.

"I said, you *fucking* moron, you're feeding me a pile of crap," Rambo repeated.

"Whoa! Hold on a minute," Brandon responded, reacting with anger. "Where the fuck did that come from? I've invited you here in good faith, along with your son and brother, I'm about to offer you all a fantastic chance to become the BMC's chief venue assessors and out of the blue you're taking a pop at me because I won't tell you where I caught a fish from. What the fuck's going on?"

"I'm asking the questions, boy," Rambo insisted. "And what I want is for you to tell everyone here the name of the water where you caught that fish."

"I'm not telling *anyone* where it came from," Brandon insisted. "What right have *you* got..."

"*Don't* talk to me about rights!" Rambo erupted, throwing his food to the ground and aggressively stepping forward into Brandon's personal space. "I *know* where you caught it from, you prick! I just want you to man up and admit it. *You* poached *our* water, you scumbag," Rambo raged, spelling out Brandon's misdemeanour. "Matt, known to you as 'Eric', owns The Pit," Rambo stated, pointing at me. "It's part of Hamworthy Fisheries and as you well know it's the best carp fishery in the UK. *I* help him run it. I'm Rambo Ramsbottom and that's my real son, Sylvester. It's why we're here under different names, you fucking idiot. We've been tracking you down ever since we found a couple of your dark pink baits in The Pit's margins and alarm bells started ringing in our heads. It's why we joined the BMC. It's why we went to the BMC roadshow in Southend. To find out for certain if someone had poached The Pit. And boy did we find out because we saw you, Brandon, up on a nice big screen, larging it, giving it all the 'UK PB' bollocks, holding one of *our* fish!" Rambo let out a hollow, evil laugh. "We already know what you've done, you fucking clown. Don't insult our intelligence by trying to wheedle out of it, hiding behind all this 'no publicity' bollocks! We're here," Rambo rumbled ominously, like thunder before a storm, "to sort this nonsense out once and for all, boy."

"Hey, gents! Please, can we all *calm* down," Simon insisted, intervening. "I'm not sure what's happened here, you've obviously got some kind of grievance, er, Rambo, whether real or imagined I'm not sure, but let's all try and cool down and sort this out in a civilised manner?"

"'Imagined?'" Rambo queried, with an incredulous laugh. "Have you not been listening to a word I've been saying? He's poached a well-known fish from our water. I can show you previous photographs of it. It's called Pugwash and it's been in The Pit for nearly thirty years!"

"Enough! Get the fuck off my water now!" Brandon screamed, squaring up to Rambo and ignoring his Higher Associate's advice. Maybe it was because it hadn't come via WhatsApp. "I don't know what sort of stroke *you're* trying to pull, coming on here and accusing me of this shit, but it ends now."

"Oh, it's going to end, all right, boy. You can't bluff your way out of this one," Rambo snarled, dispensing some advice of his own. "You must have had help to poach our water and I need to know who it was. I want the name of the shithead who took the photo of you and the fish. Tell me who helped you *or...*" Rambo's face contorted into a countenance issuing a severe warning of impending physical retribution.

"Or *what*, old man?" Brandon sneered, laughing and backing away out of Rambo's reach. "You're fucking kidding me, aren't you? *You* threatening *me*! I can bench press your body weight with one arm."

Brandon's boast was like water off a duck's back as far as Rambo was concerned. "It's decision time, boy," The Terminator with Tackle stated, standing firm. "Tell me who helped you poach The Pit or I'm going to *make* you tell me."

There was a brief pause as Brandon weighed up his chances. Watching him from only a few feet away, sensing his body language and reading the look on his face, I had a strong feeling it wasn't going to be a case of 'Punched-son revisited'. Brandon definitely looked up for backing himself.

"Come on, then, Mr *Realtree*," Brandon said, mimicking Neo's 'bring it on' hand gesture to Agent Smith in the Matrix. "Show me what you've got."

I'm not too sure if the hand thing meant anything of significance to Rambo – I had never noticed a Complete Matrix Trilogy box set in his house – but what I did know was 'Mr Realtree' was an incitement to riot to one so kindly predisposed towards British Army camo. In fact, it was the verbal equivalent to a giant red flag being waved under the nose of the prize bull the farmer affectionately called 'Rambo'.

My churning guts, now on spin cycle, told me the time for talking must be over.

Fuming and with afterburners fully ignited, Rambo exploded off the blocks, Usain Bolt-like, and hurled himself, headfirst and horizontal, into Brandon's powerful torso, lifting the BMC founder member clean off his feet. (Think best ever rugby union hit and then double it.) As the two of them flew through the air in Sylvester's direction, the youngster wisely took sharp evasive action and side-stepped the co-joined human missile allowing it to whistle past him and out on to the swim's platform. With an approximate combined weight well in excess of two hundred kilos, the Rambo and Brando Mk1 Rocket soon deferred to the laws of gravity and crashed back to earth – smack bang in the middle of Sylvester's set-up. Several cracks went off like shotguns – whether vertebrae, carbon or fractured metal, or a combination of all three, was hard to tell – as Pup's rods and my birthday gift rod pod were utterly decimated by human bulk.

Incredibly, surviving the hit, Brandon managed to push Rambo and various shards of shattered fishing tackle up and off him – he used *two* arms, the fucking liar – and almost instantaneously staggered to his feet. The bench-pressed Rambo, having been flung on to his stomach after a full three sixty degree roll, couldn't recover so quickly and was only up on one knee by the time the BMC founder saw his chance to go for the kill. Brandon waded over to his opponent and aimed a potentially devastating kick at Rambo with a wild swing to his head. For a split second, I thought Rambo might be done for until I saw Brandon's leg stop well short of its intended target. Amazingly, Rambo had caught Brandon's kick with both arms, and now, thrusting upright via the power of his thighs only, lifted the not-quite-as-muscled-as-the-rest-of-him kicking leg high in the air, pushing it ever upwards. Brandon hopped a couple of times on his single standing leg to try and compensate, failed miserably, overbalanced and fell backwards right across the wooden stake-lined split level border between the dug-out flat section of Willow Tree swim and the naturally inclined bank. Brandon's coccyx crunched sickeningly – from my viewpoint, 'satisfyingly' – against the mini wall of upright wooden stakes.

"Go on, Dad! Finish him off!" Sylvester screamed, throwing a lusty haymaker into the gloomy evening air in his excitement.

Not wanting to disappoint his only son, and like a tiger leaping on its prey, Rambo pounced on Brandon, his leading and full load-bearing knee landing directly on the BMC founder's solar plexus, simultaneously crushing his back even harder against the unyielding wooden stakes. Standing two yards away, I heard the air whoosh out of him like a punctured airbed. The next sound I heard was the one aurally depicting someone's nose being shattered by a massive fist, which, funnily enough, was exactly what had happened. Rambo's straight right caused vermilion blood to flow copiously from both of Brandon's horribly distorted nostrils. In contrast to the somewhat lively bleeding, the rest of Brandon's body slumped into a state of inaction. Unperturbed by the inert gory spectacle before him and not finished yet, Rambo bent down and grabbed hold of Brandon's bull-like neck in a stranglehold grip and hauled the groggy BMC founder upwards on to his feet.

With Rambo's vice-like forearm tight under Brandon's Adam's apple, the back of his head locked against Rambo's chest, Brandon was struggling to breathe and began coughing and spluttering. Large goblets of thick blood and mucus came snotting out of his nose and mouth, like a succession of monkey afterbirths, on to the sleeve and front of Rambo's Realtree jacket.

"Get me the bankstick that's in the barbecue, Sylvester," Rambo ordered his son.

Face beaming with delight and admiration at his father's fighting prowess, Sylvester rushed up to the barbecue, removed the stainless bankstick from the coals and returned with its point glowing red hot in the twilight.

"There you go, Dad. Enjoy," he said, handing over the branding implement.

Still gripping Brandon's neck with one arm, Rambo offered up the glowing point with his other hand and waved it hypnotically under Brandon's nose, the red radiance from it making swirling patterns in the growing darkness.

"That didn't take long, did it? Not for an old man," Rambo stated, his voice full of the delicious inflection of victory. "Right... Now everything's under control, let me tell you what's going to happen next," Rambo continued, his voice softer and menacing. "If you don't give me the name I want this thing's on its way down your ear canal, boy."

"Please! Please stop him!" Simon implored me, retching and almost being sick. "This is awful. I can't stand violence. Please make him stop."

I pulled a 'nothing to do with me, mate' face. The Rambo Show was on now and I was merely a viewer in the audience along with everyone else. My one caveat to that was my coming up with a useful idea. Then I might intervene.

"He only has to tell us the name and then it *will* stop," Rambo said, as if it was the most reasonable request in the world.

"No!" Brandon grunted, defiant with what little energy he had left. "Not telling you. Put it in my ear. Had worse put inside me," he said, managing to splutter his resistance in as few words as possible. "Show the police again."

"For fuck's sake! Get me his phone," I shouted at Simon, stunned by Brandon's disobedience and, I presumed, the indication of sexual abuse he was claiming to have endured in the past. "Let's see if there's another way to end this."

An idea had come.

Simon nodded and although Brandon wriggled pathetically as the Higher Associate searched the pockets of his shorts, he was no longer a viable threat. Battered and hardly able to breathe his resistance *was* futile.

"There you are," Simon said, dry heaving. "I hope to God you find what you want so you can get out of here and go," Simon petulantly frothed as he handed me Brandon's phone.

"Hold on a minute, Simon," I replied, snatching the device from him. "We're not the bad guys here. You're being led up the fucking garden path as well, pal. I don't see how poaching a water fits in with the BMC's carp fishing etiquette remit, do you? Or trumpeting a snide fish at a BMC slide show."

Simon's eyes lowered in defeat and I started to scroll through the phone's contacts list, scouring it for Pit membership names. It was a long list to work through.

"Hurry up, Matt. I don't want the trail to go cold, if you see what I mean," Rambo cajoled, waving the now dull bankstick in the air as if he was conducting Ramsbottom's Torture Concerto in F-sharp major.

"Okay. Just give me a sec. I'm going through all Brandon's contacts for a Pit member's name."

Fervently, I continued to run down the list to the end. Shit! Nothing. There were no names or initials giving away or hinting at a Pit member's name. Keeping silent, I tried to think clearly. Perhaps our mystery traitor was listed under an alias, I reasoned. Much like we had all changed our contact details on our phones to match false names. If so, I was fucked. How would I ever know what the false name could be? It could be anything. Starting to feel rising panic and mindful of Brandon's seemingly heroic/stupid claim he could take a red hot bankstick in the ear canal and the legal ramifications should he do so – to my mind, two guys fighting was a whole different ball game to wilful torture – I restarted at the beginning of the contacts list. More in desperation than any sense of hope, I discarded my earlier Pit members' names tunnel vision and focused on the notion of an alias. To my stupefaction, the second name on the contacts list, which wasn't a proper name, rather a three-worded phrase, popped out at me.

'Agent of Fortune' was the contact. Deep inside my head, a cog whirred and located into a larger cog, rotating it and moving a lever. A couple of conversations and a trivial piece of knowledge instantly came to mind and made a satisfying 'snick' as everything neatly interlocked together. I had made the vital connection. Feeling pleased, and sure I had cracked it, I mentally patted myself on the back. Not many people would have made the association. Now all I needed was verification.

With a heart rate rapidly escalating, I tapped on Agent of Fortune and looked at the mobile number. It didn't ring any bells, but then it was unlikely to, infrequently used mobile numbers rarely stick. Taking out my own phone, I rapidly made my way to its contact list and started working through The Pit member's mobile numbers. Not that one. Not that one. Not that one. Yes! That one! I checked the number, checked it again and then checked it one more time.

"Got the bastard!" I said, punching the air with a fist formed around a phone. "I know who it is! You can let the fucker go now."

"Good work, boy!" Rambo declared, releasing Brandon who collapsed to his knees, coughing up more blood and spitting it out on the ground. "Who the fuck is it?"

I told him the name of the culprit.

"I *knew* it was a member." Rambo looked down with disgust at the crestfallen BMC founder. "Feel like telling us why you two hooked up and started dating?" Rambo asked Brandon.

"My back's killing me. I'm in agony. Can hardly breathe," Brandon gasped. "Call an ambulance. For fuck's sake someone dial nine nine nine."

"'Now that's not what I asked, is it?" Rambo answered, putting his foot in the small of Brandon's back and easing him flat to the floor.

"Arggh! Stop it!" Brandon screamed as Rambo directed more weight through the boot clamping him to the floor.

"Tell me."

"Arggh! Please! Okay, okay. I wanted a big fish. A real big UK fish. To promote the BMC," Brandon groaned.

Rambo thrust out his lower lip. "Let's skip on, shall we? Forget the fish, and the aspect of the commercial use of a carp capture being unethical, and let's move on. What's the BMC really all about? What exactly are you two up to?"

"Get off! Please get off! My legs are going numb!"

"Don't go all melodramatic on me, Brandon. Fucking hell, I've been with men who've said that because they haven't got any legs left, the poor bastards. They were proper men, not fucking 'look at me' show off wankers like you. Why you and him?" Rambo demanded once more, pressing harder. "What's he getting out of it? What are *you* getting out of it?"

"Argggh! No! He only helped me get the big fish. Nothing else."

"You're lying, Brandon. What's the maggot at the centre of the BMC? The one not even Simon, a Higher Associate, knows about!"

"He's got this thing. The maggot. It's been bugging him for ages," I explained to Simon, matter-of-factly.

"Oh," Simon answered non-comprehendingly, his face pale and sallow, much like the colour of the now visible rising full moon.

Rambo leant hard into Brandon's back. "Tell me,"

"Arggh! No! Ask him. Let him tell you. It was his idea," Brandon grizzled.

"Did he steal Matt's bait and rig from his bivvy?" Rambo asked, ignoring Brandon's request.

"Who?" Brandon said in confusion.

"Eric. Did he steal *Eric's* bait and rig from his bivvy on The Pit? That special new rig you've got tucked away in your rig box. The one Sylvester... 'Jacob' saw in your bivvy."

"I don't know where he got it. Sent me a photo. Please! The pain! Tied it up myself. Never seen anything like it. No bait. Never sent any bait."

"I'm getting bored," Rambo declared, perhaps sensing he wasn't getting anywhere and a fresh approach was needed. "Go and pack up, Matt. First your gear and then come back here. Keep hold of the phone, we'll need it. Sylvester, you pack up my stuff and then come back here as well. On your way back get the rig from Brandon's kit. I'll keep an eye on these two. Simon, sit. On the chair," Rambo instructed.

"Now look..."

"The fucking chair, Simon!" Rambo said, pulling a moon-lit Glock from his clothing.

"Jesus!" Simon screamed, starting to retch again, only in fright this time rather than through squeamishness. "All right! I'll sit on the chair."

"I'll need a dust pan and brush to clear my stuff away," Sylvester said wistfully, shining his recently donned head torch on the remnants of Pup's Prodigy GT3s.

"And look at this!" he said holding up a twisted metal component from his rod pod. "My birthday present from Uncle Matt. Es ist kaputt!" he said, dejectedly.

"Casualties of war, son. There are always casualties of war," Rambo said, sombrely. "At least in this case they can be replaced. If only that were always true," he added, ruefully.

Rarely have I packed up with so much gusto. I suspected I wanted to get off the water as much as Simon wanted us to leave it, although there were a few things I intended to say to the Higher Associate to set the record straight before we did leave. As I 'skirted about', as one Vimeo carp fishing video uploader put it, I couldn't help but wonder why the recently disclosed Pit member had done the dirty on us. Whatever his reasons, they were intrinsically linked to what lay at the rotten heart of the BMC. Rambo's imaginary maggot feasting on the puerile core.

Barrowing my stuff back to the van in the dark, it was clear we were only half done. Rambo had tried all he could to extract information from Brandon, short of ramming a red hot bankstick down his ear canal, and had decided to acquiesce to the law of diminishing returns. To be fair, the BMC founder had proved to be a gutsy performer under questioning and had bravely defied his victor. Rambo had wisely acknowledged this, knowing full well when to stop flogging a dead horse, and had called time on the theatrical red hot bankstick – a visual prop I was convinced he never intended to employ. He realised a new source of information was needed. One much closer to home, now we knew whose door to knock on.

With two sets of kit safely stowed, myself and the carp fishing prodigy, Sylvester, returned to Willow Tree. Simon was sitting quietly on the lad's stalking chair trying to avoid looking at Rambo's Glock, while Brandon crept gingerly up and down the swim, trying to manipulate and loosen his damaged back. The BMC founder looked a sorry sight to behold by moonlight and even worse under closer inspection by torchlight, with a bloody misshapen nose and swollen blackened eyes. The way he moved was most odd looking, resembling an eighty-year-old shuffling geriatric sewn inside an elaborately constructed muscle suit. In silence and with haste, Sylvester and I packed up his kit, the last object to go was the stalking chair on which Simon had been obediently sitting.

"That's it," I said, returning from the van for the last time. "We're all done and loaded."

"Good," Rambo said, the Glock still held in the right hand hanging by his side.

"Thanks for the invite, guys," I said to our two hosts. "Sorry it turned out so horrible, but you have to admit it was self-inflicted. You mess with Rambo at your own peril," I said, truthfully.

"You've got what you came for. Please go," Simon said, pleadingly.

"We'll be on our way soon enough, don't worry," I said. "Before we do, I'd like to say a couple of things." With little choice, Brandon and Simon offered no words of contradiction despite it being evident they weren't exactly enthralled at the prospect of me lecturing them.

"This isn't going to take long, is it, boy?" Rambo asked warily, apparently not so keen either.

"No," I assured him. "All I want to say before we go is, despite joining the BMC purely as a vehicle to find out who helped Brandon poach our water, and, next on the list, to unearth the maggot at its core, we genuinely liked what the BMC had to say. The BMC's remit, its mission statement, is a good one. The concept of using WhatsApp and Higher Associates, a one-off payment for life membership, a carp fishing etiquette, a rolling back of commercialism are all worthy ideas. Carp anglers have taken to it. Lots of carp anglers. It could have been a real force for good if it had stayed on track. I know, Simon, you really believed in it. Believed in Brandon. Now you know he's not quite as squeaky clean as he said he was, your opinion might differ. I don't know, it's for you to decide. I suspect a bit of poaching will be the least of it. We'll find out soon. Maybe the whole thing will turn out to be built on a pack of lies." I let my words sink in. "The thing that pisses me off is you've blown it. You had a once in a lifetime chance to change things for the good and you blew it. Once word gets out, the BMC will be yet another failed carp fishing organisation to add to the list."

"We'll still carry on," Brandon mumbled through puffy lips. "Who's going to care what you say? Who will believe you?"

I laughed, hiding my regard for Brandon's, admittedly, misplaced drive and determination. "When we find out the real reason why the BMC was started, I shall personally blow it wide open. I'll be on to every magazine and website you can think of. You won't survive the shit I'll throw at you."

"Do you have to?" Simon asked, an air of sadness in his voice. "If me and the Higher Associates took it over and got rid of Brandon and anyone else involved in the bad stuff? If we promised to keep it clean and stick to the mission statement?"

I raised my eyebrows. A crack in the ranks! At last Simon was thinking for himself and seeing Brandon for what he really was. "It's possible, I suppose. We'll have a think. I've got your number. I'll be in touch once I know the full story."

"Done?" Rambo asked.

"Done!" I confirmed.

"Let's go! Oh… one last thing, Brandon," Rambo said, halting in mid-stride. "We'll keep your phone for now. I don't know if you've got any other way of contacting our fellow acquaintance, but I'd rather you didn't. I like doing surprise visits, not that he's going to appreciate it! My advice, I'll tell you to your face because you haven't got a phone to get a WhatsApp message, is to get yourself to A & E. Say you slipped down the bank, fell face first into a tree and landed on your back. By the time you've queued up and waited to be seen we'll have already made our little visit." Rambo turned to Simon. "The keys to the padlock, boy," he demanded, pointing the Glock at him. "We'll leave them in the lock." Simon silently handed Rambo the key.

"Is that thing even real?" Brandon sneered.

"Real! Where would I get a real gun like this from?" Rambo said, turning back and laughing. "This is a BB gun!"

We left the pair of them to it and returned to the van for the last time. I started her up and with some relief we pulled out of the gate Sylvester had previously opened and commenced the journey home.

"Top session," I said, as I accelerated away. "Not that I'll be back for another one in a hurry."

"I really enjoyed it!" Sylvester enthused. "Apart from my gear getting damaged at the end."

"You fished well, Sylvester," Rambo said, ruffling his son's spiky blond hair. "And you played your part well. I was proud of you. Don't worry about your rod pod, I'll get you a new one exactly the same and I'll replace Pup's rods for him in case he ever needs them."

I switched my eyes from the road momentarily to catch sight of Sylvester's proud grin.

"While we're handing out the medals, well done for taking out Brandon," I said, addressing his father. "That was one hell of a fight!"

Rambo sniffed. "Nice to know it's still there if required." A few seconds passed and I wondered if Rambo was rerunning the fight through his head, a trait very familiar to someone like myself. "You were good, boy," he continued. "Working out our traitor. Brandon wasn't going to give me any more, you know. He was a gutsy fucker, if nothing else." From the corner of my eye, illuminated by the street lighting, I saw Rambo's brow furrow. "How did you know it was Eccentric Ed?"

I was pleased Rambo had finally asked as I was dying to tell him. "Well," I began, keen to disclose my methodology. "Obviously, I didn't want you to shove a red hot bankstick down his ear canal, much as I disliked him, because of the situation it might create if he went bleating to the law like he threatened. I guessed you didn't, either, so I was hoping for another way out of it by looking through Brandon's phone. To begin with, I searched it for any Pit members' names or initials and found nothing. Then I wondered if a member's number might be hidden under an alias for security reasons. For example, the phone ringing when someone like Simon might see the screen, or just as a general precaution because Brandon was up to something shady on the QT. Like I said to you at the time, I was certain Simon wasn't party to any of the bad stuff. Maybe very few within the BMC are party to the bad stuff. It might boil down to it just being Brandon and Eccentric Ed using the BMC for their own designs with every other fucker, founder member and Higher Associate completely in the dark."

"Makes sense," Rambo concurred.

"It was a real shot in the dark, to be honest, even more so trying to find it. The alias could have been anything. Any reference whatsoever. Anyway, I began looking through the list again with fresh eyes, bricking it because I knew we didn't have a lot of time and, close to the beginning, thanks to alphabetical fate, I found a contact number under 'Agent of Fortune'. It clicked into place there and then."

"How?" Rambo asked, bemused.

"Earlier on this evening I'd asked Brandon who wrote the Daily Directives and he'd been a bit evasive and edgy in answering. 'Just some guy we got in', he'd said, or words to that effect. I could tell he didn't want to discuss it. That was one conversation. The other was the time I came round to see you when you'd caught Frankenstein. Do you remember me asking if you got the reference within the last Daily Directive we'd received?"

"Vaguely," Rambo answered. "You said it was a play on an old rock song or something."

"That's right. The Daily Directive was, (Don't Fear) The Cleanser – Black Mirror Cult, a play on (Don't Fear) The Reaper by Blue Öyster Cult. Now, and here's the bit where a slice of pop trivia helped me nail Eccentric Ed, the track was taken from the album called Agents of Fortune. Once it had popped out at me, all I had to do was compare the number I had on my phone for Eccentric Ed to the one on Brandon's for Agent of Fortune. They were the same. Eccentric Ed must be the one who writes the Daily Directives! Problem solved, traitor nailed! Bang in the bottom lip!"

"You see, Sylvester," Rambo began, shaking his head in disbelief. "That's why me and Uncle Matt make such a good team. I would never have worked it out…"

"And I would never have been able to beat up Brandon," I added.

"Awesome!" Sylvester declared.

"Are we really going to have to go round and see him as soon as we get back?" I asked. I'd had enough excitement for one day.

"Got to be done, boy. We'll grab a few hours kip in the van and ambush him at home first thing in the morning. I just need to make sure he's not fishing. I'll send out a few texts in a minute and find out."

"Any ideas on what the maggot might turn out to be?"

"Not sure," Rambo admitted. "My guess is if Eccentric Ed is involved it's got to hinge around money."

"I wonder how he knew I wasn't in my bivvy?" I asked, thinking aloud. "And how come Brandon could fish The Pit without anyone seeing him?"

Rambo never answered. He was texting on his phone, engrossed. Five minutes later a message came back.

"Rob. He's not on The Pit," Rambo informed me.

I drove on in silence. Ten more minutes passed before Rambo confirmed Eccentric Ed wasn't on The Lake either.

"Good! That's a bit of luck. Get Sophie to send us his home address," Rambo directed.

I phoned Sophie's mobile on the van's hands free system and asked her to look up Eccentric Ed's home address from the membership file I kept at home. As she read it out to me, Sylvester tapped the details directly into my sat-nav.

"How's it going?" Sophie asked, after reading out the address.

"All right," I answered, not wanting to go into details.

"Why do you want his address?" she pressed, smelling trouble.

"We need to pay him a visit," I replied.

"Has he been a naughty boy?" she asked, her intuition cranked up to a Delkim '6'.

"Sort of."

"You haven't got any hand grenades with you, have you?" she asked in alarm.

"No!" I said, indignantly "I'm not going to blow anything up this time. Jesus! That was years ago!"

"Just checking. I know what can happen when you and the lummox get on the warpath against Syndicate members."

"He *can* hear you, you know. He's sitting right next to me."

"Good!" Sophie snapped. "By the way. We've had a wedding invitation come in the post the other day. It's for the marriage of a Peter and Daisy and it's in Venice! We have to RSVP as quickly as possible so they can arrange our flights."

"Fantastic! That's from Pup the boilie guy," I explained. "He said he would pay for me, you, Rambo and Steffi to fly out to Venice for the ceremony and he would cover the accommodation costs as well."

"Gosh! Really? How wonderful! I've always wanted to go to Venice." Sophie's tone changed from delight to one of perplexity. "On the invitation, it also asks, and I don't really understand this, what size Murano glass piece *I* would like as an attendance gift from the happy couple. It asks me to stipulate if I want six, eight or ten inches."

"I'll explain later," I said, hastily. "Start looking for a new outfit and shoes to go with it. Something sophisticated and elegant, bearing in mind the fact you might have to get in and out of a gondola while wearing them."

# Chapter 18

Trying to sleep wedged in the van's driving seat wasn't much fun, particularly as both Rambo and Sylvester were out like a light and snoring. In between snoring, Sylvester made tiny, intermittent sighs and occasionally blew air out through pursed lips making a 'put-put-put' sound. His father, the louder snorer, although not prone to making other noises, often shifted in his sleep, the redistribution of his weight sufficient to gently rock the van. Every sound and movement was adding to my increasing sleepless frustration and it left me to contemplate how any angler could ever share a two-man bivvy. The odds had to favour one or the other murdering his cohabiting angler at some point during a session – whether through interrupted sleep or carp-catching jealousy. I would have to ask The Bookie if his firm had any hard data to back up my theory.

As time crawled by, Rambo and son's night-time sleeping idiosyncrasies began to consume my whole world. The more I tried to ignore them, the more they managed to permeate my skull up to the point I was convinced the pair of them were sleeping rent-free *inside* my head.

I looked at my watch. Half three. Fuck's sake!

I screwed my eyes shut – an act only succeeding in amplifying the snoring – Sylvester started put-put-puting and the van gently wobbled once again. The night seemed destined to stretch out forever in front of me, never to end, as I sat caught in purgatory within the confines of a white tin box on wheels.

Sylvester had fallen asleep very early on in the journey to Eccentric Ed's house. Everyone knows kids can sleep on a washing line and Sylvester had proved the point. Despite his head leaning against the bulk of his father, he had remained completely oblivious to the sound of Rambo's voice – one which had loudly and vigorously informed me what fresh hell lay in store for Eccentric Ed. Once we had parked on the street opposite to Eccentric Ed's marvellous house, at one in the morning, and Rambo had set the alarm on his phone for five hours later, he had instantly dropped off with ease. Used to snatching sleep in a foxhole while under constant enemy shelling, dropping off when shoehorned into a van's passenger seat was a doddle for him. I, on the other hand, hadn't been able to get comfortable at all and had shuffled and wriggled and shifted in a vain attempt to manoeuvre my body into a position sufficiently agreeable to induce a bit of shut-eye. So far, I had been doing this for over two hours with zero success. If I didn't nod off soon my brain would turn to mush through sleep deprivation, ooze out my ears, run down the van's seats and ruin the upholstery.

I looked at my watch again. Three thirty-five. Fuck's sake!

I told myself to forget the time, ignore all the distractions and *concentrate* on going to sleep. Almost simultaneously, I dismissed the notion as a ridiculous concept. *Relax*. Think about something else, I thought, which at least was a step in the right direction. Distraction was what was needed as forerunner to sleep as I had to sidetrack myself from the snuffling pigs to my left. With this in mind, I looked over at Eccentric Ed's Audi Q7, sitting on a driveway the full width of the double garage behind it, and tried to guess how many bedrooms the property adjoined to it might possess. More than four, less than seven. Let's go for five and a study. Next. Value? Now that was more interesting. I could guess and then browse Zoopla on my phone for a similar property and see how accurate I had been. I plumped for nine hundred and fifty thousand and found an almost exact property, two hundred yards further up the road, which had sold for one and a quarter million last year. Christ! Property prices, eh? Pretty soon, a decent cardboard box would set you back five grand. More if situated in a desirable location – like a shop entrance.

Getting distressed, and now a bit mentally disorientated, I moved on to wondering who chose the ever-changing eclectic mix of weekly specials available in Lidl stores. Last time I had been in one it had consisted of waffle makers, flip-up motorcycle helmets, oil-filled radiators, decorative plant climbing aids, cat scratching posts, denim shirts and bow saws. Maybe whoever it was did it with the aid of a pin, a blindfold and a giant catalogue listing every in stock globally-available retail item.

My brain began running away with itself. Had a motorway service station washroom attendant ever sought an industrial injury claim for hearing loss caused by high powered commercial hand dryers? What was the most socially embarrassing act from the following: Still laughing out loud at Dad's Army catchphrases, picking your nose while driving a battered car with over two hundred thousand miles on the clock, dancing to YMCA by The Village People – and knowing all the moves to spell out the letters in the title – or audibly breaking wind at a dinner party just as the hostess serves starters? What *was* the highest possible sustainable percentage of all retail outlets being coffee shops in any given town centre? To be a genuine alternative comedian today, did you have to be a fat, right-wing northerner wearing a suit telling mother-in-law and Englishman, Irishman and Scotsman jokes? If the CEO of a company earned four hundred times as much as the lowest paid employee, did it mean he was working four hundred times harder, was four hundred times better or was four hundred times greedier? If someone punched you in the face in a weightless environment, say an orbiting space station, would they be able to hit you harder, or not as hard, as on planet Earth? And if money was the root of all evil, what was the name of the plant that grew from it?

I looked at my watch again. Three forty-five. Fuck's sake!

How come time dragged so much when you didn't have rods out? Two day session – gone in the blink of an eye. Inside this van for five hours – a couple of billion years, at least. It was ridiculous. I turned my head to the left to gawp at the

194

two sleeping beauties, dappled by street lighting, who were seated next to me. Not only were they asleep, but they were managing to look comfortable doing it! Bloody cheek!

Annoyed, I let my eyes wander further afield within my purgatorial prison and, on noticing it, stretched over and grabbed my BMC beanie hat from the passenger shelf, put it on and pulled it tight over my head. To my pleasant surprise, I found a significant gain in doing so. The snoring was muffled and less obtrusive, plus I could rest my head against the driver's side window in a bit more comfort as the hat cushioned the glass's unyielding surface and minimised its coldness on my head. I closed my eyes, folded my arms tightly about myself and tried to let my mental diatribe go.

"Wake up, boy! He's coming out the house!" Rambo barked.

Startled from a deep sleep, I lurched upright in my seat, banging my wrist violently against the steering wheel. The sharp pain brought the world into sharp focus and to my disbelief I saw the van's digital clock display a time of a few minutes turned eight. More with it now, I looked out past first Sylvester's and then Rambo's head and, sure enough, there was Eccentric Ed closing the front door after leaving – and I could be pretty categorical about this – his million pound plus house.

"I'm looking forward to this!" Rambo assured me, opening the van's door with pugnacious enthusiasm. "Come on, you two. Time for the final push. Let's find out once and for all what the fucking maggot is!"

Clambering out my side as instructed, I ran round the front of the van to catch up with Rambo and Sylvester who were already across the road and on the far pavement.

"Oi! I want a word, boy" Rambo shouted ominously to the BMC's Daily Directive scribe.

Eccentric Ed had made contact with the Q7's ergonomic door handle and the look of panic on his face, as he saw a blood-splattered Rambo in Realtree marching towards him, suggested he was considering the possibility of jumping in his sixty-grand car and making a dash for it. Unfortunately for Ed, his thought process had been too slow, or fear had constrained his mind, and Rambo was now virtually upon him. The holder of both a Lake and Pit ticket – shortly to be forfeited without recompense – seeing the game was up, meekly let his hand slide off the Teutonic door opening mechanism.

"Sir Rambo!" he half boomed, his voice lacking its usual bombastic sonic quality. "What a pleasant surprise. Master Ramsbottom as well and… Matthew?" he asked, squinting at me with only vague recognition.

"Yeah, it's me, Ed. I'm in the BMC. We *all* are," I confirmed, pointing to the badge on my identity-muddling beanie.

"Indoors or out here?" Rambo asked, drawing up alongside Eccentric Ed. "I'm not bothered."

Eccentric Ed shifted his gaze on to the mass of dried blood plastered across

Rambo's jacket, a garment now only inches from his fetching and, for the moment at least, contrastingly blood-free expensive coat.

"Brandon's," I told him. "He's *not* well."

Eccentric Ed scanned his little piece of suburbia, as if considering the impact an external altercation might have on his neighbours and his social standing with them.

"Let's go indoors, gentlemen. I'm sure we can deal with this civilly."

"I wouldn't bank on it," Rambo answered, a cold smile on his lips.

By way of response, Eccentric Ed's face lightened a few shades on the Dulux 'Complexions' colour chart.

"Come this way," he grimaced, starting to walk around the back of the Audi.

The three of us followed Ed around to the back of his house to a patio area adjoining a well tended rear garden with a flat and recently mown lawn. Traversing the patio, we entered into a large utility room via the back door. Once through the utility room, we passed into a huge kitchen kitted out with glossy brilliant white base and wall units, black granite worktops and polished glitter-flecked floor tiles. Ed flicked a couple of switches with the same hand on which his fuck off watch was hanging and LED downlights in the ceiling, LED strips under the wall units and square LED plinth lights spectacularly lit the room. Miele appliances were everywhere; hob, extract hood, double oven, microwave and coffee machine were the ones I could see and doubtless there were many more hidden away behind the base unit fascias. It was an incredible show kitchen if ever there was one. A fifty grand job, at least; almost as expensive as his car, but probably more expensive than his watch – not that I was *so* fixated on how much money Eccentric Ed had.

"Take a seat if you will," Eccentric Ed suggested, starting his charm offensive and gesturing towards the granite-topped kitchen breakfast bar surrounded by six leather upholstered bar stools. "Coffee or tea anyone?" he asked, his voice now virtually back to normal.

All three of us plumped for tea. Ed opened a wall unit door and pulled out four mugs, hooking two of his thick stubby fingers through a couple of them for transportation to a worktop.

"Oh. Helloo. Ahh, Ed, I thought you gone," said an accented female voice.

I looked up to see who the voice belonged to and saw a young Thai woman who had come into the kitchen. She was, I estimated, in her late twenties, dark-haired, petite and attractive. I diverted from her to look at Rambo who had already zoned in on me. I raised my eyebrows, sending out a damning message, and we both turned to regard Eccentric Ed.

"This is, Nee, my wife," Eccentric Ed explained, knowing we had judged him. (Guilty as charged.) "Nee, this is business, I'm afraid."

"Ahh, okay," she replied and quietly turned and melted from the room.

Ed had filled the four mugs from one of those taps capable of dispensing boiling water and was busying himself with tea bags and milk.

"Wonderful lady. My soul mate," he declared. "It's been the best two years of my life since I married her." Ed handed out the teas and sat down. "Met her on holiday in Bangkok. I have to declare it was love at first sight."

More like love at first *site*, I thought – www.thaibrides.com.

"How nice," I said, indicating it was anything but.

"Anyhow, gentleman, I suspect you're not here to listen to me pontificate on my personal life and thus it begs the question: What lies has that scoundrel, Brandon, been bandying around, Sir Rambo?" Ed asked, a grim look on his face.

"We've discovered rather a lot of things for ourselves, actually. Brandon only confirmed them… once I *persuaded* him, if you get my meaning. Unfortunately, it all adds up to you ending up in my bad books, boy," Rambo stated, sipping his tea. "And that's about as massive an understatement as I can think of." Rambo eyed Eccentric Ed with contempt. "Your 'best years' are about to come to an abrupt end."

"No! There must be some misunderstanding! I can't have that! What lies has he told you, Sir Rambo? And you, Matthew?" Eccentric Ed blustered. "I would never do anything to upset you two."

"We *know* everything, you fool," I said, spitting the words out, tired of Eccentric Ed's stupid mannerisms and speech. "You helped Brandon poach The Pit and *you* stole my bait and rig from my bivvy. You're the only guy with a double ticket for Hamworthy Fisheries and yet you cheated on us in the worst way possible. All the other members are as good as gold, but you, you're despicable. You dumped on me and Rambo and you broke the sacred rule. You went inside another angler's bivvy and stole some of their gear. *My* bivvy. *My* gear." I was trying to make eye contact with Eccentric Ed, to look into the blackness of his soul, but his head was bowed to the ground. He might have been examining the quality of the grouting on his floor tiles for all I knew. Cranking up the bile, I pushed on. "We know it's you who writes the Daily Directives for the BMC. That's how we pinned you down, 'Agent of Fortune', and we know how you and Brandon originally set up the BMC and suckered everyone in. Originally, we heard about the BMC through Luke and once we had our dark-pink-bait-in-the-margin riddle to solve, they weren't The Bookie's, incidentally, we know they were Brandon's, we joined up, went to the BMC roadshow at Southend, saw Brandon holding Pugwash and made a plan to befriend him. We've just come back from a session at Brandon's syndicate water up near Cambridge and after a little dust-up on the bank we pretty much know everything!"

Eccentric Ed's profile had been a giveaway as each bombshell had detonated, blowing his cover ever further open. Any hopes he may have harboured of bluffing his way out of the situation must have evaporated under the burning sun of our knowledge. We had him, but we didn't yet have the maggot.

"Matt's very upset," Rambo said with a lightness of touch hinting at heavy-handed retribution.

"To say the least," I chimed. "You've lost your place on The Lake and The Pit for a start. Sine die, mate. Start looking for other waters and don't dare ask for a fucking reference. You…"

"Where's the toilet?" Sylvester asked, butting in. "I well need to go."

"Out the door and first on the left," Eccentric Ed answered with distraction, pointing to the exit where Nee had disappeared.

Sylvester nodded, got off his stool and left.

"As I was saying," I resumed, watching Sylvester leave the kitchen. "You betrayed us. Big time."

Eccentric Ed made a dramatic groan and, with his head in his hands, lowered it on to the black granite in front of him.

"Oh, my God, I'm so sorry!" he cried into the worktop. "I beg your forgiveness. I've been so ruinously stupid. Please hear me out and let me explain."

"I'd *love* to hear your extenuating circumstances," I said, sarcastically.

Eccentric Ed jerked his head upwards, his face a picture of penitent angst. "I'm so sorry, Matthew, Sir Rambo. I know you must be upset. Please let me have my say."

"Go on," Rambo answered. "I could do with a laugh."

"I know it looks positively dreadful, but it's not as it seems, I promise you. You see, I chanced upon this Brandon character purely by accident and sadly it seems I am to pay a heavy price for my involvement with him, through my own stupidity and naivety," Eccentric Ed quickly tacked on the end. "We, Brandon and I, discovered we had this shared love of carp fishing when we first met through a mutual business contact. Thanks to this shared enthusiasm I, being the innocent dreamer I am, mentioned how I wished I could take carp fishing back to a bygone age. To a less commercial time, to older values, ones more dignified and in keeping with the nature of angling. And he, to my great surprise and pleasure, agreed with me! He told me he wanted to help me achieve my vision and believed if the pair of us worked hard enough we could actually bring it to fruition! Or so he said," Eccentric Ed looked up, dismayed. "Initially, the pair of us, working each other into a frenzy of altruistic anticipation, the route to an idealistic carp fishing utopia possibly lying in our hands, *our* hands, thought long and hard over how we could pitch my beautiful idea to the masses. After many weeks of rejecting unsuitable proposals, we eventually arrived at the bare bones of our ideology. If only I'd realised! If only I could have foreseen how he would change!" Eccentric Ed declared melodramatically, through the splayed fingers of both hands covering his mouth. "Once we had started in earnest, recruiting other founder members, some reliable and wonderful Higher Associates and salt of the earth foot soldiers to start spreading the word, it was then the intimidation started. He'd already told me I would have to remain firmly behind the scenes as he didn't see me as a face others would follow. He insisted he, young, muscular and vibrant should be the public face of the BMC. Then, one night, totally unexpectedly and against all previous behavioural patterns, Brandon told me he needed to catch a big fish to up his profile as the figurehead of the BMC. Naturally, I told him this cut against the grain of the BMC's agenda. In no uncertain manner I reminded him carp captures for gain were unethical. Even if it *was* to promote ourselves and that very ideal. I was unequivocal on the matter!" Eccentric exclaimed, passionately slapping his hand on the granite worktop. "I insisted we couldn't run a policy of double standards under any circumstances. The Black Mirror Cult, above all else, had to run its affairs in a manner beyond reproach. We had to be unimpeachable!" Eccentric Ed shook his head in discomposure and tears welled in his eyes. "But I was weak. He was having none of it and couldn't see the blatant contradiction in his plans. He physically threatened me. Threatened to harm me and to harm Nee, as well. He said we were in it together and I had to help and do exactly what he said. Against every sinew in my worthless body, I agreed. I hadn't the bravery or the body to deny him, not like you, Sir Rambo, and I wished to protect my dear young wife. Shamefully, ignobly and with terrible dishonour, I kowtowed to Brandon and helped him poach The Pit."

"How did you do it?" I asked, bemused by Eccentric Ed's florid tale.

"It pains me terribly to recall my vile act," Eccentric Ed replied, wiping both eyes with a bent first finger. "I smuggled him on to The Pit in my car, at night, and he kept out of sight during the day inside my two-man bivvy. The first trip was easy, no one was there, but Brandon didn't catch. What a rage he flew into. He insisted we must try again, grabbing me by the throat and spewing out expletives right into my face, roughly manhandling me and making more threats against Nee. Again, although it pains me to say it, I agreed to his demands. The next time, despite a few members being on The Pit, making it more difficult, he caught. He was using my rods, doing all the casting and baiting at night, so it looked like I was fishing, whereas I was, in truth, doing nothing at all. A mere puppet to my master. Luckily, the bite from Pugwash came early morning, while it was still dark, so he could play and land it. If it had come during the hours of daylight, I would have had to have landed it and my ordeal would have been ongoing. Once Brandon had his fish, he was satisfied. I insisted he must never go near The Pit again and, with his prize secured, he mercifully agreed. A small victory after such a dastardly deed, I agree."

"And stealing my bait and rig?"

Eccentric Ed, bent double on his stool and retched as if he was going to be sick. He was worse than Simon! "Forgive me. It sickens my soul what I've done. Physically sickens me." Eccentric Ed, who, to be fair, was certainly living up to his name, slowly straightened himself upright. He took a mouthful of tea, the mug oscillating wildly at his lips. "I stupidly, *stupidly*, mentioned how good your bait was when talking to Brandon about how Pup had quit the bait game. I had told him I wasn't too sure which port to head for having being caught in a bait-less storm. I think I had also mentioned in passing how I noticed you always left your rigs in the margin when fishing The Pit. Only The Pit, not The Lake. Now, personally, this didn't mean anything to me. I presumed it was a ritualistic thing, something you just did. Brandon, however, would have none of it. He flew into one of his rages and started screaming at me, saying he wanted to see your bait and it was obvious to him you were hiding something rig-wise. I protested as strongly as I dared, but he rode roughshod over me. He told me he wanted some of your bait and a look at one of your rigs. He said he didn't care how I got them, but if I didn't there would be serious consequences. I was so frightened, I took to spying on you, Matthew, I'm sorry to say. To tracking your every movement and invading your privacy in a terrible way. One night you left The Pit early, in the dark, and I took my chance. I can only apologise, dear fellow. Deeply, sincerely and honestly for the shameful act I inflicted upon you. You may think me pathetic, I'm sure you do," Eccentric Ed said, his voice now soft and quiet. "But the things he promised he'd do to Nee and I were shocking. Far too shocking to say."

"Go on, give us a try," Rambo encouraged, sardonically.

Eccentric Ed slowly turned his head to Rambo, had another episode of the dry heaves, ran despairing palms down the cheeks of his face and took three… slow… deep… breaths.

"He said… he said, he would brutalise both Nee and I. Sexually brutalise us. Tie both of us up and sodomise the pair of us. Me first and then her. My tiny, fragile Nee, fucked in the arse by a savage like Brandon. Oh, my God!" Eccentric Ed burst out into tears, sobbing and blubbering like a two-year-old who had lost a favourite toy. "The thought of it! And he was capable! Those who suffer abuse are the most likely to dispense it!"

My eyebrows were on the heaven-bound escalator on hearing that comment. Was it possible Eccentric Ed was telling the truth? Up until that point, I had been utterly convinced it was all bullshit, if acted out with a certain over-the-top élan. I could see Rambo was having second doubts as well and he shrugged at me over the top of Eccentric Ed's waterworks act. The threat he had described also hammered home the multi-faceted nature of any sexual act. An expression of love, an expression of lust, an expression of abuse and an expression of hate – all true depictions, depending on context.

"I'm so sorry, gentlemen," Eccentric Ed apologised, dabbing his eyes with a pristine white cotton handkerchief he had taken from a pocket. "How can you ever forgive me? My treachery is absolute."

Sylvester walked back into the kitchen, I had forgotten he had gone, such was my involvement in Eccentric Ed's defence speech, and dumped a mass of small packaging on the granite worktop in front of his father.

"I had a snoop round like you said, Dad, and found these in the garage. There's boxes and boxes of them. Other stuff too. Leads, line, indicators, but mainly this stuff. End tackle. Boxes and boxes of end tackle. There was this as well," Sylvester said grimly, holding up a larger packet before passing it to his father who looked at it with disgust.

I raced from my stool and went to have a closer look. Eccentric Ed had stopped crying and was studying Sylvester with horror and in anger. I picked up a couple of the small packs from the pile on the worktop. One was a pack of swivels, the other a pack of size-six hooks. The rest were packets of boilie stops, hooklink clips, sinkers, chod rigs, rig rings, silicone sleeves, lead clips and tail rubbers, all of them in identical packaging. Printed on all the pieces of card within each tiny plastic wallet containing the items of end tackle were the words 'BMC Basics', with BMC written in the same distinctive font as the sew-on badges.

"Look at this, boy," Rambo said, holding up the bigger packet Sylvester had given him.

To my consternation and intense indignation, I saw a ready-tied version of The Carper's super trick rig. This time the words 'BMC Special' were on the inlay card.

"Oh, my days!" I exclaimed as it sunk in. "You cunning fucker, Ed! You and Brandon set the BMC up as a *commercial* enterprise! All the shit about carp fishing etiquette, the cleansing of carp fishing from commercialism and giving it back to real anglers was just a front to sell punters tackle! Tackle produced by *you!*" I walked away from Rambo and turned in a little circle in the centre of the kitchen, my head kaleidoscoping with images of Black Mirror Cult branding. "It's brilliant! You give the masses the power to review the competition from the moral high ground after setting up the Black Mirror Cult, to slag them off in other words, and then introduce your own 'no nonsense, support-the-cause' brand. No need to advertise, no need to pay consultants, no need to strive for brand recognition, or develop fresh ideas by the looks of it, you've just copied what's already out there, and you make a fortune out of everyone's good intentions! It's one hell of a maggot, Rambo!"

Rambo was equally impressed at the pure snake oil salesmanship of it. "Sure is, boy. No one's thought of getting a brand out there this way round. Very devious and manipulative! You've certainly excelled yourself, Ed, you hideous prick."

I was secretly hoping Eccentric Ed was going to say how he would have got away with it too, if it hadn't have been for that pesky kid, but my Scooby-Doo fantasy never materialised as Eccentric Ed kept his mouth resolutely shut.

"If only you could get a bait range going as well, eh?" I goaded. "Our bait and Brandon's dark pink one would have been a great addition to the BMC's commercial package." I laughed, coldly. "How's it going trying to analyse our bait? Not too good? What a shame! You haven't even sent it to Brandon yet, have you? It's still being analysed, isn't it? Not so easy as copying a rig, is it?"

"I'll cut you in," Eccentric Ed boomed, brushing aside my taunt and breaking his silence. "Both of you. The Black Mirror Cult Company is owned by myself and Brandon and is held within an offshore dummy corporation. Sixty-forty split. We'll give you ten per cent each from our respective shares. Make you directors. No one will know. You let this go, turn a blind eye and permit us to launch the BMC Basic range later this summer, and you won't regret it. I'll pull your rig if that's what you want. Keep it to yourselves. And your bait." Eccentric Ed looked up at me. "You're right. Mick the Bait's not getting anywhere with it. He might have come up with Brandon's dark pink boilie, but he can't unpick yours." Eccentric Ed waved a dismissive hand. "Not a problem. BMC Basic on its own, without a bait range, will be the biggest carp fishing end tackle brand in the world by next year. Then we expand into other areas. We'll clean up. We're talking millions. *Tens* of millions. The hard work is done. Not pretty, I know, but in business you need an angle. The BMC was always a commercial venture, right from the minute Brandon and I came up with the business plan. It's the best marketing idea anyone's ever come up with in carp fishing circles. As you rightly say, Matthew, we'll twist the review system to knock the other big players, I don't think we'll have to push too hard to get BMC members to do that!" Eccentric Ed said, smiling cruelly. "Then we'll introduce our own brand at very competitive prices to undercut the review-discredited competition thanks to our low overheads. *We* won't have to pay for any advertising or consultants because *we're* the BMC! We'll put a small percentage of the profits back into the Black Mirror Cult to keep all the 'believers' happy, splash a bit of cash their way to make them think everything is sweet, thus leaving the four of us to siphon off a fortune. Korda, Fox, Nash and Gardner and all their websites, DVDs, YouTube channels and consultants won't know what's hit them. Ha! They'll be bit part players once we go live! The BMC's a juggernaut, gentlemen, and it'll crush every other tackle brand before it!" Eccentric Ed, business mode Eccentric Ed, spun his head to Rambo and then to me. "What do you say? Are you both in?"

\*

I sat down in my sitting-outside-the-bivvy-in-the-sun-during-the-day chair and looked out across The Pit. The water had a bit of chop on it, caused by a fresh south-westerly, and the tiny peaks of gin-clear water glittered in the bright sunshine like a thousand night-time stars. My three rods were out, baited with our still exclusive, revolutionary, indented, dirty brown bottom bait boilie and attached to The Carper's super trick rig. One I tied myself, even if I did have five hundred ready-tied BMC Specials stacked in my garage. I was hopeful of action, but in truth I was more than happy to simply be fishing. It had been nearly a week since we had discovered the ultimate truth concerning the Black Mirror Cult and it was nice to unwind behind some rods. Not that going fishing had stopped me from wondering how things would play out in the end. Others would decide the conclusion, although the plan was for me to clandestinely contribute to the debate.

I had asked Rambo if he had been tempted by Eccentric Ed's offer and he had admitted, much like myself, for a split second the selfish allurement of taking the money had been a seductive choice. But only for a split second. How could either of us have lived with ourselves? Or enjoyed our fishing? It would have tainted our passion more than diesel-soaked fingers hair-rigging a flavourless boilie. Whether the solution we had devised was correct, well, who knew? Time, once more, as ever, would tell.

When Eccentric Ed had additionally offered Nee, as a sacrifice, to perform any sexual act on us we desired – another facet of sex, that of a tradable commodity – as well as ten per cent of the BMC's profits, Rambo had finally flipped, punching the heinous man in the stomach so hard I had thought Rambo's fist might break his spine. We had stormed out of the house, after taking two large boxes of The Carper's super trick rig from the garage – probably a vain gesture, albeit one that had felt good – and left Eccentric Ed gasping for air on his designer-kitchen floor. Once sat in the van, we had discussed a course of action. With a decision made, I had phoned Simon and told him the whole sorry story. I had the feeling he was more shocked than I had been.

"What shall I do?" he had asked, despairingly. "Everything was a lie. A complete and total lie. It's all turned to dust. My dreams have turned to dust."

"Maybe not," I had replied. "But whatever happens, me and Rambo have decided to leave it up to you and the other Higher Associates and founder members to choose. As I see it, you can either come out and destroy the BMC for good, telling its members everything was a façade, an unethical manipulation of their goodwill, or, as you suggested, you can hang on in there and try and take control from Ed and Brandon. If you can overthrow the pair of them and stop the commercial tie-in from occurring and stick to what's out there at the moment, you might be able to carry forward the dream *you* have, Simon."

The Higher Associate had been unconvinced. "How the hell am I going to do that? They won't drop the BMC products after they've spent money setting them up and manufacturing them."

"They can repackage them," I had said, dismissively. "I expect a lot of it's made in the same factory in China as all the other end tackle. They could cut their losses if they could manage to re-sell their stock to another company."

"But I've got no clout," Simon had protested. "If I threaten to take them down, I destroy what I want."

"I might be able to help," I had said. "I know someone, let's say a friend of a friend, who writes books about carp fishing. I'm going to get hold of him and when I do, I know I'll be able to persuade him to write a book about the BMC. He'll write the story of how me and Rambo uncovered the real motives behind it. It'll read like he's ghost written it for me."

"Right," Simon had responded, the hint of a possible-way-out-of-this-mess-solution in his voice.

"It'll take him a year, to write it and get it out as a paperback, so it gives everyone time. You can tell Ed and Brandon what's going to happen and let them pick the bones out of it. In just over a year's time we'll be able to see how the Black Mirror Cult fares once the truth has come out. I think it will either kill it stone dead in the water if it has gone down the commercial route, or, if you have managed to take control and run it purely on its moralistic values, it will make it stronger. Do you see what I mean."

"Yes. Yes, I do," Simon had answered.

"Good. That's settled, then. I'll leave it with you. Good luck."

The laptop, the device on which I would write my contribution, was in my bivvy, calling me to make a start on a project the likes of which I hadn't attempted in over a decade. In ten minutes, I thought, procrastinating, I'll start in ten minutes. Ten minutes soon passed – I had rods out – and knowing I really did have to bite the bullet and get started, I retrieved the laptop from under my bedchair and, sitting side saddle on it inside the bivvy, cracked it open and rested it on my legs. After it had booted up, and having opened a new Microsoft Word document, I stared at the blank white page with a blue background. The title? That was obvious enough. In a large font, I typed 'Black Mirror Cult' and centred it towards the top of the opening page. On a fresh page, I put up the heading 'Introduction', before deciding I would come back to it later, and on yet another new page typed 'Chapter 1'. So far, so predictable – Joseph Heller eat your heart out.

How to start, I wondered? At what point did this latest tale begin? After several minutes contemplation, I had the opening line of the story. With two fingers, and all the prowess of an appalling piano player attempting Twinkle Twinkle Little Star, I started typing; '"I'm glad you popped by," Pup told me…' and then fondly remembered I had a trip to Venice to look forward to.